Landscape Architecture and Digital Technologies

Landscape Architecture and Digital Technologies explores how digital technologies are reshaping design and making in landscape architecture. While the potential of digital technologies is well documented within landscape planning and visualisation, its application within design practice is far less understood. This book highlights the role of the digital model in encouraging a new design logic that moves from the privileging of the visual to a focus on processes of formation, bridging the interface of the conceptual and material, the virtual and the physical.

Drawing on interviews and projects from a range of international designers, including Snøhetta, Arup, Gustafson Porter, ASPECT Studios, Grant Associates, Catherine Mosbach, Philippe Rahm, PARKKIM, LAAC and PEG office of landscape + architecture among others, the authors explore the influence of parametric modelling, scripting, real-time data, simulation, prototyping, fabrication and Building Information Modelling on the design and construction of contemporary landscapes. This engagement with practice is expanded through critical reflection from academics involved in landscape architecture programs around the world that are reshaping their research and pedagogy to reflect an expanded digital realm.

Crossing critical theory, technology and contemporary design, the book constructs a picture of an emerging twenty-first-century practice of landscape architecture premised on complexity and performance. It also highlights the disciplinary demands and challenges in engaging with a rapidly evolving digital context within practice and education. The book is of immense value to professionals and researchers, and is a key publication for digital landscape courses at all levels.

Jillian Walliss has over 15 years' experience as a landscape architecture academic in Australia and New Zealand. She works in the Landscape Architecture program at the University of Melbourne where she teaches landscape theory and design studios. Jillian's research focuses on the relationship between theory, culture and contemporary design practice. Her most recent work investigates the potential of digital technologies to produce a new generation of urban open spaces, which feature the explicit manipulation of climatic phenomena.

Heike Rahmann is a landscape architect at RMIT University and has worked with various practices within the fields of landscape architecture and urban design in Germany, Japan and Australia. Her research explores the intersection of landscape, technology and contemporary urbanism with focus on design practice and theory. Her publications include the co-authored book *Tokyo Void: Possibilities in Absence* (Jovis, 2014), which examines notions of vacancy and transformation processes in one of the largest urban areas in the world.

Landscape Architecture and Digital Technologies

Re-conceptualising design and making

Jillian Walliss and Heike Rahmann

Routledge
Taylor & Francis Group

LONDON AND NEW YORK

First published 2016
by Routledge
2 Park Square, Milton Park, Abingdon, Oxon OX14 4RN

and by Routledge
711 Third Avenue, New York, NY 10017

Routledge is an imprint of the Taylor & Francis Group, an informa business

British Library Cataloguing-in-Publication Data
A catalogue record for this book is available from the British Library

Library of Congress Cataloging in Publication Data
Names: Walliss, Jillian, author. | Rahmann, Heike, author.
Title: Landscape architecture and digital technologies : re-conceptualising
design and making / Jillian Walliss and Heike Rahmann.
Description: Abingdon, Oxon [UK] ; New York : Routledge, [2016] | Includes
bibliographical references and index.
Identifiers: LCCN 2015021219| ISBN 9780415745864 (hardback : alk. paper) |
ISBN 9780415745857 (pbk. : alk. paper) | ISBN 9781315713526 (ebook)
Subjects: LCSH: Landscape architecture–Computer-aided design. | Landscape
design–Data processing. | Visualization.
Classification: LCC SB475.9.D37 W35 2016 | DDC 712.0285–dc23
LC record available at http://lccn.loc.gov/2015021219

ISBN: 978-0-415-74586-4 (hbk)
ISBN: 978-0-415-74585-7 (pbk)
ISBN: 978-1-315-71357-6 (ebk)

Typeset in Univers 8.5/13.5 pt
by Fakenham Prepress Solutions, Fakenham, Norfolk NR21 8NN
Printed in Great Britain by Ashford Colour Press Ltd

Contents

Preface

There has never been an easier time for designers to engage with the digital realm. Designers can now explore the creative potential of computational design, with minimal mathematical knowledge, aided by more accessible programming languages that transform designers into 'toolmakers' to customise software for their own needs. Hardware advancements offer designers autonomy to define and gather their own data, fabrication techniques such as 3D printing and CNC routing can now be accessed at minimal cost, while the emergence of open source resources offers unprecedented access to a collaborative community in which to exchange and share ideas.

In comparison to architecture, these digitally driven design opportunities have been slow to influence landscape architecture. This disparity in adoption is reflected in the projects featured in the 2012 publication *Digital Landscape Architecture Now*, where almost half of the profiled firms are architectural or art practices.[1] This observation led us to ask why is it that landscape architecture has been so hesitant to engage with a digital design practice? In asking this question, we also became inspired to look more closely for evidence of change.

For the past 3 years we have been working with leading international landscape architects and urban designers, practitioners and academics to construct a record of an emerging digital design practice of landscape architecture. This book highlights how designers apply a range of digital technologies and associated operative techniques in the conceptualisation, design, and construction of form, materiality and systems. We see the book as a work in progress, rather than a manifesto, presenting a snapshot of contemporary developments which we encourage students, academics and practitioners to analyse and debate. Crossing theory, technology and practice, the book uncovers a contemporary design practice embracing complexity and performance, well positioned to engage with the pressing challenges of the twenty-first century such as climate change and intense urban growth.

Importantly, we offer a new generation of landscape architects already engaged with digital technologies (often self-taught) much needed direction in how to meaningfully apply digital techniques and tools within the distinctive disciplinary framework and concerns of landscape architecture. For more experienced practitioners, we provide an outlook on where practice and design opportunities may develop in the next decade, offering direction for implementing and embedding the digital realm within design practice and pedagogy. And, finally, we offer suggestions on how these two generational positions may engage each other's strengths to advance and shape the discipline.

In this book, this digitally driven design practice is positioned relative to theoretical developments within landscape architecture as well as in relation to a longer theoretical and technical history of the allied design disciplines of architecture, urban design and engineering. This wider positioning recognises that changes to landscape architecture are due to internal (e.g. design discourse and precedents) and external influences such as developments in construction and in software and hardware technologies. For example, the construction industry is currently undergoing significant transformation following the introduction of BIM (Building Information Modelling), which revises construction processes into new models of collaboration conceived to offer efficiencies, cost-savings and simulation of post-construction management processes. BIM is slowly being mandated for major projects across the world, requiring design firms to adapt and revise their work practices.

We present a significant departure from the dominant manner in which landscape architecture currently engages with digital technologies as an advanced representational toolbox. We aim to shift discussions of digital technology from questions of representation and visualisation to a critical reflection on the design possibilities emerging from a digitally driven design practice of landscape architecture. There is no question that these developments will fundamentally reshape the design and construction practices of landscape architecture over the next decade, in a manner already witnessed in architecture. As Antoine Picon, Professor of the History of Architecture and Technology at Harvard's Graduate School of Design (GSD), notes:

> One can safely wager that the contrast between the respective degrees of permeation by computer culture of landscape architecture and architecture will fade in the years to come, as digital tools are about to transform the former as profoundly as they have already changed the later.[2]

So what is meant by the term digital technologies? At the most basic level, the term describes the application of digital resources crossing digital media, programming tools and software applications in the design and construction process. Two distinct concepts emerge in this context – 'computerisation' and 'computation'. Computerisation refers to applications where digital technologies form a 'virtual drafting board', while computation 'allows designers to extend their abilities to deal with highly complex situations'.[3]

This book concentrates on the definition of 'computation', introduced in two major ways. First, we focus on the concept of modelling, in particular parametric modelling (also known as relational or associative modelling). Accordingly, design shifts from an emphasis on the compositional or visual to a more procedural or rules-based approach.

Second, we introduce the role of digital tools. Through the use of proprietary software or by writing their own code or script (instructions understood by the computer), designers use computational power to apply and explore operations such as spatial modelling or the testing of particular phenomena and conditions represented by data within their design processes.

In addition, we outline how developments in hardware such as sensors, terrestrial laser scanners and fabrication techniques support new means for recording, analysing and modelling site conditions and systems, facilitate the design of 'intelligence' into constructed projects and allow for the construction of complex forms and infrastructures.

The book's structure

We have drawn extensively on the experience of landscape architects and urban designers engaging with digital technologies within their design practice. Through over 80 hours of interviews and detailed analysis of selected projects, we explore how software and hardware, applied within new theoretical framings, transform design processes, workflows, collaborative relationships and construction processes. These projects, crossing large-scale infrastructure, parks, urban squares, river edge and memorials, have mostly been designed in the past 5 years, with over half constructed or in the process of being constructed.

The practices have been strategically chosen to reflect a diversity of sizes and international contexts, encompassing some of the largest landscape architectural practices in the world (up to 100 employees) through to practices of fewer than ten people.

Snøhetta (Oslo), LDA Design (London), Arup (London) and HASSELL (Melbourne) offer the experience of large-scale internationally operating practices, some of which are multidisciplinary. ASPECT Studios (Melbourne), Gustafson Porter (London) and Grant Associates (Bath) provide examples of large landscape-architecture focused offices. Catherine Mosbach (Paris), PARKKIM (Seoul), ecoLogicStudio (London), LAAC (Innsbruck) and PEG office of landscape + architecture (Philadelphia) represent smaller design firms.

This engagement with practice is expanded through critical reflection from academics involved in landscape architecture programs that are reshaping their research and pedagogy to reflect an expanded digital realm; namely Harvard's GSD, the University of Pennsylvania's Department of Landscape Architecture, the University of Virginia's Department of Landscape Architecture and the Master of

Advanced Studies in Landscape Architecture (MAS LA) at ETH, Zurich. And, finally, these perspectives are further widened through the consideration of speciality research labs such as the University of Toronto's GRIT Lab and the University of Southern California's Landscape Morphologies Lab, together with input from the research and development-driven practices of OLIN Studio, Kieran Timberlake and CASE.

Throughout the book we introduce five conceptual framings for conceiving of a digital design practice of landscape architecture. In our Introduction we explore some disciplinary attitudes that have so far limited landscape architecture's engagement with digital technology, before introducing the defining characteristics of a digital design practice. This discussion highlights the primacy of the digital model. In Chapter 1 Topographic surface we focus on the emergence of the digital model, introduced through a discussion of the theoretical and technical influences on architectural design during the 1990s, highlighting the three influential concepts of topology, parametric modelling and performance. In parallel, we discuss advancements in hardware and software sourced from the automobile, aviation and film industries. This is followed by an examination of how landscape architects and urban designers (LAAC, PARKKIM, ASPECT Studios and Snøhetta) interpret theoretical developments and utilise software in the production of precise spatial geometries and a parametric rule-based approach to topography.

The concept of parametric design is discussed in more detail in Chapter 2 Performative systems. We explore how landscape architects apply computational design, guided by a performative theoretical framing, as operative techniques for investigating relationships between form, phenomena and systems. We begin with a discussion of performative design, introduced through Catherine Mosbach and Philippe Rahm's winning scheme for the Taichung Gateway Park competition held in Taiwan in 2011. This is followed by a more detailed interrogation of parametric modelling and scripting explored through the work of PEG office of landscape + architecture and master's-level design studios held at Harvard's GSD and the University of Pennsylvania (2014–13). The chapter concludes with a discussion on the potential of parametric modelling in offering a new approach to landscape planning.

This exploration of parametric modelling is extended in Chapter 3 Simulating systems where we introduce the emergence of environmental modelling, prototyping and robotics in the simulation of systems. Beginning with the *Gardens by the Bay* in Singapore and PARKKIM's proposal for *Danginri Thermal City* in Seoul, we demonstrate the value of embedding simulation modelling within design processes to test for performance and offer evidence-based metrics such as achieving thermal comfort levels. The possibilities of real-time data together with recording technologies such as small unmanned aerial vehicles (UAV) drones and inexpensive site sensors are then discussed as techniques for gathering and modelling site data, conducting evidence-based research on constructed designs, as well as contributing to the development of intelligent design systems. We conclude the chapter with an examination of design studios and research labs that explore physical and digital prototyping of systems such as water and material flow as part of their design processes, effectively shifting the conceptualisation of the design studio into the design laboratory.

We continue the focus on prototyping in Chapter 4 Materiality and fabrication, where we examine how material explorations and 'file to fabrication' techniques can extend landscape architecture practice into the design of components that have traditionally been considered as 'off the shelf' items. We begin by introducing the impact of 3D Global Navigation Satellite Systems in creating an automated construction process increasingly applied to large-scale projects. The 'materials first' design practice of Brian Osborn at the University of Virginia, PEG office of landscape + architecture and ecoLogic Studio is then discussed, before concluding with a detailed account of the innovative digital design and fabrication processes critical to the construction of Gustafson Porter's *Diana, Princess of Wales Memorial*.

The theme of construction continues into Chapter 5 Collaboration, where we introduce the 'data' inspired BIM construction environment that is currently reshaping the design and construction processes of the United Kingdom, Asia and the Middle East. We explore the experience of Arup, LDA Design, ASPECT Studios, HASSELL and Snøhetta as they negotiate an emerging collaborative data-driven construction process, which challenges the workflows, design, and construction practices of landscape architecture. And, finally, in Future directions we summarise the opportunities presented by a digital design practice of landscape architecture, combined with strategies for transitioning practice and pedagogy into an era inclusive of digital technologies.

This book is dedicated to Ada Lovelace and Grace Hopper – the brilliant women who could see beyond the hardware to imagine the true potential of digital technologies.

Acknowledgements

An enormous thank you extends to all the designers, academics and students that trusted us with their thoughts, reflections and, most importantly, their work.

These include Jenny B. Osuldsen, Diccon Round, Pål Hasselberg, Andreas Heier and Claire Fellman from Snøhetta; Kathrin Aste and Frank Ludin from LAAC; Andrew Grant from Grant Associates; Meredith Davey from Atelier 10; Yoonjin Park and Jungyoon Kim from PARKKIM; Catherine Mosbach and Philippe Rahm; Christian Frenzel from Transsolar; Neil Porter and Mary Bowman from Gustafson Porter; John Gould from Barron Gould; Neale Williams from SurfDev; Christian Hanley and Christopher Landau from OLIN Studio; Stephanie Carlisle from Kieran Timberlake; Tom Armour and Darren Hickmott from Arup; Neil Mattinson and David Thompson from LDA Design; Matthew Mackay and Johanna Picton from HASSELL; Geoff Heard from Fytogreen; Kirsten Bauer, Jesse Sago, Marti Fooks, Nicolaus Schwabe and Christian Riquelme from ASPECT Studio; Karen M'Closkey, Keith VanDerSys and Richard Weller from the Department of Landscape Architecture, University of Pennsylvania; Andrea Hansen, David Mah, Bradley Cantrell and Zaneta Hong from Harvard GSD; Daniel Davis, Steve Sanderson and Federico Negro from CASE; Maarten Buijs from West 8; Brian Osborn from the School of Architecture, University of Virginia; Liat Margolis from the John H. Daniels Faculty of Architecture, Landscape & Design, University of Toronto; Alexander Robinson from the Landscape Architecture Department, University of Southern California; Pia Fricker, James Melsom and Christophe Girot from ETH, Zurich; Tom Morgan from Monash University; Claudia Pasquero and Marco Poletto from ecoLogicStudio; Eduardo Rico and Enriqueta Llabres-Valls from Relational Urbanism.

We would also like to thank our colleagues: Margaret Grose, Katrina Simon and Marieluise Jonas for their rigorous editing and continuous support; Tom Harper for his graphic design input; Jack Langridge Gould, Catherin Bull and Dongsei Kim for their comments; and a very special acknowledgement to Wendy Walls for her valuable research and ongoing interest. And thank you to Sade Lee and Louise Fox from Routledge for their encouragement and valuable input. We would also like to acknowledge a publication grant from the Melbourne School of Design, Faculty of Architecture Building and Planning, University of Melbourne. And lastly thanks to Philip Goad and the late Bharat Dave who encouraged us to just write the book (rather than hold a conference). They were so right!

Introduction

Landscape architecture has a proud connection to the earliest explorations of digital applications for spatial analysis. The publication of this book coincides with the 50-year anniversary of the establishment of Harvard's Laboratory of Computer Graphics, which was influential in the advancement of automated mapping technology, which later evolved into spatial analysis and Geographical Information Systems (GIS). Despite this history of earlier adoption, landscape architecture today demonstrates a more tentative engagement with the possibilities of digital technologies. In this introduction we discuss some of the reasons behind this hesitancy, before introducing the importance of grounding an emerging digital design practice of landscape architecture within a theoretical framing.

We begin by acknowledging the innovative work of landscape architects, who over a half century ago began to explore the potential of burgeoning technologies for informing better decisions about the planning of our cities and the environment.

Funded by a grant from the Ford Foundation, Harvard's Laboratory of Computer Graphics was established in 1965 under the guidance of Howard Fisher. The Laboratory was developed to explore the potential of computer graphics in addressing the urban, social and spatial issues of the American city. Research focused on the development of modelling tools such as SYMAP (a vector model and a punch card system) that could spatialise demographic, social and ecological data into 2D digital format thematic maps. SYMAP is recognised as the first widely distributed computer package that could support geographical data.[1] Early applications of SYMAP included Carl Steinitz's 1967 design studio at Harvard's Graduate School of Design (GSD), which mapped and analysed the urban development and natural systems of the Delmava Peninsular.[2]

In 1965, Ian McHarg (also supported by the Ford Foundation) established the Regional Planning Program at the University of Pennsylvania, and in 1967 visited the Laboratory, to experience first-hand the potential of SYMAP to his emerging methods of spatial analysis. In the following year he began his extensive regional planning study of the Delaware River Basin, followed by the publication of his seminal text *Design with Nature* in 1969. During this period, McHarg tried to introduce a computer system to the program, however, students were reluctant to engage with the time-consuming punch card system.[3] At the same time, Jack Dangermond left Harvard's Laboratory to co-found Esri (Environmental Systems Research Institute), now considered the largest supplier of GIS software in the world. In a common pattern in the history of software development, research originating from universities offered the basis for commercially viable software, with Esri releasing ARC/INFO software in 1982 (including a PC version in 1986, followed by ArcView in 1991).[4]

Encouraged by the availability of ARC/INFO software, McHarg argued for the reintroduction of computers at the University of Pennsylvania in 1984, leading to the purchase of Intergraph computer system, which included three Intergraph Workstations (to the value of $500,000).[5] Dr John Radke, a visiting professor from the Department of Geography who helped McHarg to establish the computer system commented on the 'immense' analytical capabilities of the computers, stating:

> This Intergraph computer will enable us to do the type of 'McHargian' ecological land-use sustainability analysis that has, in the past, taken much longer to do with a much wider margin of error. You will be amazed at how quickly you can draw features of the landscape, move them around, and actually view, in three dimensions, a variety of design alternatives with the push of a button.[6]

Throughout the 1980s and 1990s, GIS spread across universities and practices as a digital application for integrating environmental knowledge into planning, promoted by the increasingly accessible software and guided by the academic writings of McHarg, Carl Steinitz, Stephen M. Ervin and Dana C. Tomlin.

However, the exploration of GIS within landscape architecture has weakened considerably in the early twenty-first century, considered by many designers to be too constrained within scientific positivist methodologies weighted towards inventory and analysis for land suitability. Aimed at addressing this acknowledged limitation, Esri has more recently proposed a further iteration of landscape planning known as 'Geodesign'. Geodesign is broadly considered 'design in geographic space'.[7] But techniques for integrating design practice with the geographic sciences currently remain ill-defined and ambiguous, ranging from the development of 'sketching' capabilities, either by the application of hand drawings or the ability to sketch within specific software, through to the development of collaborative processes inclusive of designers.

These proposals share conceptual difficulties in conceiving design logic or techniques for bridging design generation, data and the considerable power of the computer. But foremost, this discussion is occurring in isolation from the theories and ideas that drive a designer's adoption of digital technologies. The challenge of inserting design into Geodesign is therefore multifaceted, encompassing ideas, generative techniques, imagination and theories. It is our ambition in writing this book to show how the considerable powers of a computational approach (including the capabilities of GIS), can be applied within a creative and generative practice, and to demonstrate how these techniques can help landscape architects to explore the ideas and concerns core to landscape architecture in the twenty-first century such as designing with ecological systems, working with systems in flux or engaging with the extreme weather events caused by climate change.

Conceiving a digital design practice

Many landscape architects have difficulties in conceptualising digital technology as a creative medium. This attitude can be traced to three issues: the conceptualisation of creativity as a human endeavour; the assumption that an unmediated connection between hand and the brain evident in the act of drawing provides the most valuable insights for design; and that technology distances the designer from the real world. Underlying all of these attitudes is the problematic conflation of a tool with technique.[8] For example a pencil is no less a tool than a computer, with neither offering non-mediated technique. These attitudes are equally prevalent in practice and academia.

For instance, a 2003 survey of members of the ASLA (American Society of Landscape Architects) concluded that 'the predominant response was that computers were not intuitive and design is intuitive'.[9] The computer 'was not perceived to have significantly impacted the artistic or creative aspects of design practice', with few practitioners believing that 'the computer can improve these aspects of the profession'.[10] Even a decade later, a survey of 427 ASLA-registered landscape architects continues to highlight the attitude that technology negatively influences creativity, with design conceived as requiring 'human creativity' and 'human spontaneity'.[11]

These attitudes are mirrored within academia. Numerous publications and essays have emerged since 2000 that link creativity with hand drawing, reinforcing the association of design as a distinctly 'human' endeavour. Most prominent are Marc Treib's edited collections *Drawing/Thinking: Confronting an Electronic Age* (2008) and *Representing Landscape* (2008).[12] Such writing produced predominantly from a generation of scholars and designers educated within a non-digital era, expresses anxiety over the assumed loss of particular qualitative attributes and skills, if hand drawing is replaced by digital technologies.

These positions tend to be formed from a limited understanding of the potential of digital technologies, reducing its value to that of a 'virtual drawing board' to replicate analogue modes of representations. This perspective, observes architectural historian Mario Carpo, is aligned with historic patterns of technological change, where 'new and potentially disruptive technologies' are used to 'emulate pre-existing ones'.[13] As Karen M'Closkey states: 'If digital media are believed to be deficient, this is only because they are used to replicate hand-drawn techniques, rather than explored for the medium's inherent capabilities.'[14]

In this light, a more valuable discussion focuses upon what techniques such as drawing type, operative technique or analytical process – whether analogue or digital – might offer the designer. There is no argument that hand drawing will always have a valuable place in any designer's skills. Equally, computational design offers landscape architects analytical power and new generative capabilities that cannot be replicated through drawing. Therefore in this book we avoid the binary discussion of an either/or approach to analogue and digital techniques. Instead we focus on the areas where digital technologies demonstrate the capability to *expand* the design practice of landscape architecture.

Presently, there are few publications or essays that discuss the design potential of digital technologies to landscape architecture within practice or pedagogy. This absence is reinforced by the manner in which design projects are discussed, which emphasises the representational quality of the image and often diminishes the role of digital technologies in the generative design process, keeping such practices 'back of house' observes Charles Waldheim.[15] Anecdotal evidence suggests it not unusual for landscape architects to hand draw over digitally generated designs to present more 'pleasing' images for the client. Even when considerable technological innovation has shaped a project, there can be a tendency to privilege a particular 'artistic' framing, as is demon-strated in the manner in which the *Diana, Princess of Wales Memorial*, designed by Gustafson Porter is generally understood by the discipline.

Jane Amidon's 2005 monograph on Gustafson Porter, for example, included minimal discussion of the innovative digital scanning, 3D modelling, physical prototyping, and advanced stone fabrication techniques integral to the realisation of the memorial, beyond the scant reference to 'advanced 3-D digital imaging and stone cutting technology'.[16] This project not only utilised technologies *ahead* of architecture, but also could not be achieved without them.[17] As we explore in Chapter 4, the subsequent design development and fabrication processes of this memorial allowed the granite 'necklace' to be designed and manufactured in just 26 weeks.

How is it that such digital innovation is so quietly put aside? It is inconceivable that Jørn Utzon's design of the iconic Sydney Opera House would be discussed without referring to his collaboration with engineer Ove Arup in the design and construction of the monumental concrete shells. Yet, too often landscape architecture

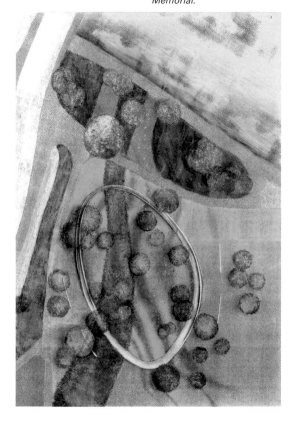

I.2a–c
Plan image and clay model from Gustafson Porter's winning competition entry for *Diana, Princess of Wales Memorial*.

design projects are written with minimal reference to materiality and construction, thereby masking many moments of innovation and technological advancement. Such accounts establish imagined limitations to practice and knowledge within the discipline itself, and are further reinforced by the types of drawing and images used to present design. Similar to textual accounts, the graphic representation of design projects, overwhelmingly emphasise the conceptual or the evocative final renders over design processes and construction details. Most landscape architects would be far more familiar with the colourful drawings and clay models of the *Diana, Princess of Wales Memorial*, shown in Figure I.2, than the extensive digital modelling required to realise the design depicted in Figure I.3.

Given these observed disciplinary tendencies to over-emphasise the conceptual and representational aspects of design, this book aims to extend the definition of creativity to be inclusive of design development, materiality and construction. Accordingly, the design projects and design studios featured, are not presented as discrete case studies, but are instead carefully sequenced, analysed and interwoven to construct a wider understanding of contemporary digital design practice. Covering a variety of typologies, these projects reveal the potential of digital technologies at all scales of design.

Many of these design projects are revisited throughout the book, allowing for a more detailed interrogation of design processes than is often presented in design

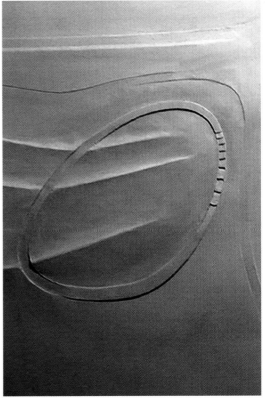

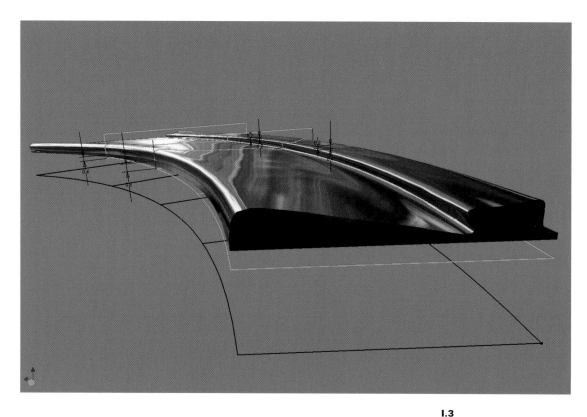

I.3
The 3D 'jelly mould' produced
from the competition clay
model by a GOM scanner,
commonly used in the
automotive and aerospace
industries.

monographs. Included are what one designer described as 'the ugly images' – that is, screen shots, un-rendered spatial models and scripting codes. We feel these are critical to fully understanding the characteristics of a digital design practice. In addition, projects are contextualised beyond the disciplinary boundaries of landscape architecture, to also consider their significance against a background of digital design theory and a sixty-year history of technological development.

Grounding a digital design practice

Technology in itself does not inspire design innovation. Instead it is the questions or intent that drives the designer in their use of technology that provides the foundation for novel outcomes. Theory, technology and design advancements therefore work concurrently. This integral relationship is well explained by Mario Carpo in *Ten Years of Folding*. Reflecting on the significant challenges to architectural form that emerged during the 1990s, Carpo comments:

> True, without computers some of those complex forms could not have been conceived, designed, measured or built. However, computers per se do not impose shapes, nor do they articulate preferences.

One can use computers to design boxes or folds, indifferently ... the theory of folding created a cultural demand for digital design, and an environment conducive to it.[18]

Presently landscape architecture operates within a weak theoretical discourse of making, which contributes to difficulties in conceptualising a role for technology, theoretically and culturally, within design processes. This weakness has not always been so apparent, heightened by the reflexive thinking encouraged by Postmodernism which inspired the realignment of landscape architecture's theoretical discourse towards 'understanding' driven by a transdisciplinary concept of landscape informed by geography, cultural studies, the humanities and the arts. This theoretical realignment, combined with the disciplinary desire to distinguish itself from architecture, has contributed to landscape architecture's isolation from the unfolding theoretical and technological innovations shaping architecture, engineering and the construction industry. More recently the performative ambitions of Landscape Urbanism, which emerged in the late twentieth century, offered a more design-focused discourse, however, its influence has manifest predominantly as a critique of urbanism, rather than a more generative stimulus.

Returning to Carpo's observations of architecture in the 1990s, it becomes clear that without a theoretical grounding to engage with technology and design, landscape architecture would continue to struggle to explore its considerable potential. Throughout our research, practitioners, academics and technology specialists consistently comment on the need for designers to have clarity of purpose in order to maximise the potential of technology. To engage with digital technologies requires new ways of thinking about design methodologies and aspirations. This is the role of theory.

Consequently, we conceive this book as an exploration of theory and praxis, grounding the featured projects against an unfolding theoretical terrain of a landscape architecture digital practice, developed in two ways.

First, we insert landscape architecture into a longer theoretical and technical history relating to digital culture, technologies, design and construction. This positioning does not diminish the distinctive attributes, practices and concerns of landscape architecture. Instead it offers an understanding of influential concepts and techniques now being adopted in landscape architecture that have their origins outside the discipline. This includes consideration of hardware and software developments such as the evolution of parametric modelling and fabrication techniques.

This contextualisation begins with the comprehensive diagram shown in Figure I.4 that documents the advancements and relationships between technological developments in software and hardware, theoretical thinking, influential design precedents and significant research outcomes. Breaking from disciplinary agendas, this diagram considers landscape architecture's more recent engagement with digital technologies as part of a longer history, beginning with the earliest codes written in the 1950s.

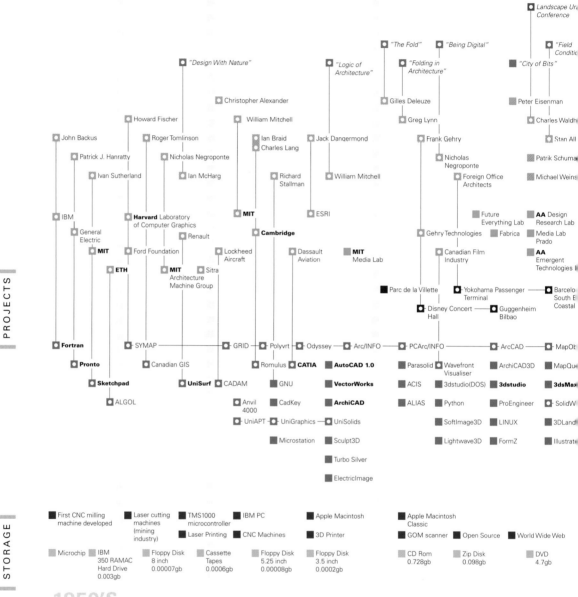

CODE **SPATIAL ANALYSIS** **ARCHITECTURAL GRAMMARS** **CONTINUOUS VARIATION**

THEORY

Landscape Ur[banism]
Conference

"The Fold"   "Being Digital"

"Design With Nature"   "Logic of Architecture"   "Folding in Architecture"   "Field Conditi[ons]"

"City of Bits"

KEY THINKERS

Christopher Alexander   Gilles Deleuze   Peter Eisenman

Howard Fischer   William Mitchell   Greg Lynn   Charles Waldh[eim]

John Backus   Roger Tomlinson   Ian Braid / Charles Lang   Jack Dangermond   Frank Gehry   Stan All[en]

Patrick J. Hanratty   Nicholas Negroponte   Nicholas Negroponte   Patrik Schuma[cher]

Ivan Sutherland   Ian McHarg   Richard Stallman   William Mitchell   Foreign Office Architects   Michael Weins[tein]

INSTITUTIONS

IBM   **Harvard** Laboratory of Computer Graphics   **MIT**   ESRI   Future Everything Lab   **AA** Design Research Lab

General Electric   Renault   **Cambridge**   Gehry Technologies   Fabrica   Media Lab Prado

MIT   Ford Foundation   Dassault Aviation   **MIT** Media Lab   Canadian Film Industry   **AA** Emergent Technologies [Lab]

ETH   **MIT** Architecture Machine Group   Sitra

PROJECTS

Parc de la Villette   Yokohama Passenger Terminal   Barcelo[na] South E[ast] Coastal

Disney Concert Hall — Guggenheim Bilbao

SOFTWARE

Fortran   SYMAP   GRID — Polyvrt — Odyssey — Arc/INFO — PCArc/INFO   ArcCAD — MapOb[jects]

Pronto   Canadian GIS   Romulus   **CATIA**   **AutoCAD 1.0**   Parasolid   Wavefront Visualiser   ArchiCAD3D   MapQu[est]

Sketchpad   **UniSurf**   CADAM   GNU   **VectorWorks**   ACIS   3dstudio(DOS)   **3dstudio**   **3dsMax**

ALGOL   Anvil 4000   CadKey   **ArchiCAD**   ALIAS   Python   ProEngineer   SolidW[orks]

UniAPT — UniGraphics — UniSolids   SoftImage3D   LINUX   3DLand[scape]

Microstation   Sculpt3D   Lightwave3D   FormZ   Illustrate[r]

Turbo Silver

ElectricImage

HARDWARE / STORAGE

| First CNC milling machine developed | Laser cutting machines (mining industry) | TMS1000 microcontroller | IBM PC | Apple Macintosh | Apple Macintosh Classic | | |
| Laser Printing | CNC Machines | 3D Printer | GOM scanner | Open Source | World Wide Web |

Microchip   IBM 350 RAMAC Hard Drive 0.003gb   Floppy Disk 8 inch 0.00007gb   Cassette Tapes 0.0006gb   Floppy Disk 5.25 inch 0.00008gb   Floppy Disk 3.5 inch 0.0002gb   CD Rom 0.728gb   Zip Disk 0.098gb   DVD 4.7gb

1950'S

I.4
Evolution of theoretical and technical innovations of a digital design practice.

PARAMETRICISM   PERFORMANCE

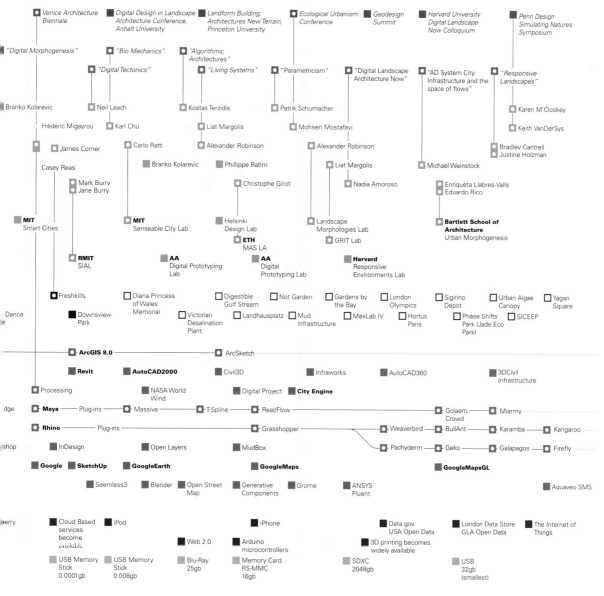

Venice Architecture Biennale

Digital Design in Landscape Architecture Conference, Anhalt University

Landform Building: Architectures New Terrain, Princeton University

Ecological Urbanism Conference

Geodesign Summit

Harvard University Digital Landscape Now Colloquium

Penn Design Simulating Natures Symposium

"Digital Morphogenesis"

"Bio Mechanics"

"Algorithmic Architectures"

"Parametricism"

"Digital Landscape Architecture Now"

"AD System City: Infrastructure and the space of flows"

"Responsive Landscapes"

"Digital Tectonics"

"Living Systems"

Branko Kolarevic

Neil Leach

Kostas Terzidis

Patrik Schumacher

Karen M'Closkey

Frédéric Migayrou

Karl Chu

Liat Margolis

Mohsen Mostafavi

Keith VanDerSys

James Corner

Carlo Ratti

Alexander Robinson

Alexander Robinson

Bradlev Cantrell
Justine Holzman

Casey Reas

Branko Kolarevic

Phillippe Rahm

Liat Margolis

Michael Weinstock

Mark Burrv
Jane Burrv

Christophe Girot

Nadia Amoroso

Enriqueta Llabres-Valls
Eduardo Rico

MIT
Smart Cities

MIT
Senseable City Lab

Helsinki Design Lab

Landscape Morphologies Lab

Bartlett School of Architecture
Urban Morphogenesis

ETH
MAS LA

GRIT Lab

RMIT
SIAL

AA
Digital Prototyping Lab

AA
Digital Prototyping Lab

Harvard
Responsive Environments Lab

Freshkills,

Diana Princess of Wales Memorial

Digestible Gulf Stream

Not Garden

Gardens by the Bay

London Olympics

Sigirino Depot

Urban Algae Canopy

Yagan Square

Dance

Downsview Park

Victorian Desalination Plant

Landhausplatz

Mud Infrastructure

MaxLab IV

Hortus Paris

Phase Shifts Park (Jade Eco Park)

SICEEP

ArcGIS 8.0 ——————————————— ArcSketch

Revit

AutoCAD2000

Civil3D

Infraworks

AutoCAD360

3DCivil Infrastructure

Processing

NASA World Wind

Digital Project

City Engine

dge

Maya ——— Plug-ins ——— Massive ——— T-Spline ——— Real/Flow

Golaem Crowd ——— Miarmy

Rhino ——— Plug-ins ————————— Grasshopper ——— Weaverbird ——— BullAnt ——— Karamba ——— Kangaroo

shop

InDesign

Open Layers

MudBox

Pachyderm ——— Geko ——— Galapagos ——— Firefly

Google   SketchUp   GoogleEarth

GoogleMaps

GoogleMapsGL

Seemless3

Blender

Open Street Map

Generative Components

Grome

ANSYS Fluent

Aquaveo SMS

erry

Cloud Based services become available

iPod

iPhone

Data.gov USA Open Data

London Data Store GLA Open Data

The Internet of Things

Web 2.0

Arduino microcontrollers

3D printing becomes widely available

USB Memory Stick 0.0001gb

USB Memory Stick 0.008gb

Blu-Ray 25gb

Memory Card RS-MMC 16gb

SDXC 2048gb

USB 32gb (smallest)

2000'S

Second, we consider the projects featured in this book against a slowly evolving theoretical digital discourse of landscape architecture that is emerging predominantly from North America. This discourse is yet to be formalised. However, through interviews and an extensive review of literature it is possible to discern some influential voices, institutions and central theoretical framings, some of which are mentioned briefly in the following section.

In their writing, design work and teaching at the University of Pennsylvania, Karen M'Closkey and Keith VanDerSys are major advocates of a digital design practice. Systems modelling, scripting and computational design, they argue, offer techniques for engaging with dynamic systems and temporality with more accuracy and precision, closing the gap between analysis and generation. M'Closkey has said:

> What distinguishes the latest technologies from previous innovations is their total integration into all phases of design and construction. It is precisely this multiplicity of roles that has allowed technology to profoundly transform contemporary practice by altering models and standards of making.[19]

In March 2015, they hosted the 2 day research symposium Simulating Natures, an investigation of how contemporary media influences an understanding and formation of landscapes with a focus on computationally enabled imaging and models. This symposium will form the basis for a thematic issue of LA+ (Landscape Architecture Plus) an interdisciplinary design journal by PennDesign, which will be published in 2016. This will be followed by the publication of M'Closkey and VanDerSys's book Dynamic Patterns: Visualizing Landscapes in a Digital Age by Routledge in the same year.

For over a decade, Bradley Cantrell has explored the potential of computational design to landscape form and systems through his research and teaching, first at Louisiana State University's Robert Reich School of Landscape Architecture, and more recently at Harvard's GSD. His research explores techniques for engaging with complex biological systems through responsive systems across a variety of scales. Cantrell's nomination as a TED fellow in 2014 (one of the first landscape architects to achieve such recognition) demonstrates his growing influence outside the discipline. In 2016, Cantrell's book, Responsive Landscapes: Strategies for Responsive Technologies in Landscape Architecture (co-written with Justine Holzman) will be published by Routledge.

Change is also imminent in academic education. Harvard University's GSD, under the leadership of Charles Waldheim, John E. Irving Professor and Chair of the Department of Landscape Architecture has introduced a more a digitally orientated curriculum, drawing on a new generation of digitally proficient academics such as David Mah, Andrea Hansen, Zaneta Hong and Bradley Cantrell. In 2012, the GSD held the Digital Landscape Now colloquium, which brought together practitioners and academics to discuss and debate the unfolding potential of digital media to landscape architecture. Many of the invited speakers feature in this book. Antoine Picon, Professor of the History of Architecture and Technology at the GSD, offers a further valuable theoretical voice, extending his 2010 exploration into the influence of digital culture on architecture into landscape architecture.[20] His 2013 article 'Substance and Structure II: The Digital Culture of Landscape Architecture' published in the *Harvard Design Journal* highlights the potential of digital tools to accentuate and work with the dynamic and unstable forces that distinguish landscape.[21]

In Europe, Professor Christophe Girot and his academic team directed by Pia Fricker offer the Master of Advanced Studies in Landscape Architecture (MAS LA) at ETH, Zurich which integrates modelling, simulation and visualisation techniques as design and research tools for landscape architecture. This program was established in 2009 to address the low level of expertise in university graduates in applying digital tools to design and practice more generally.[22] The MAS LA is the only course available internationally which focuses entirely on a digital practice of landscape architecture.

Building on this experience, Girot advocates the use of advanced 3D modelling tools and sensor-based data to develop sophisticated site models. These possibilities are a catalyst for Girot's concept of 'landscape as topology', which advocates the return 'to a more original intelligence of terrain'.[23] Topology, states Girot, 'is about design in an age of geographic information, where one must master the available tools to meet the challenges ahead'.[24]

And, finally, the research and design studios emerging from the MArch Urban Design program at the Bartlett School of Architecture provides a valuable perspective for landscape architecture.[25] The two associated research clusters of Bio-Urban Design and Synthetic Urbanism bring together Claudia Pasquero (who with Marco Poletto is co-director of ecoLogicStudio), Enriqueta Llabres-Valls and Eduardo Rico (with their background in Relational Urbanism) to explore, experiment and reflect on the potential of computational design, digital simulation and systems prototyping for engaging with dynamic landscape processes.

Before we move into a more focused enquiry, it is useful to pause and consider some defining attributes of a digital design practice shared by disciplines crossing the built environment. At the most general level, a digital design practice presents a new language and logic of design. The design processes and workflows of a digital design practice must be explicitly controlled and curated by the designer (rather than driven by the application of a singular methodology or the assumption that the computer generates the design). Some common attributes of a digital design practice include the centrality of the digital model; the application of non-linear and relational design processes; the increased role of data, metrics and performance; the new construction potential of digital fabrication; and novel collaborative opportunities.

Defining a digital design practice

3D parametric modelling is considered a defining characteristic of a digital design practice. In parametric modelling the importance of composition or geometries is replaced by the declaration of specific parameters or rules which become foundational to design outcome. This design approach shifts the focus from form as outcome to processes of formation, emphasising relationships over composition. It also significantly alters the notion of design and construction as linear and segmented methods of analysis–concept–design development–documentation–construction. Instead the modelling process encourages iterative and recursive techniques of testing and speculation where information and form is relational and linked and the consequences of change are apparent to the designer in real time.

Robert Oxman and Rivka Oxman, in their reflection on architecture's 20 years' exploration of digital design highlight the emergence of 'a digital continuum from design to production, from form generation to fabrication design'.[26] The digital model is central to this continuum, acting as 'medium that supports a continuous logic of design thinking and making'.[27] A digital continuum bridges disciplinary and workflow delineations associated with earlier design processes such as the separation of design and construction, creativity from practicality, form and systems. This revised understanding of space has permeated all areas of design and construction, shaping surveying, design processes, documentation, fabrication and construction.

These digitally driven design processes are contextualised against a larger cultural shift known as the era of Big Data. Commenting in 2010, former Google CEO Eric Schmidt stated that 'the amount of data collected since the dawn of humanity up until 2003 is equivalent to the amount we now produce every two days'.[28] The term Big Data reflects far more than quantity, instead describing data that can be considered to be 'generated continuously, seeking to be exhaustive and fine-grained in scope, and flexible and scalable in their production'.[29] Access to such information offers disciplines different modes for understanding and constructing knowledge. New relationships, patterns and knowledge can emerge from 'mining Big Data' without the need for a prior theory, model or hypothesis. Big Data, states Rob Kitchin offers the potential to shift 'from data-scarce to data-rich studies of societies; from static snapshots to dynamic unfoldings; from coarse aggregations to high resolutions; from relatively simple models to more complex sophisticated simulations'.[30]

Increased access to data and information is paralleled by an emphasis on performance shifting the attention from what a design represents, to what a design does. Design value and efficiency are central, introducing a focus on metrics, alongside form and aesthetics. This represents far more than a quest for economic efficiency, equally reflective of pressing twenty-first-century challenges including climate change, highly urbanised societies and reduced resources. However design creativity is not sacrificed to these values. David Benjamin for example concludes that data and digital design practice structures a relationship between creativity and efficiency 'that balances their different strengths'.[31] Accordingly, designers adopt a 'work flow for exploration rather than exploitation' aiming to 'search for several novel, high-performing designs rather than searching for a single best-performing design'.[32]

In parallel, processes of digital fabrication have fundamentally revised design generation and construction. Nick Dunn observes that 'this process has facilitated a greater fluidity between design generation, development, and fabrication, than traditional approaches which necessitated a more cumulative, staged process'.[33] Within a digital fabrication process, components are developed within 3D modelling software, which are then tested in scale models (produced in a rapid prototyping process) before the development of full-scale prototypes. This ability to make components or objects directly from design information, states Dunn, is a major transformative moment for design.

And, finally, a digital design practice has altered the nature of collaboration, challenging hierarchical and disciplinary power structures and developing new relationships between designers, clients and contractors. Scripting offers a shared design language that can be understood and applied across disciplines, while BIM (Building Information Modelling) presents a new collaborative model for design, documentation and construction. The concept of open source – referring to the free and public sharing of knowledge, data or codes as opposed to the use of proprietary software – is central to these modes of collaboration, promoting the constant evolution of software, data, ideas and knowledge. Open source software (including its source code) is universally available and with further testing, refinement and development by interested parties its continuing evolution is guaranteed.

Shared across landscape architecture, urban design, architecture and engineering, these five characteristics of a digital design practice provide the conceptual framework for the following chapters in which we explore how digital technologies are applied by landscape architects in speculative and constructed projects. We hope this book encourages readers to embrace the vast potential associated with digital technologies in design and making, which are already beginning to shape and redefine a twenty-first-century landscape architecture practice.

1 Topographic surface

In this chapter we explore the potential of digital technologies for designing topography. We begin with a discussion of design explorations and theoretical writing emerging in architecture during the late twentieth century. At first glance, this might seem odd for a chapter focusing on topography. However, as will soon become apparent, the transformative moments in architecture in the 1990s, form an important foundation for understanding concepts and techniques now being adopted in landscape architecture. Throughout this chapter these new cross-disciplinary concepts will be explained and contextualised within landscape architecture. This discussion should also be considered in conjunction with the time line of ideas and technological developments featured in the Introduction.

The work of Ivan Sutherland was a major catalyst for what has become known as computer aided design (CAD). In 1963, Sutherland developed the Sketchpad computer program (also described as Robot Draftsmen) as part of his Ph.D. studies at the Massachusetts Institute of Technology (MIT). His work highlighted the potential of computer graphics to be used for both technical and design purposes, while also proposing a unique method of human–computer interaction. Importantly, Sutherland's work can be considered the first example of parametric software, a concept which will be introduced in more detail further in this chapter.[1]

Following Sutherland's influential lead, developments in CAD evolved in two key directions; first, in the ambition to develop a computer graphics system for interactive drawing, and, second, in the exploration of the computer's potential to inform methods of design more directly. In the first case, computer graphic systems were sufficiently developed to be released into industry by the early 1980s – ArchiCAD became available in 1982 (considered the first CAD product for use on a personal computer, the Apple Macintosh), followed by AutoCAD in the same year.

Topographic surface   1

These two systems were adopted as industry standards for 2D and 3D drafting and technical drawings across architecture, engineering and landscape architecture throughout the 1980s and early 1990s. However the application of computer graphic systems by most designers remained limited to the translation of established representational conventions such as plans, sections and elevations into digital files; essentially drawing through a digital means.

In contrast to simply replicating the pen with the mouse, the second approach sought to explore the computer's ability to influence design generation. This work focused initially on the concept of object-based architectural grammars and spatial allocation techniques for rationalising approaches to design, popular during the 1970s and 1980s. This emphasis on the 'computability of design' in many ways mirrored the rationale approaches proposed by GIS which was unfolding in the same period. The work of Architecture Machine Group established in 1968 at MIT, which evolved into the Media Laboratory, was significant. Director William J. Mitchell produced two seminal texts *Computer-Aided Architectural Design* in 1977 and *The Logic of Architecture: Design, Computation and Cognition* in 1990. Building on the influence of geometry in determining architectural form, Mitchell conceived of architecture as a series of formal grammars that could be modified through the application of grammatical rules.

While these early object-driven design explorations had limited application to landscape architecture, this was to alter in the 1990s when architects became interested in the potential of non-Euclidean geometries, which had first emerged in mathematics during the early nineteenth century. During this period, mathematicians developed geometric alternatives to Greek mathematician Euclid's planar and solid geometries described in his treatise *Elements*. Euclid's fifth postulate proposed 'that for any given infinite line and point off that line, there is one and only one line through that point that is parallel'.[2] The publication of elliptical (or Riemannian) geometry and hyperbolic geometry challenged this postulate, and it was the possibilities of these new geometries as 3D surfaces that captivated the imagination of architects towards the end of the twentieth century.

This interest in the new potential of continuous surface combined with the emergence of a theoretical terrain aimed at addressing the tensions inherent between the two competing ideologies of Postmodernism; that of Contextualism and Deconstructivism, inspired a transformative move towards what could be considered an architectural 'digital design practice'. The writing of French philosopher Gilles Deleuze was particularly influential. His essay 'The Fold: Leibniz and the Baroque', which was translated into English for the first time in 1992, provoked spatial possibilities for envisaging concepts of complexity and contradiction, both pivotal Postmodern framings featured prominently in the work of the Deconstructionist-inspired architects.

Peter Eisenman was one of the first to explore Deleuze's essay 'The Fold' in relationship to architecture. He was pivotal in articulating 'a new category of objects defined not by what they are, but by the way they change and by the laws that describe their continuous variation'.[3] For Eisenman, the notion of the fold offered an exciting alternative to gridded space of the Cartesian order, challenging the binary distinctions of the interior–exterior and the figure–ground. The exploration of these ideas was continued by Greg Lynn who, informed by Deleuze's definition of smoothness 'as continuous variation', proposed new ways for conceptualising spatial complexities. His essay 'Folding Architecture', published as the keynote essay of a special themed issue of *Architectural Design* (*AD*) in 1993 is considered a turning point in the history of Deconstructivism in relationship to design. Lynn defined 'smooth transformation' as 'the intensive integration of differences within a continuous yet heterogeneous system' and identified the concept's value in resolving the tensions inherent between the pursuit of Contextualism, order and composition versus Deconstructivism's alternative focus on opposition, fragmentation and disjunction.[4] Significantly, smoothness could be understood as a 'mathematical function derived from standard differential of calculus'.[5]

Technological developments in hardware and software emerging in parallel provided the opportunity for architects to explore these theoretical ideas through space and form. The application of spline (understood most simply as a line that describes a curve) modellers in architecture sourced from the aviation and automobile industry was one of the most influential advancements, offering designers faster and more intuitive means for exploring calculus-based forms. These technological advancements fundamentally altered the designer's relationship to the design process, blurring the boundary between software design and the designer through a series of new generational techniques such as parametric modelling, simulating and scripting.[6]

This moment of late twentieth-century architectural design history exemplifies the intrinsic relationship between technological opportunity and theoretical ambition, with both necessary for innovative outcome. The writings of Eisenman, Lynn, Stan Allen and Bernard Cache, together with design explorations by firms such as Foreign Office Architects and Frank Gehry offered compelling demonstrations of the potential of this theoretical terrain to inspire novel architectural form. This capacity was made possible through the innovative software and hardware developments, emerging from outside the architecture professions. Mario Carpo explains further:

> So we see how an original quest for formal continuity in archi-
> tecture, born in part as a reaction against the deconstructivist cult
> of the fracture, ran into the computer revolution of the mid-nineties
> and turned into a theory of mathematical continuity … Without this
> preexisting pursuit of continuity in architectural forms and processes,
> of which the causes must be found in cultural and societal desires,
> computers in the nineties would most likely not have inspired any new
> geometry of form.[7]

Throughout the 1990s the British journal *AD* formed a critical avenue for disseminating these design approaches and ideas (and continues to be a leading avenue for advancing a digital design practice). This period can best be summarised as a move from 'the representational as the dominant logical and operative mode of formal generation' to a focus on performative and material investigations of topological geometries.[8] Accordingly, core design concepts such as 'representation, precedent-based design and typologies' are replaced by a new interest in 'generation, animation, performance-based design and materialization'.[9]

Defining theoretical concepts

By the beginning of the new millennium, theories of architectural digital design practice were becoming more articulated, distilling into defined theoretical concepts. Frédéric Migayrou's symposium Non-Standard Architecture held at the Centre Pompidou in Paris in 2003 is recognised as a defining moment, along with the influence of discourse emerging from the Venice Architecture Biennale in 2000 and 2004.[10] The three concepts of topology, parametric design and performance emerge, and are commonly acknowledged as foundational to a digital design practice. These concepts are introduced in the following section, and will be revisited in more detail in following chapters.

Topology

The concept of *topology* has its origins in mathematics and is understood as the study of geometrical properties and spatial relations which remain unaffected by changes in size and shape. For example a topological map (as distinct from a topographic map) is a simplified diagram that may be developed without scale, but still maintains the relationship to points. The London Underground map is an example where the map remains useful despite the fact that its representation shares little resemblance to a scaled plan of the Underground.[11]

Topology therefore offers a non-geometric manner in which to conceive space premised on the geometry of position.[12] Topology departs from an understanding of space as Cartesian (where each point is identifiable by fixed coordinates) to instead embrace topological properties of space that encompass surfaces and volumes. A topological approach, often described as 'rubber sheet' geometry, evolves from the application of pressure on the outside of surfaces through modifying algorithms. The resultant surface-driven architectural forms became known as BLOB or Binary Large Objects Shapes, defined as the development of a mass without form or consistency. Within this framing 'formation precedes form' with design generation emerging through the logic of the algorithm, 'independent from formal and linguistic models of form generation'.[13] This shifts design thinking from a visual or compositional judgement to a focus on relational structures represented within codes, algorithms and scripts.

Parametric modelling

The adoption of algorithms in form making introduces a *parametric* approach to design, which is considered the dominant mode of digital design today. Algorithms define a specific process which offers sufficient detail for the instructions to be followed. They are also known as script, code, procedure or program, terms which are often used interchangeably. Similarly, parametric modelling can also be referred to as associative geometry, procedural design, flexible modelling or algorithmic design. In this book we adopt the term parametric modelling. So how is parametric modelling applied in the design of the built environment?

Traditionally, design emerges through the making and erasure of marks, which are linked together by conventions. But within parametric modelling the marks of design 'relate and change together in a coordinated way'.[14] Rob Woodbury notes that:

> No longer must designers simply add and erase. They now *add*, *erase*, *relate* and *repair*. The act of *relating* requires explicit thinking about the kind of relation: is this point *on* the line, or *near* to it. *Repairing* occurs after erasure, when the parts that depend on an erased part are related again to the parts that remain. Relating and repairing impose fundamental changes on systems and the work that is done with them.[15]

However, is this an adequate explanation? Daniel Davis for example argues that Woodbury's definition doesn't explain how the relating of marks differs from other forms of parameter driven modelling such as Building Information Modelling (which will be discussed in Chapter 5).[16] He offers an alternative definition of parametric design:

> A parametric model is unique, not because it has parameters (all design, by definition, has parameters), not because it changes (other design representations change), not because it is a tool or a style of architecture, a parametric model is unique not for what it does but rather for how it was created. A parametric model is created by a designer explicitly stating how outcomes derive from a set of parameters.[17]

From these two definitions, it can be seen that a parametric approach to design places emphasis on 'describing relationships between objects establishing interdependencies and defining transformational behaviour of these objects'.[18] In short, the importance of composition, geometries or shape is replaced in parametric design by the declaration of specific parameters or rules for a design outcome. For example parameters related to landscape architecture could encompass achieving particular ecological or spatial conditions.

However, it is not simply the selection of parameters. Davis reminds us that 'the pivotal part of a parametric equation is not the presence of parameters, but rather that these parameters relate to outcomes through explicit function'.[19] In other words, the establishment of parameters within prescribed relationships.

On one level parametric design processes are highly structured, but at the same time they also encompass a high level of uncertainty and complexity. Importantly, they do not defer design generation to the computer, which instead remains within the domain of the designer. Branko Kolarevic offers a clear articulation of this approach to design generation stating:

> The capacity of parametric computational techniques to generate new designs is highly dependent on the designer's perceptual and cognitive abilities, because continuous, transformative processes ground the emergent form (ie its discovery) in qualitative cognition. The designer essentially becomes an editor of the generative potentiality of the designed system, where the choice of emergent forms is driven largely by the designer's aesthetic and plastic sensibilities.[20]

The generative potential of parametric modelling will become clearer in later discussions of design examples.

1.2
Yokohama Port Terminal designed by Foreign Office Architecture in 1995.

Performance

The third change associated with this transformative period is *performative* design. Broadly speaking, performative design shifts attention from what a design is, to what a design does. So far, out of the concepts introduced in this chapter, performative design is the least foreign to a landscape architecture audience, evident in late twentieth-century landscape architecture discourse. For example, in his Introduction to the edited volume *Recovering Landscape: Essays in Contemporary Landscape Architecture* published in 1999, James Corner advocates for the shift 'from landscape as a product of culture to landscape as an agent producing and enriching culture'.[21] Focus moves from 'landscape as a noun (as scene or object)' to instead 'landscape as verb' (how it works and what it does).[22]

Within the context of a digital design practice, appearance and performance become increasingly blurred as digital tools increase the capacity to link analysis, generation and performance.[23] At a theoretical level, the concept of 'affect' emerges, which questions 'the separation between object and subject'.[24] Borrowing from the philosophical writings of Deleuze and Bruno Latour, digital designers explore continuity, through concepts of 'active agency', where architectural affect is produced through 'continuous interaction between subjects and objects'.[25] This thinking has evolved into performance-orientated architecture, 'based on the understanding that architectures unfold their performative capacity by being embedded in nested orders of complexity and auxiliary to numerous conditions and processes'.[26] Put

more simply, 'the building *is* its effects, and is known primarily through them, through its actions or performances'.[27]

Approaches to performance in architecture have been aided by computational techniques such as scripting and simulation that provide a more comprehensive understanding of effects and outcome. While landscape architecture has been interested in performance theoretically, its resistance to these computational techniques has until recently limited its ability to explore performance as part of design processes.

The convergence of the three concepts of topology, parametric modelling and performance is evident in a number of urban design projects constructed in the late 1990s. Of most note is the Foreign Office of Architecture's (FOA) 1995 design for the *Yokohama Port Terminal* shown in Figure 1.2, which has been acclaimed as 'one of the most meaningful architectural achievements of the digital age'.[28] FOA identify two driving ambitions for the project: first, 'an interest in the *performative* approach to material practices, in which architecture is an artefact within a concrete assemblage rather than a device for *interpreting or signifying* material and spatial organisation', and second 'the construction of a model which is capable of integrating differences into a coherent system'.[29] These agendas combined in the conceptualisation of the port terminal as:

> a mediating device between the two large social machines that make
> up the new institution: the system of public space of Yokohama and the
> cruise ship flow, reacting against the rigid segmentation usually found
> in mechanisms dedicated to maintaining borders.[30]

A continuity of surface and movement offers 'smooth connectivity' blurring the boundaries between internal and external spaces. Different segments of program operate 'throughout a continuously varied form; from local citizen to foreign visitor, from flâneur to business traveller, from voyeur to exhibitionist from performer to spectator'.[31] The folding surface provides for 'creases' that offer structural strength, 'like an origami construction', challenging the conceptual separation of load bearing structure and the building envelope.[32] Of particular interest to landscape architects is that, as noted by Stan Allen, the *Yokohama Port Terminal* 'is perhaps the most convincing realisation of an architecture invested in the idea of landscape techniques working at the scale of a building'.[33] According to Allen, the scheme 'operates almost entirely on the basis of the operative techniques of landscape design and the programmatic effects of continuous topological surfaces'.[34]

Yokohama Port Terminal, together with contemporaneous urban projects in Barcelona such as *South-East Coastal Park*, demonstrates how an exploration of topological spaces facilitated by new software led to significant architectural interest in the domain of landscape architecture, which continues today unabated. As discussed in the Preface, the architectural projects that dominate the content of the 2012 publication *Digital Landscape Architecture Now* reflect almost quarter of a century exploration of surface topology, parametric modelling and performance. The concept of landscape provided architecture with productive models of synthesis offering formal continuity, performative potential and programmatic flexibility.[35]

Importantly, these new theoretical concepts for design generation coincided with what is described as 'the Direct Manipulation Boom' in technology, which reduced the necessity for designer's to engage directly with mathematical understandings of algorithms. Increasingly software interfaces offer 'tool-like operations' which modify space and form in real-time onscreen.[36] Discovery occurs through 'manipulation rather than derivation through formulas', although the formulae remains embedded within the software.[37] The digital realm is now accessible to non-specialists, allowing surfaces to be modelled in an intuitive manner, with real-time feedback or 'applied with a geometric rationale'.[38] The development of a visual language of scripting such as Grasshopper (which emerged in 2007), further progresses the designer's ability to intuitively build scripts to generate and test form without extensive mathematical knowledge. Designers are liberated from mathematics, while at the same time form making is liberated by mathematics.

Similarly, there has been a rapid evolution of hardware capacity. Personal computers and laptops were common within the design office by the early 1990s. The Macintosh Classic for instance was released in 1990, and was the first Apple product priced below US$1000. Correspondingly, data storage has increased in size and decreased in price. In the early 1980s, 3.5 inch floppy discs held just 0.0002 GB of memory. By 1994 zip discs offered 0.098 GB, increasing to 32 GB by 2012 (courtesy of the smallest USB memory sticks), while the emergence of personal cloud computing since 2006 has radically transformed file storage and sharing.[39]

All of these changes significantly altered the designer's capacity and relationship to technology. But unquestionably, one of the most significant technological developments for landscape architecture is the evolution of 3D modelling capabilities of software from vector based techniques, well suited to the design of objects, to meshes, polygons and NURBS (non-uniform rational b-splines) which are of great value to the modelling of topography.

Modes of surface modelling

Modelling (whether virtual or physical) has not featured as prominently in the design processes of landscape architecture as in other disciplines such as architecture and industrial design. A handful of designers are well known for their use of physical clay models as form generators; notably Kathryn Gustafson and George Hargreaves. In his role as Chair of the Landscape Architecture Department at Harvard, Hargreaves introduced a clay landform workshop as a compulsory part of the curriculum. To Hargreaves the physical model is invaluable in exploring the pure form of slopes, shapes and intersections, not as a measure of how these forms work within an existing site, but rather to understand their implications.[40]

Early versions of 3D digital modelling could not match the speed or form-making abilities of physical models. Initially, modelling techniques were constrained by the limitations of vectors which formed the means for the construction of objects within digital space. Represented by lines and points that have a quantity of direction and/or force, vectors operate within a 2D or 3D coordinate system. A vector-based system offers a restricted engagement with non-Euclidean surfaces with modelling techniques limited to the functions of addition, distancing, scaling and multiplication.

The open source program SketchUp (first available in 2000) offered one of the first general purpose user-friendly 3D programs, originally known for its rectilinear and 'blocky' form-making derived from the pushing and pulling of shapes and surface vectors. The linear nature of the extrusions and spatial manipulations required the user to complete extensive small operations to generate more irregular form.

The introduction of polygons and meshes within 3D modelling programs provided a more complex and 'landscape friendly' engagement with surface. Mesh surfaces are made through the joining of polygons to form geometric units, with the density of the polygons influencing the accuracy and detail of a surface. The mesh is manipulated through the modifications of points, with the smoothness of curves and geometries a factor of the number of points and lines within a mesh. This geometric

1.3a–b
Folded landscape at the *Laban Dance Centre* designed by Herzog & de Meuron with Vogt Landschaftsarchitekten in 2003.

domain establishes controls of 'faces', 'edges' and 'vertices' as the major modes of spatial manipulation. Andrea Hansen, in her article 'From Hand to Land: Tracing Procedural Artifacts in the Built Environment', highlights a number of constructed landforms, predominantly among 'architect-designed landscape projects', which read as faceted surfaces reflective of their form generation within a triangulated mesh modelling program. These include FOA's *La Gavia Park* and the design of *Laban Dance Centre* by Herzog & de Meuron and Vogt Landschaftsarchitekten, as shown in Figure 1.3.[41]

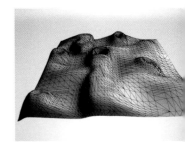

The introduction of NURBS (non-uniform rational B-spline) significantly increased the ability to work with both standard and free-form geometries. These curves and surfaces first emerged in the 1950s as engineers sought more precision in 'the description of free-form surfaces such as ships' hulls and car bodies'.[42] Pierre Bézier who worked for Renault, was influential in the development of the algorithms of uniform non-rationale B-splines, recognised in their alternative name of Bézier splines. Returning to the earlier reference of 'rubber sheet geometry', curvilinear topological surfaces can be described as NURBS. These afford the designer a high degree of control through the manipulation of weights, knots and control points. In a very few steps, designers can weight, fix or manipulate these control points, offering speed and precision in creating and understanding complex geometries in a systematic and linked manner.[43] NURBS state Antoine Picon 'are emblematic of the creative space opened up by modelling', allowing designers to interact with curves, spaces and volumes in a 'highly intuitive way'.[44]

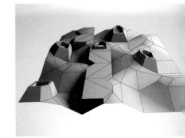

It is generally considered that polygon modelling best suits defined hard-edged objects while NURBS are more useful for curved smooth forms. However, this depends very much on which program is being used. For example the Autodesk program Maya has an extensive range of polygon editing tools alongside powerful NURBS tools.[45] In comparison to NURBS, polygon modelling offers a reduced description of a surface, which often sees designers working faster and more intuitively with polygon surfaces, before transferring their designs into NURBS modelling programs such as Robert McNeel & Associates' software Rhinoceros (known popularly by the shorter term Rhino) to produce a more detailed model. A NURBS model also offers a slower real-time speed of interaction when compared to polygon modelling.

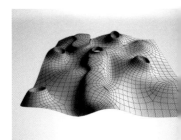

1.4a–c
Three different modelling surfaces: (a) NURBS, (b) polygons and (c) subdivision.

Sitting between NURBS and polygons are hybrid tools of subdivision that permit the merging of mesh and NURBS characteristics within the same model (Figure 1.4). Subdivision tools allow designers to use polygons for speed of modelling and to develop accurate locations for important points within a design, with NURBS then applied to add detail and 'smooth' out interstitial spaces between the polygon entities.

Some programs such as Maya have inbuilt parametric capabilities, while others such as Rhino require plug-ins like Grasshopper to perform in more parametric ways. Parametric capability (which will be discussed in far more detail in Chapter 2) includes the precise recording of command history, which offers the designer the ability to alter defined parameters. As software programs continue to evolve, this brings new capabilities and refinements to designers. Increasingly software is becoming similar, although with varying degrees of complexities. SketchUp for example is now available with a NURBS plug-in.

For a new generation of landscape architects trained within a 3D context, the digital realm offers a design platform as intuitive, creative and explorative as the clay models favoured by earlier generations. Further, the development of laser cutters, CNC routers and 3D printing and scanning hardware reverse more traditional information and production flows introducing 'dual directional' design processes.[46] Designers can transform a physical model into a digital model and vice versa, which encourages continued and faster design explorations. The cost of these fabrication techniques has also reduced significantly over the past 5 years, encouraging their application within design processes, as distinct from being used only as final presentation models. For example it is now possible to buy small CNC routers and 3D printers for less than US$1000, allowing them to be relocated from workshops and Fab labs, to be positioned directly next to the designer's desk.

In a process not too dissimilar to traditional modes of model making, a laser cut model is made through the cutting of components from a sheet, which is then manually assembled into a 3D model. Computer Numerically Controlled (CNC) milling and routing introduces a particularly valuable process for landscape architecture, replacing stepped laser cut models (which emphasise the contour rather than the slope which is referenced by the contour) with a continuous surface which offers a more accurate understanding of topography and land form. CNC milling works through the removal of material from a volume in a process similar to carving from a block. This highly accurate and detailed process is particularly useful for flatter landscapes which are difficult to understand and represent within standard analogue representational techniques such as sections and plans. In analogue sections and stepped contour model, it is not uncommon for landscape architects to exaggerate landform in order 'to see' topographic form. However the accuracy and detail of the CNC routed model offers an excellent representation of subtle surface manipulations, down to the level of a surface inscription. As shown in Figure 1.5, topography as represented in laser cut models is still influenced by the depth of material used to layer the model. This is no longer a factor within the CNC model where attention is focused on the qualities of the slope rather the exaggeration of the contour.

A 3D printer which uses a modified inkjet print head with a hardener produces a similar result. The form builds as the printer passes in successive runs, adding material in layers. This additive process produces less waste than the reductive process of CNC milling. Models are generally small. However more recently, architects have begun to explore 3D printing for fabrication. For instance, in early 2013, Dutch architecture studio Universe Architecture announced their ambition to 3D print an entire house using sections ranging up to 6 x 9 metres.[47]

Tangible User Interfaces offers a further example of digital model production. Since the early 2000s the Tangible Media Group at the MIT Media Lab has

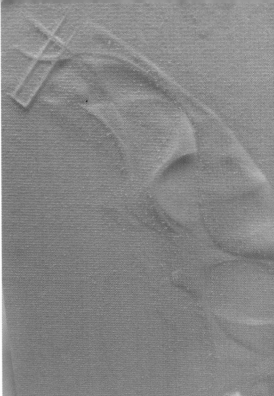

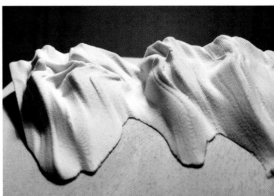

been exploring the intersection of haptic (tactile feedback) and digital modelling. Illuminating Clay (2002) followed by Sandscape (2003) combine 'dynamic sculpting and computational analysis using digitally augmented continuous physical materials'.[48] More recent software developments allow such explorations to occur with minimal cost. Conventional sand for example can be used with a Kinect scanner (developed by Microsoft as part of their Xbox game console) and customised software to establish an interface between physical modelling and a digital elevation model.[49]

This brief introduction to the evolution of 3D modelling software and associated fabrication technologies highlights the transition from vector-driven models to meshes and NURBS. In the second part of this chapter we turn our attention away from architecture to focus on contemporary landscape architecture

1.5a–c
Digitally produced
topographic models with
different level of surface
refinement: (a) stepped
terrain of the laser cut model,
(b) the smooth slopes of
a CNC routed model and
(c) a detailed 3D printed
model.

1.6a–b
Workshop laboratory at ETH
Zurich: each modelling station
consists of a sandbox, a 3D
scanner and a computer with
display monitor. Students use
the sandbox set-up during the
design process for modelling
conceptual ideas and for
presenting their design.

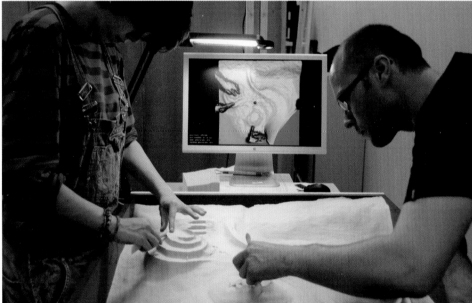

practice to explore their application of 3D modelling techniques primarily in the design of topography. Here we begin to see some disciplinary differences in the manner in which landscape architects engage with concepts of performance, topology and parametric modelling. To landscape architecture, topology represents far more than an abstract surface or a mathematical construct. Christophe Girot in his landscape-driven definition of topology identifies a three-tiered approach encompassing structure (geomorphological and infrastructural), surface (cultural organisation and production) and atmosphere (immaterial aspects).[50] As we will explore in the following section, landscape architecture's engagement with sites positioned within a cultural and ecological continuum in constant flux creates different opportunities and potential for parametric modelling.

Generative topography

As we outlined in the Introduction, landscape architecture has been reluctant to shift from the familiarity of the 2D plan into the design potential of 3D modelling. Girot comments on landscape architecture's considerable complacency in regard to representational techniques stating 'we are apparently content with a status quo that has prevailed in landscape architecture over the last forty years'.[51] For example, *Visualising Landscape Architecture*, although published in 2010, continues to champion the 2D plan as the major design representation to 'provide a basis for all further representations of the design ideas'.[52] Writing in 2008, Peter Walker observes the privileging of 'the horizontal dimensions of landscape' over the vertical, commenting that many landscape architects consider the plan 'sufficient to represent spatial relationships, grading and layout, and the disposition of plant materials'.[53]

The continuing primacy of the plan view is surprising, given that understanding topography (a distinguishing feature of landscape architecture) within 2D is particularly challenging. Not only is the plan a highly abstracted mode of representation requiring spatial literacy to interpret the information as 3D space but the aerial perspective creates considerable distance between the spatial configuration and experiential quality of the design. This is even more evident when it comes to the use of contours to represent 3D landforms, which only enables 'a trained eye to visualize the shaping of the land'.[54]

This limited use of 3D digital modelling in the discipline of landscape architecture has meant that many design firms interviewed as part of this research prefer graduates who have dual qualifications in architecture and landscape architecture. The architectural background, comments Snøhetta's director Jenny B. Osuldsen, equips graduates with a stronger understanding of 3D space.[55] Encouragingly, this weakness in landscape architecture is changing as more and more landscape architecture courses incorporate 3D modelling within their curriculum. However, to be most effective, this shift in teaching requires a more fundamental revision of design curriculum than simply 'adding' digital tools to existing representational courses.

Landscape curriculum conventionally separates design studios, technical knowledge (grading and engineering) and graphic communication. Often the introduction of digital technologies occurs within the graphic communication courses, presented as an extension of 2D representational techniques. But as Brian Osborn from the University of Virginia comments, this isolation of digital technologies from design studios makes it difficult for students 'to make meaningful connections between digital media courses and the other course work'.[56] Without direct engagement, students find it difficult to apply their new knowledge and techniques to design, which further limits their ability to discover new applications for the software on their own during the design process.[57] Significantly, this separation fundamentally disrupts the potential of 'a continuous logic of design thinking and making', which, as we discussed in the Introduction, forms a critical characteristic of a digital design practice.[58] Throughout this book, we offer guidance on how to best introduce and situate digital technologies within pedagogy to maximise its potential as a design tool. These ideas are informed by a close analysis of how digital tools alter workflows, design approaches and construction processes, combined with observations from academics experienced in this teaching.

In the following section we introduce two ways that practices have engaged with digital 3D modelling. As examples, we begin with the precise topological surface of LAAC's *Eduard-Wallnöfer-Platz* followed by PARKKIM's scheme *Mud Infrastructure*, which engages land form and dynamic water systems. Within these schemes, 3D modelling helps the designer to visualise and generate complex surfaces and forms. While producing novel and interesting form, strictly speaking these modelling approaches are not considered computational design. This difference becomes clearer through the discussion of the latter examples – ASPECT Studios' design of the *Victorian Desalination Plant* and Snøhetta's scheme for *MAX Lab IV*. Here the digital model assumes a very different role, reflective of a computational approach. The model is more formational than representational with the designers applying a rule-based parametric design approach.

Precise geometries

1.7
Landhausplatz, Innsbruck's largest public square prior to the transformation. In the foreground: the liberation monument.

In 2008, the Austrian design firm LAAC won an invited multi-stage design competition for *Eduard-Wallnöfer-Platz* (also known as *Landhausplatz*) for the largest public square in Innsbruck, Austria. Over time this site (Figure 1.7) had evolved into two disparate spaces: a small flat grass parkland fragmented by a series of memorials sited along a central axis and a car park which operated as a forecourt to the Tyrolean provincial governmental building. In a further complexity, a subterranean garage was constructed under 80 per cent of the space. The new square needed to address the conflicting language and meaning of the monuments, in addition to developing a social space for a square that had no active edges.

LAAC proposed a bold sculptural topographic form, with the ambition to 'use new geometries in new ways'.[59] No community consultation was undertaken, with the designers instead believing that innovative form would 'influence people and their use'.[60] Inspired by the metaphysical painter Giorgio de Chirico's reflections on power and freedom, particularly *Place de Italia* (1913), the designers also looked to the potential of shadow and light to develop a complex surface, which positioned the user as a 'protagonist on a stage'.[61]

The competition entry was developed using Maya software, permitting the designers to work quickly and intuitively to explore multiple iterations of the surface. The 3D

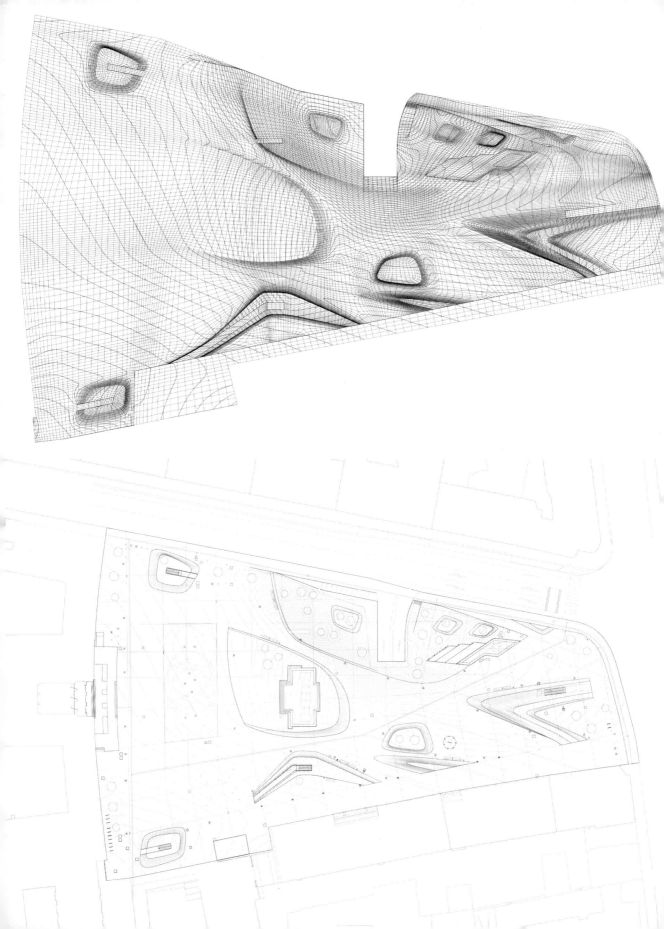

1.8a–b
LAAC's 3D modelling process: The scheme was initially designed using Maya software (a) then further refined in Rhino and developed into documentation using AutoCAD (b).

1.9a–b
Unidirectional lighting at night produces a uniform bath of light, without delineating a set path. The decision to not light the façade of the government building further reinforces the primacy of the topographic surface at the front of the government building.

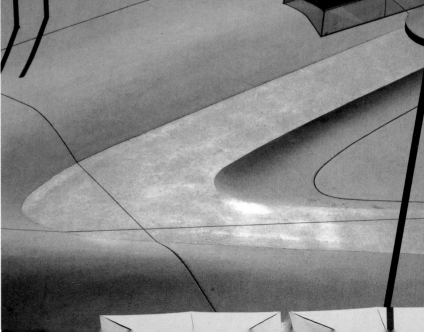

1.10a
The new surface transforms the base of the large memorial into a continuous surface that sweeps over the top of the car park entrance and into a flat multi-functional area featuring a large fountain in summer.

1.10b–c
The ambition to develop a transformative topography extends throughout the detailing, apparent in the subtle changes of concrete texture to reflect different performance parameters offering places for people to sit, skate and walk.

model offered a clear articulation of form, including the ability to understand light and shadow. The subdivision tool was used to create denser polygon meshes on the chiselled edges of the forms, while maintaining smooth NURBS surfaces in other areas. After winning the competition, the design was further evolved using Rhino. Working with more detailed site data from the surveyor, a higher level of accuracy was introduced into the curves, junctions and tangents that comprised the complex surface. The Rhino model was eventually taken into AutoCAD to produce the sections and details required for construction.

The modelling process aided the designers in conceiving a continuous surface which operates as a tactic for engaging with the ambiguous language and meanings of the existing memorials, particularly the large central memorial constructed by the French military government (as occupying power) at the end of the Second World War (1946–8). Conceived in recognition of the people who lost their lives in fighting for the liberation from National Socialism, the memorial's design problematically replicates the fascist language of the Tyrolean provincial governmental building.

Topographic surface

LAAC's approach exemplifies the concept of Lynn's 'smooth transformation', discussed earlier in the chapter.[62] This continuous topological terrain offers a 'contemporary and transformative base for the memorials',[63] dislodging them from their central axis and defusing the symbolism of the main monument by absorbing part of its stairs into the topographic surface. This spatial move disrupts the fascist highly symmetrical design language while creating more prominence for the other memorials found on the site, including the menorah that references the murder of four Jewish citizens of Innsbruck during Kristallnacht.[64]

Initial reactions to the constructed square were tentative, with many older residents dismayed by the absence of grass.[65] Very quickly the potential of the new geometries were recognised by the skating community, locally and internationally. Their enthusiastic use of the square however raised issues concerning liability. In 2011, the Free *Landhausplatz* site was established on Facebook, in response to potential threats to ban skating. This lobby resulted in two shifts. First, the square's reclassification from a public square to the status of 'street without cars' which shifted liability to the user, and, second, a negotiation with skaters to develop a 'behaviour codex'. This codex establishes the square as 'a place for urban encounters and not a skate park' and aims to 'find compromise and not prohibition' to allow all uses in cooperation.[66] This agreement includes not skating on sensitive areas such as the front of the government building and the top of the memorials. The success of this negotiation is reflected in the following statement from the Free *Landhausplatz* site: 'let's do everything together to get the *Landhausplatz* as a central meeting place where everyone can do anything, as long as it does not harm anyone else'.[67]

The intent to promote new use through innovative geometries inspired a more profound renegotiation of civic space, including the revision of regulations and acknowledgement of civic responsibilities, which perhaps would not have occurred if the designers had undertaken a more predictable community consultation process. Invariably these processes edit out possibilities and innovation leading to a compromised position after all interested parties assert their, often polarised, views. Alternatively, aided by the considerable form-making capability of 3D modelling, and influenced by theoretical concepts of topology and performance, the designers produced a novel form that not only instigated change but also heightened the ambition for public space.

LAAC's interest in performative topological surfaces can be further expanded to incorporate considerations of ecological performance in the landscape. It is generally understood that water management is one of the most dominant rationales for topographic manipulation in landscape architecture. In the following example, we explore how the South Korean-based design firm PARKKIM combines 3D modelling with dynamic hydrological processes to develop their scheme *Mud Infrastructure*.

Landform systems

This project is the winning proposal in a 2009 design competition for a 2km long and 100m wide park in the Yanghwa area of the Han River. Initiated by former mayor Oh Sehoon as part of the second phase in the Han River Renaissance, the competition aimed to revitalise the river's embankment system into a new public park. Under Oh Sehoon's leadership Seoul heavily invested in citywide design-led urban regeneration processes, unprecedented in the Asian context. In this aspect, the Han River Renaissance project is the first of its kind in South Korea to allow landscape architects to conceptually lead the renewal of a major infrastructure as opposed to the engineering-focused solutions that dominated the city's development until well into the 1990s.

While this was a great opportunity for the profession, most competition proposals merely resurfaced the existing levee and introduced new circulation routes. In contrast, PARKKIM embraced the challenges by reconceiving the new park as *Mud Infrastructure* – a responsive infrastructure that facilitates use even during the time of flooding. The project embedded hydrological principles that would allow the project to operate at any time during the year, while also addressing the massive amount of sediments deposited after the floods.

1.11a–b
Initial topographic explorations of path and slope gradients conducted in Rhino.

1.12
Mud Infrastructure reconceptualises the river's edge from highly engineered concrete levees into a dynamic landscape.

The site was challenging. The Han River is 1 kilometre wide as it runs through the centre of Seoul and is notorious for its dynamic hydrology and destructive floods that have profoundly shaped the city for centuries. Influenced by both daily tidal changes and high precipitation during the yearly monsoon season, the conditions change the river from shallow waters with extensive mudflats to deep and dangerous currents in early summer. This condition is amplified by the extreme concentration of slit and grit deposits, built-up from soil erosion in the mountainous areas further upstream, resulting in extensive costs for cleaning infrastructure along the river including parking lots, paths and highways. For instance, after the flood in 1990 sediments of between 0.1 and 1.5m deep covered most of the flood plain, requiring cleaning costs of approximately US$7 million.[68]

Addressing the existing levee structure that dominates the entire embankment along both sides of the river was a major issue for the design. Introduced in the 1960s to mitigate the destructive floods that would destroy vast areas of the historical city to the north, as well as threatening new residential developments to the south, the levees were constructed as a massive concrete infrastructure consisting of three terraces. Each terrace level contains a maintenance path that runs parallel to the river and is separated by a steep concreted slope. While the structure is partially

1.13–14
Mud Infrastructure inundated by flooding in early summer and covered in winter snow. Note that the path system remains usable during the floods.

successful in controlling floods, its linear and even slopes heavily facilitate the accumulation of deposits. Thus, PARKKIM's proposal challenges the existing layout by forming a new topographic surface that engages with the hydrological dynamics and sedimentation processes. Similar to LAAC's scheme for *Landhausplatz*, 3D modelling played a central role in creating a continuous geometry that offers a seamless flow line from the lowest water level to the higher embankments.

Driven by the three considerations of sedimentation, program and circulation, the designers reconstructed the new surface as a series of slopes with a variety of lengths and inclinations ranging between 4 and 13 per cent. A pathway system graded to a maximum slope of 5 per cent was designed to intersect these slopes and provide barrier-free access to the entire park. The shallow slopes not only support better accessibility and circulation in the park but are conceived to be beneficial in removing excessive sedimentation built up after storms. Achieving a smooth overall surface required careful cut-and-fill operations, as extending the terraces out beyond the existing shoreline was deemed unfeasible.

These basic grading principles were first laid out in plan before being translated into Rhino to construct and test the entire landform in 3D. Although a relatively small practice, PARKKIM is very accepting of the potential of a 3D modelling program such as Rhino as a primary design tool to test and refine ideas. They consider the adoption of digital technologies as a necessary step in elevating their practice to an international level. These tests allowed the designers to control the modulation of the edge condition to respond to the fluctuations in water levels. A series of landforms which would encourage the formation of eddies were introduced to increase water circulation during a flood event, thereby preventing the build-up of sedimentation. In other parts the reconstruction of the concrete edge with a 'new riprap shoreline actively encourages sedimentation to build up new habitats for fish and birds'.[69] The new landform profiles subsequently define the program development and divide the park into various activation zones including a plateau, a riverine theatre overlooking the river and adjacent Seonyu Island, and wild hills with diverse undulating topography which form the entrance into the ecological area.

Initially only conceived as schematic design, the landform further evolved after the competition following consultation with a hydraulical engineer, who advised that the eddies be further exaggerated and the irregularity of the shoreline increased. The engineer was also required during documentation to testify that the proposed tree clusters would not have an adverse impact on the water flow and the river system. During this phase, the Rhino model was taken into AutoCAD for further detailing of the contour plan and to develop documentation drawings.

Although more advanced digital techniques would have allowed the designers to engage with the potential of parametric design and the simulation of these highly complex and dynamic environmental systems, *Mud Infrastructure* was not designed to accurately reflect the dynamic flow conditions, mainly because the yearly water and velocity levels were considered too unpredictable to produce reliable data.

However, since its completion in 2011 the park has been inundated multiple times and has already proved to be successful in preventing excessive sedimentation while also providing secure access to the park during the flood events as seen in Figures 1.13–14.

To some extent PARKKIM's design process resembles a basic approach to 3D modelling, where an initial design concept is explored, tested and refined within a 3D realm. This differs from LAAC's engagement, where the digital model assumes the primary mode for exploring and generating form. The manner in which PARKKIM currently operates, employing graduates proficient in digital techniques, to complement and extend the abilities of the two directors, is common in many landscape architecture firms. These design processes are reflective of a discipline in transition, positioned between a new generation increasingly comfortable with designing directly within 3D space and an earlier generation more familiar with analogue techniques or physical modelling. For example the celebrated landforms of the northern park at the London Olympics site were initially designed by Hargreaves Associates and LDA Design using physical clay models which were then explored in more detail through 3D Rhino models.

In the final part of this chapter, we move from the discussion of a digital model as a technique for exploring, generating and testing topographic form, to a rule based approach that fundamentally introduces a new logic to a design process through the potential of computational design.

Rule-based topography

Parametric modelling or a 'rule-based' approach to design is still quite rare within landscape architecture design practice and teaching. Interviewed practitioners and academics struggled to nominate examples of built projects generated through parametric modelling, beyond the design of components such as paving. In this chapter's final examples, we introduce two parametric approaches to topographic form making applied to the design of infrastructural landscapes. These complex large-scale schemes, which require designers to address specific parameters such as balancing cut and fill and the consideration of visual, hydrological and ecological implications, provide perfect scenarios in which to apply a rule-based approach to design. The first example by Australian firm ASPECT Studios applies what we define as a conceptual parametric approach in their design of the *Victorian Desalination Plant*, while the second example by Snøhetta demonstrates a more precise rule-based approach in their design of the *MAX Lab IV* in Sweden.

Before beginning this discussion, it is useful to consider how a rule-based approach to design is approached in the landscape architecture curriculum. There is much academic debate within architecture and landscape architecture concerning when and how to introduce parametric design (including the ability to script or code) to students. This design approach requires a particular type of abstract

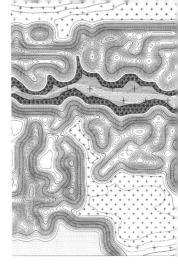

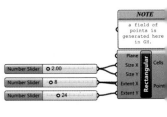

1.15a–c
The land form *Wash* presented in plan and final model, together with a Grasshopper definition used as part of the form generation.

Topographic surface

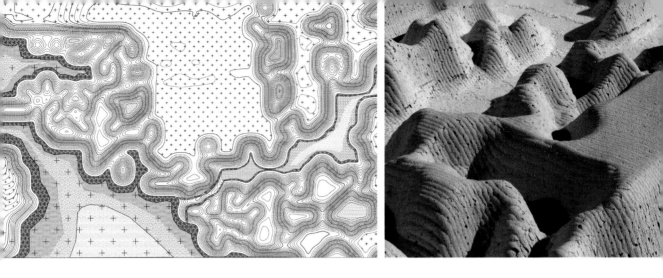

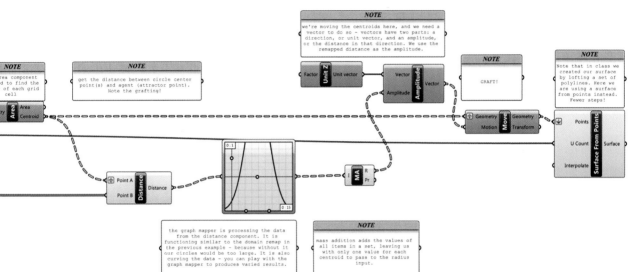

procedural thinking that is new to design education. The few landscape architecture courses that do introduce these concepts, do so in later years, instead focusing on 3D modelling such as Rhino (without a parametric emphasis) in the earlier years. However, in the University of Virginia's landscape architecture master's program Brian Osborn introduces a rule-based approach to topographic form generation as part of the very first foundational studio.[70] In this studio, students begin with investigations of the characteristics and meaning of common landform typologies such as the hill, valley, ridge, cave, swale, scarp and hoist. Students explore how these physical forms are influenced by factors and processes including geology, geomorphology, hydrology, erosion and vegetation, along with investigations of their spiritual and symbolic significance. This work is presented through topographic plans, sections, laser cut models as well as written cultural analysis. The second phase requires the application of the knowledge or 'rules' gained from students' typological studies, considered through procedural (another term for parametric) modelling, using the Grasshopper plug-in with Rhino (Figure 1.15). Students are

Topographic surface

encouraged 'to play' through the choreographing or scripting of new landforms that respond to the rules that they have uncovered. In the final stage, students use CNC milling to produce a 3D model which is used as a mould to cast final models.

Returning to earlier definitions of a parametric approach to design, we can see how this sequence of exercises explores the 'transformational behaviour' of land form, moving from the conceptualisation of shape (for example hill or valley) into an understanding of the rules which establish these topographic formations. Osborn considers a rule-based approach to topographic form a highly relevant development for landscape architecture, establishing links between form, forces and performance. He states:

> Digital techniques prompt a shift from the modelling of form to the modelling of behaviours and interactions – where landscape form is the iterative mixing of material tendencies and variable design inputs. In the context of teaching, I like that this prioritises a rule-based approach to design and one that is dependent on the interaction between form and the forces acting on it. Digital techniques encourage students to think of the landscape in if/then conditionals. If wind gusts from this direction, then debris and sediment will accumulate in this way. Because we can also think of the landscape, and ecology, in terms of sets of behaviours and interactions, parametric software becomes an ideal tool for working with landscape media.[71]

How then does an emphasis on formation rather than composition manifest in a complex design process for a built work, which requires an engagement with multiple, and at times conflicting, design parameters? Australian firm ASPECT Studios' design approach for the *Victorian Desalination Project* demonstrates the merit of a parametric process in the development of one of the largest and most complex infrastructural works in Australia.

Conceptual parametrics

The *Victorian Desalination Project* was conceived as a public service to provide a secure water supply to the Melbourne metropolitan region in response to climate uncertainty and challenges of decreasing precipitation. It was designed to produce up to 150 gigalitres (GL) of water a year, with the potential to extend to 200 GL. At the time of its design, it was considered the 'largest public sector investment in water infrastructure in Australia' and 'the world's largest Public Private Partnership (PPP)' with a contracted capital cost of AU$3.5 billion in 2009.[72]

Constructed in a scenic coastal environment in south-eastern Australia (Figure 1.16), popular with tourists, development of the desalination plant resulted in debate concerning its scale and cost. To diminish the environmental impact, the competitive tender process included strict evaluation criteria, including the

1.16
The *Victorian Desalination Project* was envisaged as a 'green and climate change conscious' infrastructural project that includes extensive revegetation in the 225 hectare coastal park and construction of the largest green roof in the southern hemisphere.

1.17
The Maya model operated within engineering, architectural, and landscape constraints and allowed the designers to manage what the landscape architects described as the 'tyranny of scale'.

mitigation of visual intrusion and noise; protection of the coastal and marine environment and the recreational values of the adjacent coastal reserve; and the maintenance of 'the highest level of health, safety and aesthetics throughout the delivery and operation of the Project'.[73]

The integration of the infrastructure with the surrounding landscape, including a vast infrastructural plant measuring over 20,000 square metres, was central to the success of the winning bid led by an international consortium of engineers and architects, including the Melbourne-based landscape architects ASPECT Studios. Within this process, the visual impact of the scheme did not form the dominant design parameter, instead offering just one of many criteria that the designers responded to. Unlike many design approaches that seek to visually hide or mask the presence of infrastructure within visually and ecological sensitive sites, this project aims to integrate the project within this unique environment by extending the dunal landscape and conceiving the site as a landscape experience. Thus, the topographic form of the *Victorian Desalination Project* is conceived by the designers as a spatial experience in its own right, emerging as 'playful and really interesting … not just a boring and pragmatic thing'.[74]

ASPECT Studios played a pivotal role in negotiating the integration of the architectural and engineering agendas with the complexity of existing topography, ecology, drainage lines and visual implications. Developing their own 3D model in Maya (Figure 1.18) based on terrain information provided by the civil engineers, offered the essential overview for understanding how all of the components related to each other. As will be discussed in more detail in Chapter 5, this model was the only representation that could communicate the entirety of the project to the client, and also informed the development of BIM documentation.

As a parametric software, Maya provides history-based modelling which includes the precise recording of command history. This permits the designer to

1.18a–c
Testing iterations. The relationship between architectural infrastructure, landform and visual experience was tested from selected geo-referenced locations up to 10km away. The aim was to reveal at certain locations the green roof of the architecture (and not the infrastructural plant) without compromising the visual and spatial integrity of the topography.

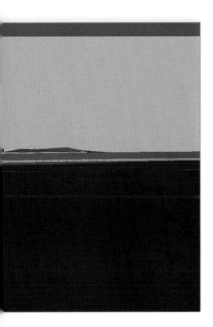
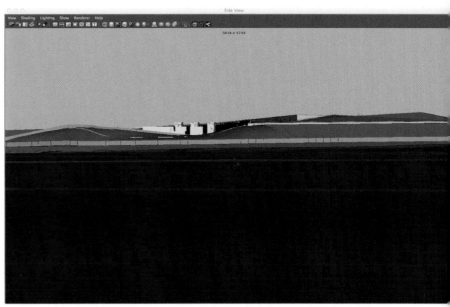

set and change parameters within a non-linear design process to quickly work through multiple iterations with real-time feedback. As already discussed in relation to LAAC's design for *Landhausplatz*, Maya's polygon surfacing tools offers the designers fast generative modelling of topographic form. The software's origin in the animation and film industry introduces other useful digital tools, including the setting up of animations to document the development and experience of design iterations. The designer's intent to develop a multifunctional landscape, combined with the versatility of Maya software led to a design process that mixes intuitive exploration of form with a rule based design approach which we define as a 'conceptual' example of parametric modelling.

In detail, ASPECT Studios were working with two defining constraints: first, the navigation of the visual experience and blending of the infrastructure with surrounding conditions from set locations, defined by the client. And, second, a careful management of cut-and-fill volumes, which the engineering firm, as lead consultants, had committed to during the tender phase and which was considered essential to maintain from a cost control perspective.[75]

Importantly, the model allowed the designers to work concurrently across multiple scales; testing the impact of their proposals from accurately located GPS points, while also understanding the experience of space at a more immediate level. The landscape model provided the ability to interrogate the intersection of the architectural form and the surrounding topography to a high level of detail. Within conventional representational methods which rely on multiple sections and 2D contours, these 'very fine movements' would be extremely difficult to comprehend.[76] The screen shots shown in Figure 1.18 highlight the advantages of the Maya model to the designer in visualising and understanding the complex relationship between architecture, infrastructure and landform. Working side by

side, architects and landscape architects could design directly within the landscape model, understanding in real time the ramifications of design decisions.

The Maya model proved invaluable in developing an iterative work flow, allowing the designers to work through multiple possibilities while simultaneously understanding the implications of their design on cut-and-fill volumes. Parametric drivers (such as gradient and slope sequence) were established on top of the rough mounds provided by the civil engineers. Form could then be manipulated and tested through the pushing and pulling of points. For example a tool extension scripted in Maya's embedded language MEL, provided immediate visual clues whenever slope gradients exceeded the set values. An additional command established in Maya permitted the landscape architects to run 'cubic metre volume calculations' alongside their topographic modelling explorations.[77] While not calculated in real time, this process, states designer Jesse Sago, 'was as close as possible to obtaining a real time review with the existing technology'.[78]

Revisiting Osborn's earlier quote on 'if/then conditions' which emphasises landscape form as the iterative mixing of material tendencies and variable design inputs, we can see that through the introduction of parametric components into the modelling process, the designers could develop more complexity and accuracy in conceiving the experience and performance of the topography. This modelling process provided ASPECT Studios with enormous confidence in responding to the parameters established by the engineers, in addition to the ability 'to spit out

1.19a–b
Balancing the extensive cut and fill generated by the infrastructure was a critical design parameter. The engineers provided calculations of fill, recommended locations for earth mounds, together with prescribed heights (and at times side profiles) to which the landscape architects responded. The landscape architects could still move the tops and crown lines to explore different configurations in line with design criteria. The proposed dunal forms in this scene are designed to blend into one continuous dune and are colour coded to test their form and alignment from a range of scales and perspectives.

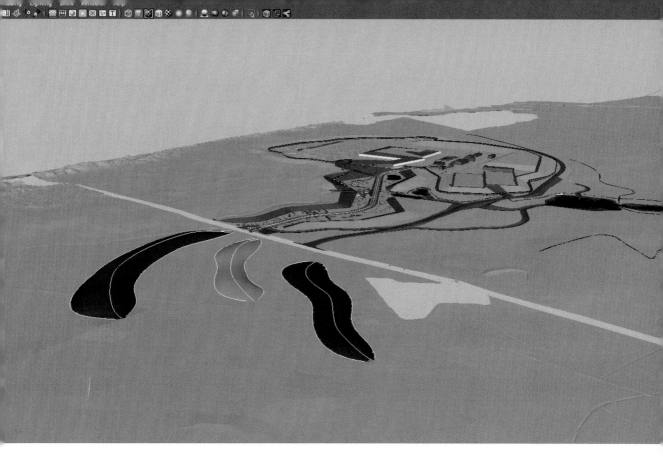

fast visualisations to the people who had to approve their work'.[79] Most importantly, it provided the landscape architects with a detailed understanding of what they had produced, 'as every bit has a purpose worked out in 3D'.[80] The ability to understand and manipulate the intent of the topographic landform fundamentally shifts the landscape architect's position within a large-scale infrastructural project. The landscape architects are now integral to the design itself, no longer limited to screening infrastructure (predominantly through vegetation) after all the major design decisions are completed.

The design process also offers a very different mode of interactivity between the designer and the media to that experienced in 'paper-based' interactions. Whereas a designer interacts directly with the shapes and forms drawn on paper, within a digital design process the designer 'interacts with, controls and moderates generative and performative processes and mechanisms'.[81] As the landscape architects observe, this process 'fundamentally changes the way that designers play with the forms they are working with shifting the way they see them, experience them and think about them'.[82]

In the following section we continue the discussion of the potential of parametric modelling to the design of topography through an examination of Snøhetta's scheme for *MAX Lab IV* in Sweden. As we established earlier, there are very few examples of constructed landscape architecture projects that have been generated through parametric modelling. Snøhetta identified that the particular challenges presented by the *MAX Lab IV* project – the use of topographic manipulation as a design strategy to support the dispersal of surface vibrations – offered the perfect opportunity to explore a rules-based design approach. The *MAX Lab IV* project therefore forms an extremely important precedent in understanding an emerging digital design practice of landscape architecture and consequently we offer a detailed analysis of their design process and reflections.

Rule-based parametrics

The MAX (Microtron Accelerator for X-Rays) Lab IV is a new facility for synchrotron radiation-based research at the University of Lund in southern Sweden. The project is developed in collaboration between the University and the Swedish Research Council and upon completion in 2015 will provide the brightest source of synchrotron light in the world. Constructed on a 19 hectare greenfield site just north-east of Lund, the lab consists of two storage rings, a linear accelerator, office buildings and surrounding landscape. In order to achieve the precision and high quality of light in the synchrotron, one of the major challenges of this project was to create a stable atmospheric environment that controls vibrations, temperature and humidity.

The design of this highly specialised facility began with a design competition in 2010 that asked four shortlisted entrants (3xN, FOJAB, Grimshaw and Snøhetta) to develop design schemes for both the architecture and landscape. The project was given to the Swedish architects FOJAB who commenced design development by the end of 2010. But while each of the shortlisted teams addressed both the architectural and landscape requirements, the jury remained undecided on the winner and eventually invited Snøhetta landscape architects to collaborate with FOJAB architects (although without a clear agenda on how the two offices would work together at such a late stage). When Snøhetta started their designs in January 2011, it was already decided that construction

1.20
Screen shots from an animation used to test the experience of the proposed dunes for the *Victorian Desalination Plant* (from the road).

would commence in April, leaving them only 4 months to develop their design from concept to construction. For a project of such high stakes, this constitutes a remarkable and challenging condition in regard to collaboration and the incorporation of necessary specialised expertise.

Both teams considered it unfeasible to simply merge the two competition entries together, leading Snøhetta to establish a new design approach to the landscape. While the team originally started the new design with conventional landscape architectural considerations such as balancing cut-and-fill volumes and storm water management it soon became clear that the mitigation of surface vibration that had been discovered and researched in detail only a year before the project started, would provide the most valuable constraint to push the design forward into new territories.

Working with sensitive equipment and procedures that require utmost stability in atmospheric and spatial conditions, it was feared that the nearby motorway E22, located fewer than 100 metres to the west of the site, and a local road to the east, could negatively interfere with the magnets in the storage rings and the beamlines. Simulations had demonstrated that very small irregularities in the road's surface produced by twigs, stones and ice had the potential to disrupt the workings of the facility.[83] In addition to these hard-to-control external factors 'new emerging technical possibilities' would place further demands on the facility in regard to the accepted tolerance in atmospheric interferences.[84] Needless to say, the architecture would contribute a major role in controlling the vibrations through various material and construction techniques in a manner that would conceive that 'the building is a part of the machine'.[85] But there were unavoidable challenges and limitations as to what the architecture could achieve as the Detail Design Report outlined:

> Isolating buildings from external vibrations could be quite demanding, considering the wavelength of the low-frequency vibrations. Isolating floor from roof and outer walls is, however, a relatively simple means. Damping of the floor could in fact be contra-productive. Damping materials are weak and thus might increase vibrations in the low-frequency part of the spectrum, which is responsible for the major contribution of the displacements.[86]

In addition, the lack of terrain movement in the slightly sloped agricultural landscape so typical for Sweden's southernmost province Skåne was seen to potentially further extrapolate and distribute the vibrations. While the constraint caused severe concerns for the client, they became the major source of inspiration for the landscape architects, leading designer Jenny B. Osuldsen to reflect on the discovery of the vibration issue with great enthusiasm, stating 'This is so interesting! This is a fantastic parameter we can work with.'[87] It became clear that the landscape design required a rule-based design approach, reframing constraints into opportunities to inform and drive design explorations. Osuldsen comments 'Even though I had no idea how this process would look like I knew it was really essential to work in 3D and parametrically.'[88]

Here we see clearly the value of digital technologies in inspiring a fundamental shift in design culture, both theoretically and practically, encouraging the designer to explore the creative opportunities immanent in constraint-based modelling. The vibrations properties defined parameters that could translate into spatial definitions, such as length, location, orientation and direction and offered a rational for the form making and mass balancing (Figure 1.21). The designers began by establishing a grid of points (using Rhino and the plug-in Grasshopper) on the site. This grid was applied on a smoothed terrain surface that maintained the existing curvature of the site which stretched from the higher points in the centre, where the storage ring is situated, through to the lower lying roads on both sides. This allowed the designers at a later stage to consider the intersections between the new landform and the existing uneven topography. While the wave lengths were defined as a fixed parameter, their orientation, location, direction, amplitude, frequency and slope gradient could be varied and tested through adjusting the input units and mathematical functions in the parametric model.

The alignment of twenty tangents with the circular form of the synchrotron that would emulate the movement of the electrons in the storage ring and the light in the beamlines formed the starting point for the new topography. Waves were then added along these tangents to scatter the surface vibration, starting with a length of 10 metres closer to the facility and extending beyond 40 metres by the end of each tangent. Early experimentations began as a creative endeavour but with increasing refinement and understanding of relational attributes, additional constraints could be scripted into the model for more control and feedback.

Testing the design

The construction of the 4 metre deep floor slaps indented to stabilise the soil beneath the two storage rings (the largest 528 metres in circumference and the smallest 96 metres) required extensive earth excavation that was then available to construct the undulating landscape. Working with the 3D model facilitated close collaboration with the engineers in Lund to review the balancing of mass volumes. Their recommendation further refined design considerations, such as identifying the optimum wave amplitude at a maximum 4.5 metres to achieve the overall mass balance.

Parametric modelling allowed the designers to rigorously test and control their topographic explorations. Using Grasshopper, a series of small definitions (another term for script or code) were developed to test the performance and experience of the emerging topography. One definition established a slope gradient to a maximum of 1:4 (determined as the steepest possible grade for maintenance and an effective grade for managing storm water run-off). When applied to the model, the definition introduces changes of colour whenever the slopes exceeded the set gradient parameter, providing Snøhetta evidence of their form and decision-making process.

Other definitions aided the resolution of proposed and existing site conditions without compromising either the strong geometry of the design or the site context. This was particularly valuable for resolving the edge conditions, maintaining

1.21
Beginning with the premise that the impact of vibrations could be reduced through the addition of terrain movement and the maximisation of the land surface through a waved topography, the design process started with the exploration of long waves between 10 and 40 metres radiating out from the synchrotron. This length was defined by the researchers as the most problematic for the smooth operation of the facility, adding more chaos through reverse waves and formation of topography.

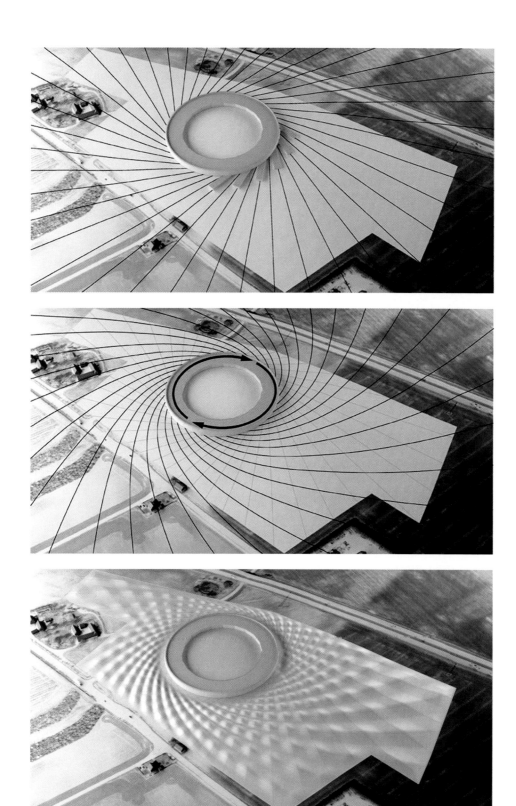

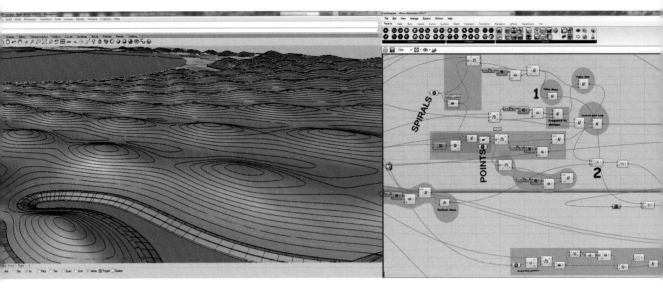

existing trees and inserting the plazas and roads into the design. The environmental performance of the design was tested using Kangaroo, a live physics engine plug-in (that operates in Grasshopper) that visualises physical behaviours in the modelling environment through particle simulation flow.

In earlier models which featured only one set of tangents, the animation highlighted where landforms would create dams, and revealed difficulties in guiding water towards the constructed wetlands. A definition was also developed to test how the topographic form interacted with the major wind conditions of this exposed site. The resulting model (Figure 1.23) highlighted where the topography created wind shadows and was used to inform the location of tree planting. Through additional definitions the designers could have explored the relationship between planting design and wind modulation in more detail. However, the quantity of trees necessary to achieve an effective windbreak was not acceptable for the client, requiring Snøhetta to dramatically reduce the number of trees. Thus, despite wind being a crucial factor in Skåne for most of the year this exploration was not pursued further.

The topographic form therefore evolved constantly through the testing of variations engaging with parameters such as vibration dispersal, drainage, wind and slope. The digital model was regularly sent to the engineers to test and validate the design against the vibration patterns and to provide feedback on how the landforms could further increase dispersal performance. Simulations suggested that a series of parameters, such as larger sized hills applied at an angle; smooth, rolling landforms composed of both hills and valleys; and finer patterns would achieve higher quality outcomes regarding the displacement of vibrations.[89] Since previous research had demonstrated that the more chaos added to the surface, the better the scattering of the vibrations, it was decided to add a second set of tangents intersecting with the first set, to create more surface variations (Figure 1.24a).

The application of two similar sets of tangents, as recommended by the engineers, produced a rigid landform that could not accommodate run-off. This then inspired the application of a twisting second set of waves to create more

1.22a–b
Testing the water run-off from the proposed topography using a Grasshopper definition to highlight areas of poor drainage.

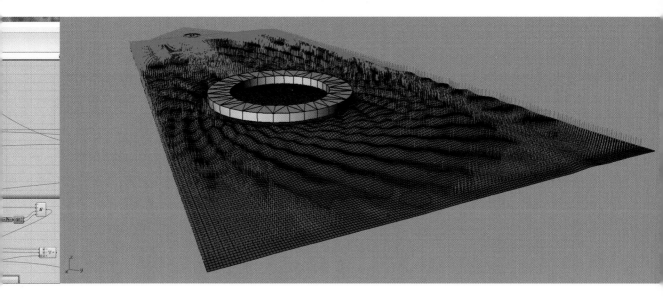

1.23
Working with Grasshopper to test the topographic form's interaction with the wind conditions. The surface colour of the model changes depending on exposure to certain wind speeds.

flexible spiral shaped surfaces which formed the final topographic form. During this parametric design process, Snøhetta navigated a balance between developing sufficient surface undulation to address vibration performance, while maintaining other important qualities such as maintenance, ecological considerations, micro-climatic factors and the user's perception of the designed landform. For example in some moments the designers elected to not perfectly drain the site, instead encouraging the water to pool to create evocative ephemeral ecosystems.

The interrogation of the user experience of the proposed landscape can be achieved in many formats, for example as discussed earlier ASPECT Studios utilised digital animations as a preferred tool to visualise and explore the landform for the Desalination Plant. In contrast, Snøhetta drew on printed 3D models, which became an essential communication and decision-making tool. Test models at 1:2000 scale were printed for weekly client meetings to check even the slightest changes in patterns, wave amplitudes and surface intersections (Figure 1.24b). More detail models at 1:200 accompanied these larger scale models to further visualise and test the intricacies of the curvature. Snøhetta also kept a second set of printed models as a record of their design explorations and decision-making process.

As discussed earlier in this chapter, the use of physical modelling in the exploration and testing phase of design has not been a feature of landscape architecture design. The availability of CNC routing and 3D printing which favour the representations of the slope and smooth surfaces, paired with a rapid production time, make physical models more relevant to the landscape architectural design process. As Osuldsen reflects:

> I don't think that we would have ever been able to achieve that [the weekly models] if it was not based on a 3D model that we could plot because it is now so fast to plot it. So you can test, and run models, and change it again in a really fast way. The site is large and if we should produce that in an old-fashioned cardboard model, I don't think we would have tested the idea because it would be too hard.[90]

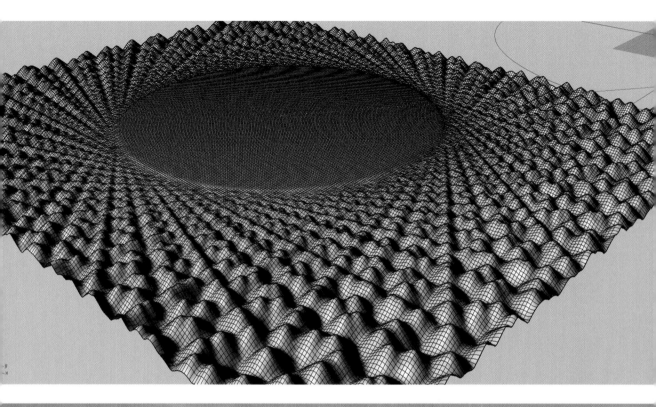

New design processes

For Snøhetta, the *MAX Lab IV* became an important exploration in the possibilities of parametric modelling in landscape architectural projects both as an intellectual and practical endeavour. Their experience highlights an extremely flexible modelling process where designers can respond quickly to new information, qualities and observations. Consequently, the designer becomes less precious with their ideas and open to new explorations. As Pål Hasselberg, an architect involved in the *MAX Lab IV* comments 'You don't think about it. You just try to do it.'[91] Without this approach, changes to the large-scale complex landform manipulation of *MAX Lab IV* would have been extremely time-consuming, leading to less exploration and experimentation in form generation.

Snøhetta's experience also highlights the new conceptual demands that parametric modelling places on designers as they depart from linear segmented workflows into non-linear design processes. It could be assumed that a rule-based or a procedural approach to design is accompanied by a clear linearity of operation. This process however must be controlled by the designer (as distinct from the assumption that the computer generates the design). As Branko Kolarevic commented earlier, 'The designer essentially becomes an editor of the generative potentiality of the designed system, where the choice of emergent forms is driven largely by the designer's aesthetic and plastic sensibilities.'[92] Hence the designer must now operate in a far more explicit and formal manner than what is commonly associated with more traditional models of design processes.[93] We discuss the differences in these design processes in far more detail in Chapter 2.

The ever expanding potential of software, combined with the increased capability of the designer to code, places more importance on understanding workflow and efficiencies. For instance Snøhetta could have developed a script to receive real-time feedback on cut-and-fill balance. Instead, they adopted a more intuitive exploration guided by defined parameters and responding to the mass calculations provided by the engineers. To engage with real-time feedback was as much a liability concern, as it was a workflow consideration, since it would require multiple scripts to run simultaneously. Pål Hasselberg, comments 'you could put everything into one magical script but that would become so complex that sometimes it's hard to work with, because it is calculating everything at the same time'.[94] The more factors added to the script, the more complex the modelling process, as each parameter has to be managed to 'make sure that they don't interfere with one another'.[95] Thus, in some cases it may be more valuable to work on one parameter at a time. This requires the designer to understand and to control modelling processes to ensure it works best for design intent.

In the future, other research laboratories such the ESS (European Spallation Source) further to the north will join *MAX Lab IV* to form a new Science City to provide world-class facilities in scientific research and innovation in Lund. In light of the growth plans and the international significance of the developments in the region, the *MAX Lab IV* was conceived to 'be an eye catcher' in the landscape.[96] As

1.24a–b
Digital model testing a more chaotic landform. 3D printed models formed an important tool for the design exploration, communication with the client and an important record of the design process.

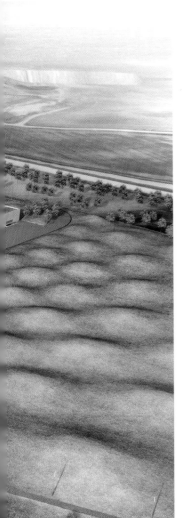

1.25a–b
MAX Lab IV under
construction (2014) and a
rendered view of the final
design proposal including the
wetlands in the foreground.

1.26a–b
Experiencing the undulating wave
landscape during snow and a rendered
summer view. Figure (a) also shows the
integration of existing and new planting
within the landform system.

shown in Figures 1.25 and 1.26, this was achieved. Osuldsen comments that while in a programmatic sense the design of *MAX Lab IV* was 'not at all what the client was asking for', the landscape design now forms 'an iconic part of the project – not just visually but also functionally'. Thus the opportunity of a rule-based design really lies in detecting a significant parameter and to use this as leverage to 'lift landscape off just the practical stuff'.[97]

The parametric process therefore offered Snøhetta more possibilities to advance their relevance in projects where clients have only a marginal understanding of landscape performance. As Osuldsen states in many of their projects clients only require the most basic deliverables.[98] In the case of *MAX Lab IV*, the parametric modelling process, combined with new technologies such as 3D printing, empowered Snøhetta to expand the complexity of their design, while also offering clear demonstration to the client of the systemic, performative and experiential qualities of the final design.

Conclusion

Many of the concepts introduced in this chapter such as parametric modelling and scripting may still remain confusing and foreign to some readers. To engage with the potential of digital technologies is to understand a new language, new workflows, design processes and theory. This understanding will continue to develop over the course of the book as we expand on these major concepts and developments in more detail. The most critical knowledge to take from this chapter is the understanding that design logic, knowledge and processes change with computational design, and that the digital model is core to this revision.

The topographically driven design examples discussed in this chapter present four different roles for the 3D model in the design process. In their design of *Landhausplatz*, LAAC worked directly with their 3D model to digitally sculpt precise and novel landforms that responded to very specific conditions and constraints inherent in the site. In contrast PARKKIM in their design for *Mud Infrastructure*, generated an initial design concept in plan which was then explored, tested and refined within a 3D model. In these examples, the designers explore form through 'tool-like' operation which modifies space in real time onscreen. Surfaces are modelled intuitively, with the algorithmic formulae remaining embedded within the software, and as a consequence the designers are not actively applying a rule-based design approach.

In the later examples we see a major change in design logic and in the role of the design model. Emphasis is now placed on the 'design' of the model which becomes the primary space of exploration and generation. Working with the versatility of Maya software, ASPECT Studios' design process mixes more intuitive exploration of form with a rule-based design approach, including the testing of very particular parameters such as slope gradients. We define this hybrid of techniques as a 'conceptual' example of parametric modelling.

The final example of Snøhetta's approach to the design of *MAX Lab IV* offers a far more explicit application of rules, encouraged by the design brief which required the topographic form to disperse surface vibrations. The vibrational properties provided a clear parameter that could translate into spatial definitions (such as length, location and orientation) offering the foundations for developing a topographic form. The performance of this emerging topography was iteratively tested against criteria ranging from drainage, wind and slope gradients to its ability to minimise vibrations, using a mix of bespoke scripts and open source plug-ins. Importantly, the designer requires a far more precise design thinking than what is commonly associated with more traditional design processes, explicitly curating the generational potential of the parametric model.

In the following chapter, we continue a focus on parametric modelling and performance, with a closer interrogation of its value to a contemporary design of practice of landscape architecture.

2 Performative systems

The ambition to develop design practices responsive to dynamic systems assumes a major focus for landscape architecture in the late twentieth century. Inspired by the discourse of Landscape Urbanism and the increasing influence of ecological thinking, landscape architects began to privilege the performative attributes of landscape as exemplified in Field Operations' winning entry for the 2001 Fresh Kills design competition. We suggest it takes a further decade before the process-driven ideas so central to Field Operations' scheme are explored through computational techniques. In this chapter we focus on this transitional moment where landscape architects in both practice and teaching begin to uncover the potential of computational techniques for engaging with fluid and dynamic systems, further encouraged by the challenging and unpredictable conditions of climate change.

The winning scheme for the Taichung Gateway Park competition held in Taiwan in 2011 presents an early precedent for the application of a performative theoretical framing explored through the computational (computer fluid dynamic modelling) in the design of a large park. The winning entry *Phase Shifts Park* designed by Catherine Mosbach and Philippe Rahm, manipulates the conditions of atmosphere and lithosphere to propose a twenty-first-century urban park shaped by technological and biological performance. The jury heralded this design for a former airport site as a 'creative and visionary proposal', which combines microclimatic studies with innovative landscape design to propose 'a new thinking approach' and 'potentially a new design paradigm'.[1]

Specifically, the designers' response demonstrates the evolution from the generalities of sustainability and a 'green' discourse to a more rigorous engagement with data and metrics where design decisions are linked more precisely to achieving particular performance outcomes within the constructed landscape design. This

2.1
The Orographic Hills scheme,
Flux City Studio.

development can be considered a further evolution of the theoretical discourse of Landscape Urbanism which first emerges in the mid 1990s. As discussed in Chapter 1, Landscape Urbanism challenges landscape architecture to shift focus from what a landscape looks like or represents to instead an emphasis on what a landscape does (performance). Correspondingly, designers became interested in the design of dynamic systems, processes and relationships.

However, a major shortcoming of Landscape Urbanism is that the dominant design techniques adopted in its exploration, namely the diagram and the map – have limited capacity to engage dynamic systems (social, ecological and economic) directly within design processes. James Corner's Field Operations winning entry for *Fresh Kills* for example defines the park as an unfolding set of diagrammatic interrelations projected over a 30-year period, accompanied by montage images suggesting how spaces may evolve. These projections are notional, guided by generalised ecological concepts and broad assumptions of change over time. Bowring and Swaffield observe the 'diagrammatic challenge of emergent systems lies not so much in the problem of representing individual subjectivity, but in representing probability'.[2] In arguably the most extreme interpretation of Landscape Urbanism, OMA and Bruce Ma's winning design for *Downsview Park*, Toronto (1999) presented the following formula to guide the park's evolution:

> Grow the park + manufacture nature + curate culture + 1000 pathways
> + destination and dispersal + sacrifice and save = low-density metro-
> politan life.[3]

This design process was remarkable for its extreme open-endedness, divorced from broader political, social and economic processes. At the time, jurors and many design theorists celebrated the scheme as 'a stimulating expansion of landscape architecture's emerging theory of design generated by ongoing process rather than established form'.[4] But the subsequent difficulties in the park's imple-mentation expose weaknesses in proposing such a vague process. As Alissa North concludes:

> It is clear that a theoretical strategy paired with a conceptual graphic
> does not provide a clear enough image for many participants involved
> in large public works to understand, visualize and coalesce behind a
> project's trajectory.[5]

Six years after winning *Fresh Kills*, James Corner suggested that Landscape Urbanism required 'reconsideration of traditional conceptual, representation and operative techniques', including 'entering the algebraic, digital space of the computer'.[6] Similarly Chris Reed and Nina-Marie Lister in their 2014 edited publi-cation *Projective Ecologies*, identify the potential of 'flow modeling, scripting and processing software' as offering 'time-based platforms for representing and programming change and evolution'.[7] Philip Belesky comments further on the value of these approaches to landscape architecture, noting:

> Unlike plans or diagrams, a computationally-defined design emerges from a series of generative rules that form a dynamic system. By creating rules that account for the temporality, uncertainty, and dynamism of landscape systems we can begin to make these phenomena truly operative within the design process.[8]

In this chapter we explore the potential of computational techniques for embedding the relational and temporal qualities and behaviours of dynamic systems directly within design processes. While in Chapter 1, our exploration of Snøhetta's parametric modelling demonstrated the possibilities of generating novel topographic form through a series of prescribed parameters (slope, vibrations, wind, drainage), the examples discussed in this chapter present a different emphasis on systems. Unconstrained by a relationship to architecture or infrastructure, these projects foreground dynamic systems and phenomena as the actual starting point for design. Here we reveal how the behaviours or performance of systems directly informs design generation and offer further evidence of the characteristics of a landscape architectural approach to parametric modelling. We begin with a detailed analysis of *Phase Shifts Park* the winning scheme for the Taichung Gateway Park competition.

The performative park

Phase Shifts Park, as its very name suggests, engages with Taiwan's fluctuating climate which creates difficult conditions for inhabiting open space. The design was developed by French landscape architect Catherine Mosbach and Swiss architect Philippe Rahm, with further input from local Taiwanese architect Ricky Liu. Their scheme (which has become known post competition as *Jade Eco Park*), interrogates the specific environmental conditions of the former airport site at two scales – first, the island of Taiwan's position within a sensitive environmental area, shaped both by a continuously moving seismic zone and Kuroshio, one of the largest ocean currents in the world. And, second, the park's location on the foothills of a sub-tropical mountain, where processes of deforestation, steep slopes, high pollution, humidity and the compacted soils of a former airport site, create challenging conditions for open space.

Designing across these scales, the design proposes to 'give back the outdoors' to the public by developing exterior spaces 'where the excesses of the subtropical warm and humid climate of Taichung are lessened'.[9] Mosbach notes that presently, 'Taichung is unbearable outside, in the sense of modern comfort; after an hour spent outside, people are sweating as they take refuge in malls where there is air-conditioning.'[10] The park therefore proposes a healthier and more comfortable

outdoor environment, which develops through the superimposition of two overlapping strata; lithosphere comprising soils, topography and rainwater, and atmosphere encompassing heat, humidity and pollution. These layers shown in Figure 2.2b draw on the respective expertise of the designers.

While the notion of developing a healthy park is not new, and is evident throughout history including Haussmann's vision for Paris and Olmstead's Central Park in New York, the explicit performative agendas explored by Mosbach and Rahm are novel.[11] Rahm observes that over the course of the twentieth century, attitudes towards the health-giving benefits of open space have altered.[12] Developments in medicine such as antibiotics have reduced the primary role of open space in maintaining a healthy population. Contemporary challenges of climate change and increasing pollution levels have contributed to a resurgence of interest in the performative potential of open space in the city, revisiting for example late nineteenth-century aspirations for fresh air.

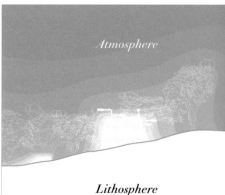

As we will explore in more detail, this design approach differs from more historic responses through a direct manipulation of external conditions such as wind, humidity, planting, materiality and topography to fulfil particular performative aspirations. Consequently, the design provokes philosophical questions regarding the relationship between biological and technological performance, and the ability of humans to influence environmental conditions.

Atmosphere

Atmosphere understood as the material of air has long been a focus of architecture, designed and regulated through physical and material techniques. Schemes from the 1950s and 1960s such as the *Air Architecture* projects by Yves Klein and Wemer

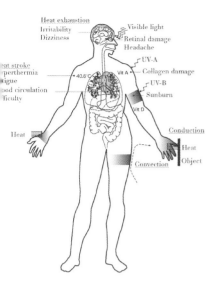
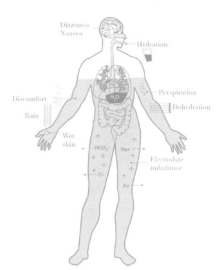
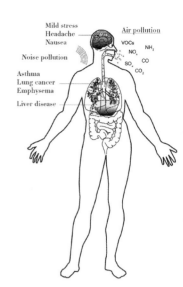

2.2a–c

Competition drawings:
(a) rendered perspectives featuring climatic interventions (pink=cooling; blue=dehumidification, grey=depollution), (b) lithosphere-atmosphere diagram and (c) diagrams depicting the effect of heat, humidity and pollution on the human body.

Rugnau and the Buckminster Fuller proposed *Dome over Manhattan* (designed with Shoji Sadao) offered provocative explorations of atmosphere, proposing new forms of architecture with minimal building envelope.[13] These speculations questioning the environmental and social politics of air quality, the bio-politics of atmosphere and the individual's relationship to modified environments, have resurfaced in a new generation of architects working within the contemporary context of climate change such as Philippe Rahm, Sean Lally and David Gissen.[14]

Philippe Rahm's interest in atmosphere lies in its performative potential. He aims to embrace climate within the domain of design, as distinct from controlling climate from a functionalist perspective to achieve optimum efficiencies. Yet, until the Taichung Gateway Park competition, his work remained largely conceptual. For instance *Digestible Gulf Stream* presented at the 2008 Venice Architecture Biennale proposed an asymmetrical thermal landscape of different spaces and activity, fluctuating between two temperature poles of 24 and 16 degree Celsius respectively.

The Taichung Gateway Park Competition provided the opportunity to explore climatic ideas at an urban scale, while maintaining a focus on the human experience. This intent is signalled in the diagrams featured so prominently in the competition entry that depict human physiological reactions to heat, humidity and pollution (Figure 2.2c). Representations of a normalised body in relationship to constructed form are an attribute of Modernist architecture, evident for example in Ernst Neufert's *Architects' Data* book (1936) and Le Corbusier's *Modulor Man* which feature 'harmonious measurements to suit the human scale'.[15] These representations, which continue in the tradition of Leonardo da Vinci's *Vitruvian Man*, position the mathematical proportions inherent in the human body as the source of measurement to universally apply to architecture and other designed elements.

Rahm's depiction of the body in relationship to 'its biological affections by the environment', offers a significant departure, instead highlighting the impact

Performative systems

Masterplan Composition
•
Heat map on site

*Wind velocity
3.0 m/s*

*Wind velocity
0.0 m/s*

North Wind Speed Simulation

warmer

colder

colder

warmer

colder

colder

warmer

Warm

Cool

Influence of North Wind from Simulation

warm

cold

cold

cold

cold

cold

cold

warm

warm

cold

cold

cold

warm

warm

•
Devices

Cooling Devices Location Plan

Masterplan Composition
•
Humidity map on site

*Wind velocity
5.0 m/s*

*Wind velocity
0.0 m/s*

**South West Wind Velocity and Vector
Simulation**

more humid

drier

more humid

drier

more humid

drier

more humid

Humid

Dry

**Influence of South West Wind and Basins
from Simulation**

humid

dry

dry

humid

dry

humid

humid

dry

dry

humid

dry

•
Devices

Dehumidifying Devices Location Plan

Performative systems

North Wind Velocity and Vector Simulation

Influence of North Wind and
Surrounding Roads from Simulation

Depolluting Devices Location Plan

that environmental conditions have on the inhabitation of space.[16] This emphasis is consistently repeated throughout the competition imagery, subsequent documentation and all interpretative material.

Mapping the climatic variations of the site through computational fluid dynamics simulation (CFD) formed the starting point for the conceptualisation of the atmospheric strata. This modelling develops an understanding of the fluctuating conditions of heat, humidity and pollution, including the impact of the future architecture on the park's edges. The models were developed by German firm Transsolar who used ANSYS Fluent software combined with weather data from the Taiwanese central weather bureau's measuring device located close to the site.[17] From their models, the designers developed three graduation climatic maps that documented the intensity and variation of heat, air humidity and atmospheric pollution (Figure 2.3). These maps were overlaid and intersected to create a diversity of conditions, conceived as a series of Coolia, Dryia and Clearia 'climatic lands'. Rahm emphasises that this approach is not a Modernist or functional response. The aim is not to modulate conditions, for instance making the hotter areas cooler. Instead the scheme maintains and even extends the graduation of conditions, increasing qualities where areas are naturally cooler, less polluted and less humid. Consequently, this tactic is more than a pragmatic response, instead reflective of Rahm's interest in designing space through voids, particles and atmospheres

2.3a–c
CFD simulations documented the effects of the three parameters of heat, humidity and pollution on the existing site conditions and informed the development of three thematic masterplans.

rather than lines and forms. A polarity of conditions is established, with hot spaces necessary to establish cool ones thereby 'creating spaces by acting on difference'.[18] Space emerges through the transformative boundaries of atmospheres and conditions, not as hard spatial delineations. This concept extends into the graphic representation of the park as points and dots, where space is communicated through a graduation of light and colour rather than sharp demarcation of form.

The Coolia, Dryia and Clearia establish an atmospheric structure for the park as shown in Figure 2.4, with circulation systems conceived to link similar climatic lands. These distinctive climatic conditions offer the rational for siting major program and activities. Sport, for example, is sited within areas of low pollution and humidity, water games placed in high humidity areas and indoor programs located within areas experiencing the most extreme heat and pollution. The design team originally proposed a more critical approach to programming, suggesting for example smoking rooms and skating parks in the more urban polluted areas. However, the clients were understandably wary of actively programming for 'bad' conditions, and this strategy was not pursued.[19]

Beyond programming, the climatic lands offer concentration points to explore the conditions of atmosphere and lithosphere concurrently. This is discussed in the following section, where a range of park stratifications are proposed as material spaces in the design of the lithosphere.

Lithosphere

In a complementary balance to Rahm's interest in atmospheric conditions, Catherine Mosbach's design practice is characterised by an interrogation of the ground condition. With a background in science (biology, chemistry and physics) combined with landscape architecture, Mosbach's signature projects such as the *Bordeaux Botanic Gardens* and the *Louvre-Lens* museum park share a detailed engagement with biological and cultural conditions encompassing scales from the microscopic to the larger environmental.

In her conceptualisation of lithosphere, Mosbach draws on the Deleuzean concept of the 'fold' (introduced in Chapter 1), along with the idea of 'folding' associated with geological 'fault', to literally and figuratively develop a topography that operates simultaneously as a process of recovery, protection and documentation.[20] The topography unfolds and transforms as a series of creases, hollows and bumps structuring spaces, views, circulation and most importantly capturing rainfall and over land flow to encourage infiltration and the recharging of the groundwater. These surface folds, influenced by parameters of drainage, soil porosity and the biological performance of vegetation, orchestrate the spatial and ecological organisation of the topographic surface.

An interrogation of water infiltration, achieved through an understanding of porosity metrics, was therefore highly influential in the proposed topography (Figure 2.5). Different gradients of porosity combined with soil features and

2.4
The 'Climatic Lands Structure' emerged through the intersection of the thematic masterplans developed from the simulations. Importantly, the design maintains a graduation of site characteristics to create diversity of microclimatic and programatic conditions.

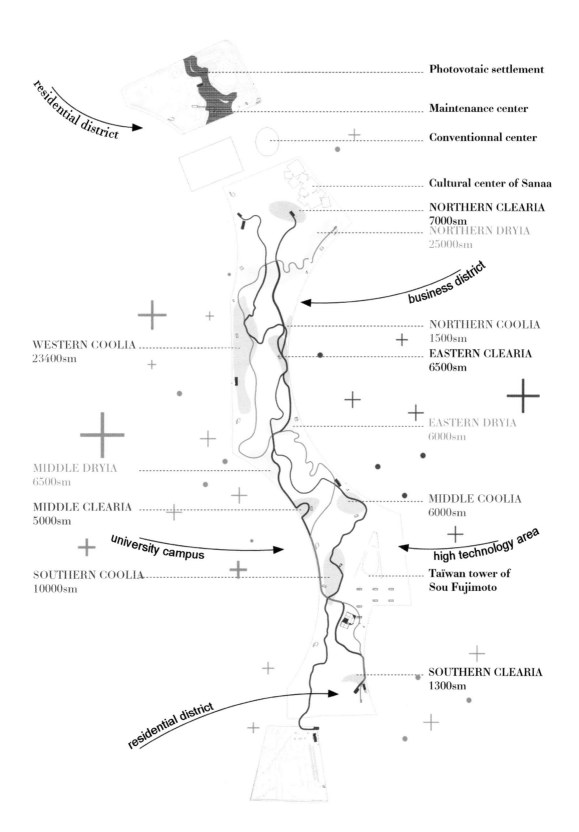

residential district

Photovotaic settlement

Maintenance center

Conventionnal center

Cultural center of Sanaa

NORTHERN CLEARIA
7000sm

NORTHERN DRYIA
25000sm

business district

NORTHERN COOLIA
1500sm

EASTERN CLEARIA
6500sm

WESTERN COOLIA
23400sm

EASTERN DRYIA
6000sm

MIDDLE DRYIA
6500sm

MIDDLE COOLIA
6000sm

MIDDLE CLEARIA
5000sm

university campus

high technology area

Taïwan tower of
Sou Fujimoto

SOUTHERN COOLIA
10000sm

SOUTHERN CLEARIA
1300sm

residential district

bushes   90%

high grass   80%

short grass   60%

smoothie soil   40%

mixed surface   20%

hard surface   0%

surface materiality established a 'coefficient of surface runoff'.[21] 'Hollow ground', for example is capable of 80 per cent porosity, and offers maximum absorption of water during tropical storms. During drier moments, these open areas provide large flexible spaces for hosting open-air activities, while in extreme-weather events over 80 per cent of the park retains up to 20 cm of water, alleviating flooding in surrounding urban areas (Figure 2.6). When dry, the topographic beds can be used for walking and picnicking, contributing to the sensation of walking over large meadows or during times of monsoon, crossing the ocean, along a dry path. The designers believe that this dynamic engagement with water 'gives rhythm to the park both by its available recreational influences' and its capability to 'morph' from dry to monsoonal period.[22] Planting within this folded topography is extremely detailed, designed to optimise soil porosity, contribute shade, transform air quality, develop places of identity, repel mosquitoes, and in the case of wetland planting, filter waste water through phytoremediation. Maintaining a continuity of landscape and circulation throughout the long thin linear park was equally important, leading to the submersion of bridges and tunnels crossing the park into the ground plane (Figure 2.7). Rhino formed an important technique for evolving these more complex shapes and spaces, where 'the plan and the section' proved 'incomplete tools'.[23]

This continuity of movement is developed further through a feature green corridor crossing east to west through the park to link the university campus to the technological campus. Accessible day and night, this green corridor is 600 metres long and 80 metres wide and is designed with a particular mix of soil and vegetation to develop an 'aire de tranquilisation zone' which encourages the fast filtering of water into the surface.[24] A digital light installation was developed to represent in real time the powerful variations in the ocean's surface currents recorded by satellites offshore from Taiwan, including the dynamic Kuroshio current. A grid of 2 metre by 2 metre LED lights designed within the pebble surface introduces 'a fine marine chart in scale' readable from the adjoining residential and commercial towers. Unfortunately this concept has not been realised in the final design.

Strategically inserted into the complex topographic surface are the 11 climatic lands that further amplify the intersection of the lithosphere and atmosphere. In a new type of twenty-first-century garden, the climatic lands mix artificial and natural artifices to heighten the comfort levels of external spaces. This is achieved through a detailed understanding of plant capabilities and the use of devices to cool, dehumidify or depollute spaces.

Climatic devices

The climatic devices are arguably one of the more controversial elements of the park, no doubt viewed by some as unwelcomed technological insertion into nature. The devices offer 'a contemporary extension of traditional furniture of parks', operating like the pavilions, grottos, trellises and niches found in older parks, and providing a texture of sensory experiences of refuge, delight and interest.[25] These

2.6
The park's topographic surface is designed to maximise water infiltration developed through the interrogation of surface materiality, gradients and soil features. This diagram references the level of porosity throughout the park, with bushes offering the highest coefficient of surface runoff.

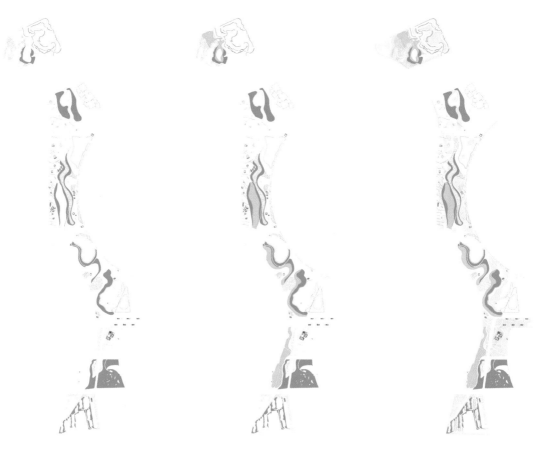

General extension area
17% of the park
Most of the time

Average extension area
25% of the park
Heavy rain

Special extension area
80% of the park
Exceptional event

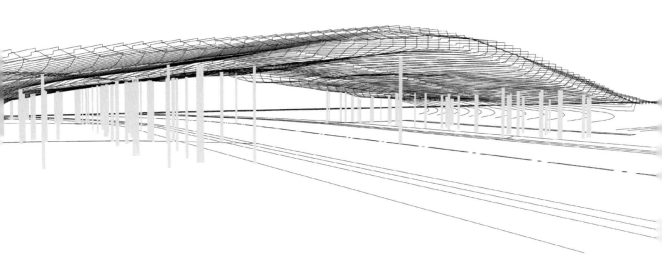

devices shown in Figure 2.8 are designed to augment the existing conditions offering a 'toolbox' of approaches including ultrasonic speakers to keep mosquitos away, artificial water devices such as rain fountains for evaporative cooling, dry clouds for removing humidity from the air, depollution techniques and passive cooling techniques.

The devices work in conjunction with detailed planting and spatial strategies to establish a complementary intersection between technological and biological performance. For open-space design, this approach is novel. Manipulating external climatic conditions was a new challenge for Rahm. External conditions are constantly changing and need to be understood as a factor of graduation rather than absolutes. He comments that 'in previous work the decision about temperature was not mine', but was determined by regulations, ambitions for energy consumption or comfort indexes.[26] In the case of the park, the design team always proposed a 'graduation of place' with wind speed the only parameter that could be definitively controlled by the devices. Standing under the Anticyclone meteor (Figure 2.10) for instance it was possible to experience a reduction of temperature by up to 6 degrees in June, producing a temperature of 29 Celsius compared to 35 Celsius in surrounding space. This reduction however is not a baseline standard, instead always relative to the fluctuating external conditions.

The devices are designed to minimise their use of energy, with power provided by 7000 square metres of photo-voltaic (solar) energy. An interesting tension emerged regarding the conceptualisation of air-conditioning within a park. The design team sited the solar panels in a consolidated field of high solar access, located away from the devices. The client however wanted the solar panels placed more directly near the devices so they would be understood as green and sustainable.[27] Eventually, the air-conditioning machines were replaced with passive cooling techniques (illustrated in Figure 2.10) that duct air 3 metres underground in a natural cooling process.

These technological interventions are supported by detailed planting regimes, featuring plants with particular performative attribute (Figure 2.9). For heat reduction, *Acer serrulatum Hayata* were selected for their large and dense canopy which provides maximum shading, for pollution the conifers *Calocedrus formosana* were nominated for their ability to absorb particulates from air, while for humidity *Ficus microcarpa* were chosen for their capacity to capture water by arial roots.

Interpretation panels are proposed throughout the park, offering detailed explanations of how the design modifies the environmental conditions. Probes containing climate sensors are planned at 50 metre intervals. This layer of 'intelligence' will send real-time weather data recording pollution levels, solar radiation, air velocity and air temperature and noise to a computer room found in the park's northern section. Climatic data will be used in three ways: graphically depicted in three interactive maps within the park; informing the intelligent running of the devices (to minimise power usage) and as information sent in real time to a smart phone application.

2.6
Diagrams indicating the park's response to rainfall. During heavy rain 25 per cent of the park is covered in water extending to 80 per cent in periods of extreme rain.

2.7
Rhino modelling of bridges and tunnels.

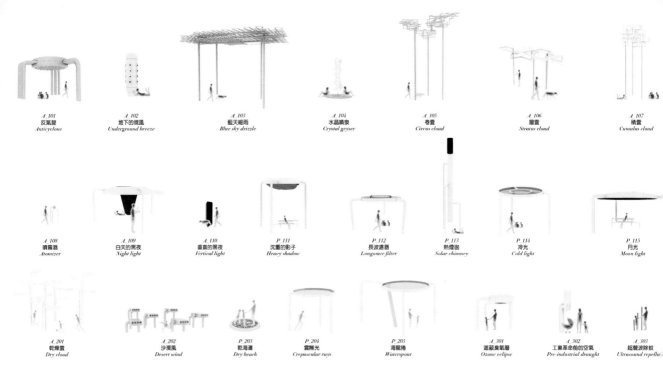

The smart phone application, establishes a new mode of interaction between the public, open space and its climatic performance. Visitor's access real-time climate data (heat, humidity and pollution), with the application suggesting different activities that best respond to the dynamic microclimate. The system can operate in a predictive manner – recommending, for instance, areas of low pollution for elderly people or parents with children, or alternatively provide readings of a nominated location along with suggested activities to match these conditions.

The Climatorium (visitor centre) offers a further feature, materialising atmosphere into a unique interpretative experience of climatic phenomena. Three 'exhibitions of atmosphere' form the major content, displaying very precise conditions. The Coolium matches the real-time Alishan temperature (6.2–14.6 C) and Jade Mountain cloud intensity, two mountainous areas of Taiwan where the effects of climate change will be first registered. The Dryium replicates the real-time humidity of Taichung's driest day of 21 November, while the Clearium offers the real-time temperature and cloud intensity of Taichung before the Industrial Revolution (1832). No interpretation or exhibition display is found within these rooms, with the visitor instead immersed in atmospheric conditions.

With the park on schedule to be completed in autumn 2016, the designers are yet to experience the final effect of their overlapping strata of atmosphere and lithosphere. The park as concept and constructed space offers an important provocation of the performative role of open space within an era of climate change, inspiring philosophical reflection (by the designers, critics and the public) on the relationship between biological and technological performance. Throughout the design process, the design team sought to improve performance efficiency through

2.8
The tool box of climatic devices proposed in the competition entry.

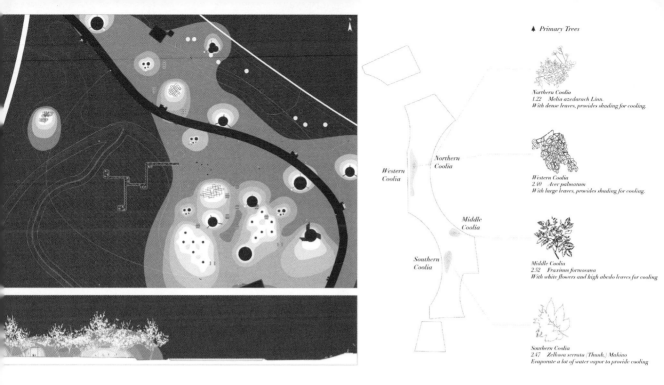

Primary Trees

Northern Coolia
1.22   Melia azedarach Linn.
With dense leaves, provides shading for cooling.

Western Coolia
2.40   Acer palmatum
With large leaves, provides shading for cooling.

Middle Coolia
2.52   Fraxinus formosana
With white flowers and high abedo leaves for cooling

Southern Coolia
2.47   Zelkowa serrata (Thunb.) Makino
Evaporate a lot of water vapor to provide cooling

2.9a–b
Planting was carefully chosen for its biological performance in regard to cooling, dehumidification and depollution.

multiple strategies and scales.[28] Mosbach observes 'we are staging fertile combinations of ingenuity and biological performance of soils, plants, micro fauna and micro flora. This is a first on an urban scale.'[29] To work with performance in the design of external spaces is a completely different technical and conceptual challenge to the more controlled and defined parameters associated with architectural spaces and environmental systems.

On reflection, Mosbach prefers the term 'perfomations' to the term performance which comes from the contraction of 'perfomance' and 'formation'.[30] This model proposes an association with 'bodily experiences [bodily evolution] with bodily choices [cultural evolution]', suggestive of a more integral relationship between artistic practices and scientific perspectives.[31] This focus on relationships extends into the modelling of park, with Mosbach preferring more plasticity to consider in additional detail how fluid systems – encompassing plants, animals and humans influence environmental conditions. She continues: 'Said in another way, this is the question of the container and of the contents and that the contents continuously remodels the container – that is, one lives and by living causes to evolve where one is living.[32] Mosbach therefore is more interested in reciprocal relationships, 'than how the technologies perform'.[33] Rahm offers a different perspective, seeing no difference between trees and machines.[34] He is more comfortable with the interaction between the natural and artificial, such as the potentially surreal experience of the park visitor uncovering a strange machine within a wild forest.[35]

Underlying these differences between the designers are two distinctive directions for engaging with computational design, systems and performance; Rahm's interest in simulating systems (atmosphere) and the active manipulation of

15th June 1pm	21st July 4pm

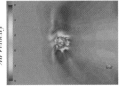

Air Temperature: 35.4 °C
Relative Humidity: 50 %
Humidity: 18.3 g/kg
Air Velocity: 0.5 m/s

Air Temperature: 28.9°C
Humidity: 20.7 g/kg
Air Velocity: 1.5 m/s

at 1pm 15th June
while the ourdoor temperature is at 35°C
people can enjoy cooled air with temeprature of 29°C underneath Anticyclone

Air volume 9000m3/h

its performance which suggests a more predictive modelling approach, compared to Mosbach's focus on fluid and dynamic systems that draws on their behaviours and performance in a generative process.

These two positions shape our discussion of parametric modelling and landscape architecture over the next two chapters. In this chapter we continue to follow Mosbach's interest in dynamic systems, beginning with a revisiting of the definitions and characteristics of parametric modelling presented briefly in Chapter 1, with a greater reflection on how the process redefines a logic of design.

2.10a–d
The anticyclone climatic device works with the principles of passive cooling to reduce its energy needs. When the external temperature in June reaches 35 degrees it is assumed that people will experience a temperature of 29 degrees when standing directly under the device (a). Constructed prototypes of the climatic devices on site (b–c).

A parametric system

Some might argue that parametric modelling is more applicable to architecture than landscape architecture, given architectural form displays a stronger rationale in geometry, pattern and mathematical concepts. Landscape architecture's interest in dynamic systems, relationships and processes make it an equal candidate to explore the design potential offered by parametric modelling. In the following section, we discuss in more detail how parametric modelling offers a new design thinking, which establishes different relationships and interactivity between the designer, process and information.

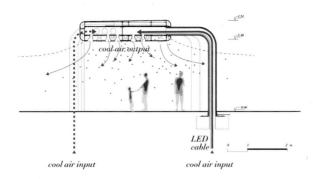

cool air output

cool air input   cool air input

LED
cable

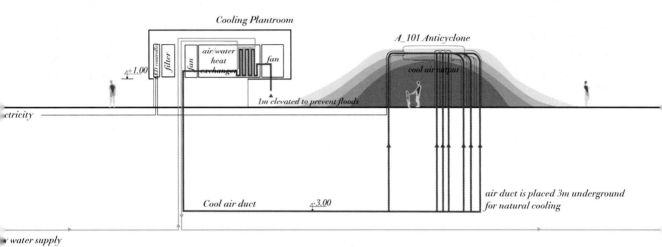

Cooling Plantroom

A_101 Anticyclone

air/water
heat
exchanger

filter   fan   fan

cool air output

+1.00

1m elevated to prevent floods

ctricity

air duct is placed 3m underground
for natural cooling

Cool air duct   +3.00

r water supply

Antonio Gaudí's use of a hanging chain as an analogue model in the design of the Colònia Güell chapel in 1896, is commonly cited as an early example of architectural parametric thinking.[36] His model was produced almost a century before the Parametric Technology Corporation released the first commercially viable parametric software Pro/ENGINEER in 1988.[37] In relationship to architecture, Rick Smith's collaboration with Frank Gehry in 1991 is considered an important milestone in digital design practice. Smith, who had considerable expertise in the Dassault Systèmes CATIA, worked with Gehry on the *Barcelona Fish* project, which is identified as one of the first times that CATIA software was applied in an architectural project. In 2001 Gehry Technologies developed a modified version of CATIA for architects, known as Digital Project 2004.

In the decade since, architecture has embraced the design potential of parametric modelling, with its influence evident in practice and pedagogy. While slower to engage, the relational attributes of parametric modelling offer landscape architects great scope for exploring dynamic relationships between systems and form. It does however require the application of a different type of design logic to what is more familiar to many landscape architects.

A parametric design process differs from the more accustomed segmented design and planning processes in landscape architecture that frequently position the generation of a design concept *after* the synthesis of extensive site analysis.

In Chapter 1 we highlighted how parametric modelling requires the designer to operate in a far more explicit manner in terms of knowledge and process than what is commonly associated with more traditional models of design processes. Rivka Oxman in her 2007 article 'Digital Architecture as a Challenge for Design Pedagogy: Theory, Knowledge, Models and Medium' offers a valuable analysis of this new design logic. She highlights that Donald Schön's influential cognitive research on 'designerly thinking' from the 1980s, which emphasised 'reflection in action', was predicated on a visual reasoning.[38] Working with 'paper-based' design thinking, Oxman states that Schön characterises visual reasoning as a process of 'talk back' or a 'dialogue with the materials of the problem' informed primarily by visual representation.[39]

While many might argue that Oxman's critique of Schön's is too simplistic, nonetheless her subsequent critique of how a digital design process offers a different mode of engagement is valuable. Digital media states Oxman brings different influences to design thinking, exemplified by parametric modelling which establishes new forms of interactivity between the designer, process and information. Within this design process, cognitive processes of design are conceptualised as 'our ability to formulate, represent, implement and interact with explicit, well-formulated representations of knowledge', where design processes move from implied to explicit knowledge.[40]

Establishing the most influential parameters is an example of this explicit knowledge, which shifts emphasis from the compositional (visual judgement) to a focus on the formational (relational structures). Accompanying this shift is the introduction of 'recursion' into the design processes. Recursion is an important concept for engaging with complexity, considered a 'method of defining functions in which the function being defined is applied within its own definition'.[41] Or in other words 'the output of applying function becomes the input of the next iteration'.[42] Correspondingly, designers replace the development of different conceptual variations with an iterative process of testing, where new knowledge informs subsequent design iterations, updated in real time. While some would argue that all design has iterative qualities, within a recursive approach form emerges as a product of information and performance, with the resultant design process structuring relationships between concepts of creativity and efficiency.[43]

Architecture has been engaging with this design logic of explicit knowledge for almost 20 years. It is useful for landscape architects to understand the debates shaping this longer exploration of parametric modelling. Patrik Schumacher, a partner at Zaha Hadid Architects, is one of the most provocative and outspoken supporters. He considers parametricism the next contemporary architectural style following Modernism, signalling 'the end of the transitional phase of uncertainty engendered by the crisis of Modernism and marked by a series of short-lived architectural episodes that included Postmodernism, Deconstructivism and Minimalism'.[44] Many critics highlight the similarities in formal outcome evident in parametrically driven buildings, supporting Schumacher's framing of parametrics as a style. For example

Mario Carpo comments that 'the normal mode of use of today's parametricism allows for such a limited range of variations that all end-products of a given design environment tend to look the same, regardless of their degree of customization'.[45]

Carpo's observation of the similarity of outcome is one reason why landscape architects may be reluctant to engage with parametric modelling, viewing it of less relevance to a site-based design practice. But Daniel Davis's research suggests the framing of parametric modelling as style places undue emphasis on the model's outputs. Conversely Davis argues that the relationships constructed and maintained within a parametric model are of far more importance, and it is within this definition that the value to landscape architecture becomes more apparent.[46] He continues:

> For architects, parametric models purportedly improve the designer's ability to make changes, thereby improving their capacity to design. In theory a designer can modify a model's parameter and see the design change almost instantly. As such, parametric models have come to be understood in terms of their outputs; a method for producing tools, or making parametricism, or creating design representations that change to parameters. This focus on what parametric models do suggests a separation between creating and doing, a separation that underplays the significance of creating and maintaining a parametric model.[47]

Davis argues that 'the presence of explicit relationships linking parameters to outcomes' not only disrupts this separation between 'maker' and 'user', but also acts to 'distinguish parametric models from traditional manual tools and from other forms of design representation'.[48] Parametric models, states, Davis 'merge making and using to the point of indistinguishability'.[49]

A major point of contention is whether the designer is responsible for their own parametric models, including designing their own codes or scripts (as reflected in Davis's comment on the merging of 'maker' and 'user') or alternatively applying circulating scripts which potentially traps design within 'a predetermined set of ideas, cultural projections, and aesthetic agendas contained within these inter-faces'.[50] However, as we explore in the following section, designers are increasingly engaging with scripts and code.

Scripting

There is much overlap in the use of the terms programming, coding and scripting, and they are to a point interchangeable. All share the base definition of being a series of instructions in the form of algorithms or rules, which explain precisely how to do something. However there are differences in the scale and characteristics of their application. Some define programming as the development of the overall logic of a program whereas coding is the interpretation of this logic into a coding

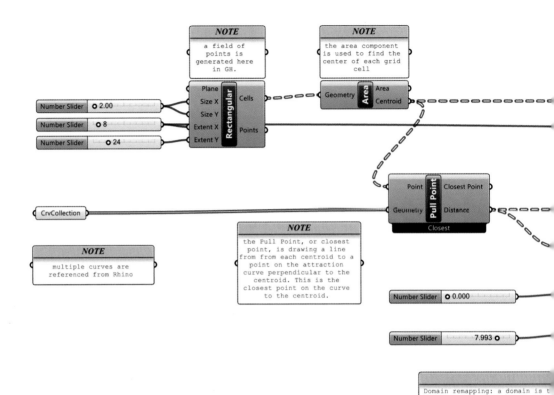

NOTE
a field of points is generated here in GH.

NOTE
the area component is used to find the center of each grid cell

Number Slider   ○ 2.00
Number Slider   ○ 8
Number Slider   ○ 24

Plane
Size X
Size Y
Extent X
Extent Y

Rectangular

Cells
Points

Geometry   Area   Area
Centroid

Point   Closest Point
Geometry   Pull Point   Distance
Closest

CrvCollection

NOTE
multiple curves are referenced from Rhino

NOTE
the Pull Point, or closest point, is drawing a line from from each centroid to a point on the attraction curve perpendicular to the centroid. This is the closest point on the curve to the centroid.

Number Slider   ○ 0.000

Number Slider   7.993 ○

Domain remapping: a domain is t
take our list of distance
porprtionately to new values
instance). In this remapping we
are larger

language, which is compiled (meaning the source code is translated into a computer readable machine code that can be executed). Scripting operates at a smaller scale such as the development of a set of instructions for running a function in a particular language, or for bringing together two different applications. Unlike coding, the computer reads the script and executes it every time. For our purposes, we will use the terms coding or scripting interchangeably.

As we discussed earlier, to think in code or to script requires explicit procedural thinking where the designer generates rules, which produce certain representations, as distinct from directly authoring the representation.[51] Coding is increasingly becoming part of many disciplines and professions, as the nature of the work force changes. Jeannette Wing, vice present of Microsoft research states that, by the middle of the twenty-first century, the ability to break a problem down into a form that a computer can evaluate will be considered a core skill in the manner of reading and writing.[52] The ability 'to abstract, compartmentalise and synthesis' will be valued in a vast range of jobs as technology transforms future employment.[53]

There are many different programming languages available, each with their own syntax and grammar. Most architectural education programs now feature coding within curriculum, some as early as the first or second year of study. A

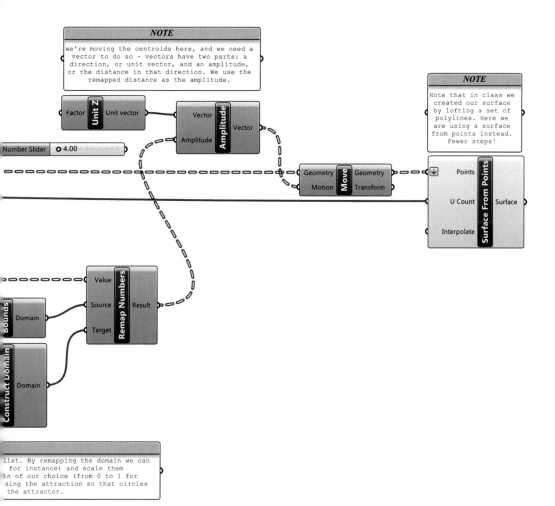

NOTE

we're moving the centroids here, and we need a
vector to do so - vectors have two parts: a
direction, or unit vector, and an amplitude,
or the distance in that direction. We use the
remapped distance as the amplitude.

NOTE

Note that in class we
created our surface
by lofting a set of
polylines. Here we
are using a surface
from points instead.
Fewer steps!

Factor Unit Z Unit vector

Number Slider ○ 4.00

Vector Amplitude Vector

Amplitude

Geometry Move Geometry
Motion Transform

Points Surface From Points
U Count Surface
Interpolate

Value Remap Numbers
Source Result
Target

Bounds Domain

Construct Domain Domain

list. By remapping the domain we can
for instance) and scale them
in of our choice (from 0 to 1 for
sing the attraction so that circles
the attractor.

2.11

An example of a Grasshopper
definition illustrating the
concept of components
(doing actions) and
parameters (data).

range of different software can be used to generate a parametric model. For instance Maya, CATIA and Pro/ENGINEERING develop 'history-based' models where features, parameters and constraints used to design the model are recorded in the order they were applied within a history tree. Software such as Grasshopper, GenerativeComponents and Houdini use 'visual scripts' which record inputs and outputs in highly visual flow chart, while the scripting interfaces of CAD programs operate within a 'textual programming' context.[54]

Two types of programming languages are commonly used within architecture, landscape architecture and urban design. The first is a textual language, biased towards procedural programming, which underpins Maya (Maya Embedded Language), 3ds Max (Maxscript), ArchiCAD (GDL), AutoCAD (AutoLISP), Digital Project (Visual Basics), Processing (Java), Revit (Visual Basic and Python), Rhino (Visual Basic and Python) and SketchUp (Ruby). The second is a visual language which favours declarative or data flow programming, found within GenerativeComponents, Houdini, MaxMSP and Grasshopper.[55]

Grasshopper (formerly known as Explicit History) is one of the most popular visual programming languages in design practice and teaching. Grasshopper creates generative algorithm programs through the concepts of components and parameters. The resultant programs are often described as definitions. Grasshopper was conceived by David Rutten at Robert McNeel & Associates in 2007 and requires Rhinoceros 3D to function. Components are framed as 'doing' actions (or functions), while parameters contain data – thereby storing information. A component requires the data or parameter to perform an action. The node-based design of Grasshopper presents a more accessible scripting language for designers than syntax bound language, allowing users to manipulate and design the script through elements that are graphically depicted.

With the emergence of visual programming language such as Grasshopper, coding becomes less about mathematics and more directly about design exploration. Malcolm McCullough explains further:

> This kind of code is by you, for you – and it is fun…It adds a whole extra level to design thinking. First you set up some rules for generating forms, then you play them to see what kind of design world they create, and then you go back and tweak the rules. With a bit of interface technology, even just a few simple button sliders, you can tweak almost as quickly as you play.[56]

In addition, Grasshopper offers a range of plug-ins, designed to address a particular issue. For instance the plug-in Geco creates a live link between Rhino/Grasshopper and the environmental analysis tool Autodesk Ecotect; Diva-for-Rhino runs daylight, thermal, glare and solar radiation simulations and Kangaroo offers a live physics engine for developing interactive simulations such as water flow. Plug-ins are constantly evolving, as designers respond to specific design issues. Davis and Peters comment:

> The process of development is similar to the computer-programming techniques of scripting, but unlike scripts these plug-ins are packaged as small pieces of software and themselves become part of the design environment.[57]

The free distribution of plug-ins shifts the development of software 'for' designers by companies to instead designers directly influencing the digital design environment, in response to emerging challenges. Software modified by the designer, comments Mark Burry, offers far more room for speculation with 'the tool user (designer) becom[ing] the new toolmaker (software engineer)'.[58] The open circulation of scripts encourages new collaborative processes which are 'under constant evolution and catalysed by sharing at a scale never before seen'.[59] Davis and Peters state 'this represents a significant shift in authorship away from the isolated teams of highly talented programmers towards end use collaboratively shaping their own environment'.[60]

Scripting has led to the emergence of a dedicated role in the design office for the 'toolmaker'. This role is increasingly common in architectural practice, and emerging in some landscape practices such as OLIN Studio in Philadelphia. This large practice of over 90 people has a dedicated Director of Technology, Christian Hanley who is responsible for evaluating and implementing emergent technologies into office and design processes. Currently six staff have high digital capacity (including the ability to script and make tools). How to best make use of this knowledge and expertise is a challenge to the organisation of practice. Developing an explicit role for a toolmaker is one such way. Within the OLIN structure, a toolmaker works closely with project teams to encourage the wide application of digital tools, which can enable the design process to gain and maintain momentum.[61] Importantly, this involves the transference of knowledge and capacity across the practice.

'Visualiser' Chris Landau develops packages of useful tools for his colleagues that can be used in Grasshopper and Rhino. In working with these tools he tries to strike a balance between learning new software and developing the craft of what he already knows.[62] For instance, Landau developed tools for the design of an urban plaza as part of a major development in Shanghai, shown in Figure 2.12. These tools performed operations ranging from importing and populating the scene with 3D trees and people through to the creation of schematic planting massing and the development of a customised algorithm for a unique canopy structure based on simple curve inputs. The tools emerged during the design process, allowing the team to understand the design from within the model and to make iterative changes based on this knowledge. Toolmaking, states Landau, helps to not only work faster and smarter but also provokes a more critical reflection of design processes.[63]

Currently the strongest evidence of scripting in landscape architecture is the increasing interest in the visual programming language Grasshopper. This curiosity is being driven by the newest generation of landscape architects. In university computer labs across the world it is not unusual to see landscape architecture students playing with Grasshopper. It is still very rare for scripting to be incorporated into landscape architecture curriculum with most students either self-taught, drawing on the extensive on-line resources, or learning through Grasshopper courses taught in architecture programs.

The Master of Advanced Studios in Landscape Architecture (MAS LA) program at ETH is one program that does teach programming within curriculum. However the Director Pia Fricker highlights the importance of students understanding how programming is applied within professional practice. She comments that students have little problem in creating their own programs, but far more attention is required in helping them critically reflect on programming and its value in design practice.[64]

In direct response to this need, the MAS LA program now features a 3-day intensive workshop called 'Theoretical Programming' which is held in a mountain hut in the Swiss Alps. Through a combination of lectures and role play, students are introduced to the larger context of programming encompassing object-oriented,

automata-based and genetic programming, along with concepts such as spring systems, shape grammar, Lindenmayer systems and agent systems.[65] Importantly, the ETH teaching team includes a computer specialist who provides valuable theoretical background and input in helping students to learn techniques for communicating a design to an IT company. At the end of the workshop, students in groups of four, must 'communicate a complex design problematic to a programming consultant'.[66]

Landscape architect Andrea Hansen shares Fricker's belief in the vast potential of coding for landscape architecture. Many of our existing processes, comments Hansen, are becoming obsolete, with scripting offering exciting new possibilities to work in a more engaged analytical manner. She believes that landscape architecture's ability to reduce from the abstract to make concrete decisions offers a unique position for engaging critically with Big Data and coding.[67] In 2014 Hansen took a sabbatical from her practice and teaching at Harvard's GSD to more fully engage with coding. In the same year, she was awarded a Code for America Fellowship, and with two others worked with the city of Atlanta to develop 'civic technologies'. Projects included working with Atlanta government officials to develop the Atlanta Court website allowing residents to gain more access to municipal court operations.[68] Through her research-driven practice Fluxscape and her teaching, Hansen continues to explore the potential of open source data, coding, web platforms and data visualisation to promote 'a unique internet-based approach to urbanism that is tailored to the rapidly changing technologies and culture of the twenty-first century'.[69]

In the following discussion we examine in more detail the explicit design processes that guide a parametric modelling approach through a closer look at the work of PEG office of landscape + architecture.

2.12
Tool making contributing further complexity in a 3D model.

Landscape and parametric

For nearly a decade, Karen M'Closkey and Keith VanDerSys from PEG office landscape + architecture have explored the potential of pattern as a means for engaging form and system. They observe a distrust of pattern within landscape architecture because pattern is often regarded as an applied surface unresponsive to site. Yet, they argue, patterns are essentially about relationships, offering a 'diagram of process'.[70] The legibility and coherence of patterns, writes M'Closkey, 'carry the potential to bind together landscape's utilitarian and aesthetic functions; systems and composition; performance and appearance; matter and signs'.[71] Correspondingly, an interrogation of pattern can reveal 'the structure of nature without looking like "nature"', providing an 'understanding of the operations and attributes of systems'.[72]

Parametric modelling offers PEG a valuable technique for exploring repetition and temporality, pattern and process. They acknowledge that architecture's 'part of whole thinking', which emphasises components, repetition, aggregates, units and blocks, offers a simpler translation into computational design than landscape architecture. However they consider parametric modelling consistent with the dynamic media of landscape architecture, stating 'as a generative design tool, this type of modeling enables the possibility of new relational and organizational structures, which close the divide between analysis and formation'.[73] Parametric modelling can be considered a further evolution of the major conceptual and visualisation models used by landscape architects to materialise change in the landscape.[74] These models, identified by M'Closkey and VanDerSys, include: Simultaneity, achieved through the superimposition of multiple images (evident in composite mapping) to convey a shifting landscape over time; Successional sequential drawings to represent changes in landscape composition over time; and Episodic such as notational drawings featured in Lawrence Halprin's eco-scores.[75]

The following discussion of PEG's scheme *Bellwether*, also submitted for the Taichung Gateway Park Competition, offers clear demonstration of the formal logic driving their Grasshopper definition (reproduced in Figure 2.13) which structures the parametric modelling process.

PEG's design shares many similarities with Mosbach's approach to lithosphere, introduced earlier. Both focus on Taiwan's extreme environmental volatility, which is simultaneously one of the wettest places in Asia, while experiencing extreme drought conditions. Whereas Mosbach interrogated the performative capability of the ground plan through manual calculations of porosity and permeability, PEG apply a computational approach to explore the forces (quantity and quality) of water and their relationship to topography, with real-time feedback. This computational approach, comments PEG, facilitates an exploration of 'how patterns (organisational and temporal) could harness, direct and index the extreme climate volatility associated with global warming and rapid urbanisation' at the level of human experience.[76] Beginning with a parametric model (constructed with

Rhino and Grasshopper), the designers modelled the extant stormwater quantities provided within the competition brief. They state:

> These amounts were combined with the existing topography and roadway widths to determine the values for modelling surface drainage into the new park area. These values were also used to infer levels of surface water pollution entering from the edges since the quality of the flow would be proportional to road width and associated car traffic. The hope was that this approach would give us a means to visualize the density and distribution patterns of both water quantity and quality.[77]

The competition brief did not offer accurate metrics, only providing broad quantities of water runoff allocated to six zones of the park. The water flows and pollution levels were established within the parametric model by applying a 'scale of relativity without true metrics'.[78] This reveals an important characteristic in what a landscape architect values during the modelling process, compared to the more empirically driven disciplines of environmental science and engineering. VanDerSys explains further:

> we could run a true hydrological model…but I am not looking for a descriptive model –but instead a decision making model that opens up opportunities but it still gives me some basic characteristics – where there are already conditions of flow that we need to dampen, collect or do something with.[79]

The contour information provided in the brief was transformed via a point cloud into a mesh. Working with Grasshopper, the slopes of the mesh were deconstructed into a series of vectors, where the length of the line (which was a product of the degree of angle – the steeper slope, the longer the line) presented concentrations within the field. The ability of vectors to represent force and flow make them a useful representational technique, sharing similarities to hachure representations of topography that apply shading in short disconnected lines to indicate slope direction. Through a simple script, the vectors were sifted into three grades of colour, with the colour and length of line now indicating intensity and direction of water flow.

This design process transformed original contour information into zones of collection and consolidation, highlighting eight zones to further interrogate for their capability to retain and collect water. In the next stage, the capacity of these zones was explored through the input of different rainfall and drainage scenarios (reflective of variable weather conditions) to test the dynamic relationship between environmental forces and form. These explorations identified sites of intensifications, which formed potential areas for the designers to intervene.

Reflecting on this design process, we can see how PEG's active construction of the parametric model is in fact the design process. Each transformative operation is an example of generational analysis, linking information and outcome. Through an explicit process, the designers consciously manipulate information, functions and representations to reveal underlying behaviours and dynamic processes. PEG explain further:

> parametric software enables the modelling of numerical information in terms of force, quantity, and direction (such as in water or wind flow) in order to generate organizations that are intrinsically relational; that is, entities are defined by virtue of their association or proximity to other elements. Consequently, the affiliation between form and process is inherent in recursive models; changes made to any one entity have a reciprocal effect on neighbouring entities.[80]

VanDerSys stresses that the parametric modelling does not produce 'form', which instead emerges through consideration of other influences. The fields of collection identified during the modelling process for instance evolved into an analogy of the atoll reef ecosystem, comprising two repeating geometries of a 'reef' and 'lagoon' system. Constructed of 'large, arc like tapered figures', the higher reef areas provides the primary controlled and maintained areas of the park, structures circulation (cars, bikes, people and water) and program (forest and occasionally flooded fields).[81] The circular low-lying lagoons (identified in the parametric exploration) fluctuate as adaptable zones able to absorb extreme alterations between drought and flood, including acting as reservoirs to collect water or alternatively, when dry, providing space for temporary events.

A further examination of patterns and their relationship to forces and material conveyance advanced the scheme. The plug-in Paneling Tool for Rhino was used to interrogate attractors and repellents, with the designers looking for repeated geometries that could be subdivided and aggregated together to create an overall organisation.[82] This geometry shown in Figure 2.14 produced a repetitious form that adds structure to the spaces located between the activity zone of the reef and the more volatile depressions of the lagoon. The final scheme presents a legible tiered structure for the park, which accommodates and registers the conditions of change created by dynamic water flows and the cycle of flooding and drought.[83] In a final layer, a series of smog 'urchins' designed to address pollution was proposed along the alignment of the former runway site (Figure 2.15).

PEG's exploratory design process, considered against Snøhetta's approach for the *MAX Lab IV* (discussed in Chapter 1), begins to clarify a landscape architectural approach to parametric modelling. In a major distinction to architecture which assumes a more abstract spatial topological surface, landscape architecture positions topology simultaneously as surface, system and materiality. For example, PEG focus on 'complex *topological* properties – those described as relationships among a variety processes flowing through a landscape'.[84] This definition aligns

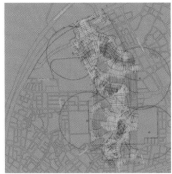

■ To isolate the x & y vectors, deconstruct and reconstruct the mesh vectors by removing the z vector

■ Rotation around the normal to get the tangent to the slope. The normal is the perpendicular direction to the tangent at the same point.

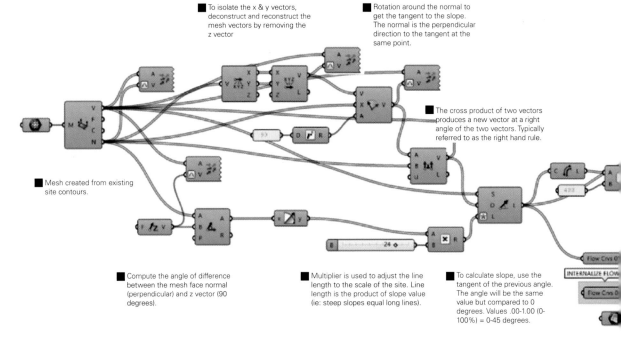

■ The cross product of two vectors produces a new vector at a right angle of the two vectors. Typically referred to as the right hand rule.

■ Mesh created from existing site contours.

■ Compute the angle of difference between the mesh face normal (perpendicular) and z vector (90 degrees).

■ Multiplier is used to adjust the line length to the scale of the site. Line length is the product of slope value (ie: steep slopes equal long lines).

■ To calculate slope, use the tangent of the previous angle. The angle will be the same value but compared to 0 degrees. Values .00-1.00 (0-100%) = 0-45 degrees.

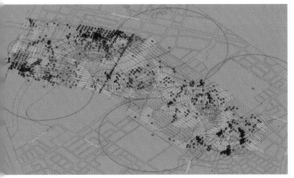
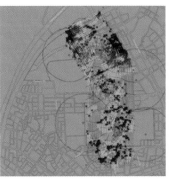

2.13
Grasshopper definition which informed PEG office of landscape + architecture's scheme *Bellwether*.

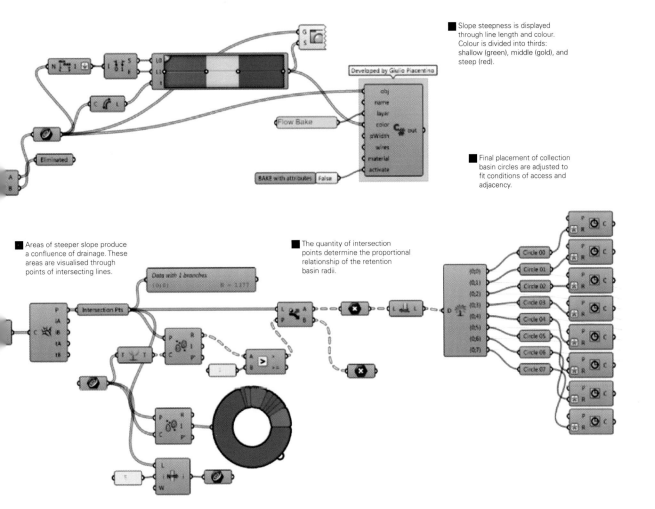

■ Slope steepness is displayed through line length and colour. Colour is divided into thirds: shallow (green), middle (gold), and steep (red).

Developed by Giulio Piacentino

■ Final placement of collection basin circles are adjusted to fit conditions of access and adjacency.

■ Areas of steeper slope produce a confluence of drainage. These areas are visualised through points of intersecting lines.

■ The quantity of intersection points determine the proportional relationship of the retention basin radii.

Collection voids

Wetland

Field

Forest

Building

Smog urchin

N

0 75 150   300

Forecast:

Local
Flooding

Forecast:

Extended
Drought

Forecast:

Smog
Warning

2.14
Masterplan highlighting the
spatial organisation of high
and low areas, including
the subdivided geometry
which adds further structural
definition for the site.

2.15a–c
Pathway following the high
atoll during periods of flood
(a) and dry periods (b).
A series of smog 'urchins'
to address pollution aligned
along the former runway
site (c).

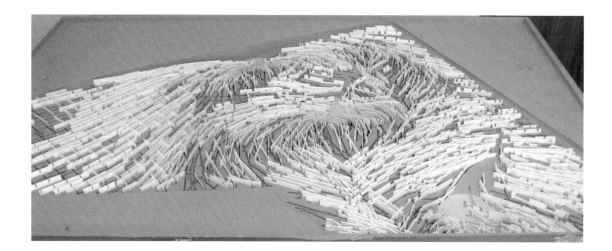

with Christophe Girot's concept of a landscape topology which encompasses the physical interrelation of complex surfaces with forces and changes in the environment'.[85] Topology states Girot 'is about the intelligence of a site perceived and shaped by society topically'.[86] The model is central to a topological design process, displacing the 'highly abstract programmatic plans' and 'dreamlike images' that have dominated landscape architecture in the past 20 years and diminish our understandings of terrain.[87] Through topology, states Girot, 'design questions and works with the model first before reverting to any image'.[88]

Consequently the parametric modelling process focuses on constructing and interrogating relationships, behaviours and forces between landscape attributes, heightened by the ability to introduce data reflective of dynamic change into the modelling process. PEG's process demonstrates the parametric model's role as a generative tool, as distinct from a descriptive or a predictive model. As VanDerSys comments 'you don't model things, you model relationships'.[89] Consequently the construction of the parametric model forms the critical design process requiring the designer to explicitly identify and define parameters and to maintain functions during its construction. The model therefore operates as a medium 'between analysis and formation', closing the problematic divide between site analysis and design generation that is evident in linear design processes.[90]

Most importantly, the model offers a testing of systems and relationships but this process rarely translates literally into form. Girot et al. describe this modelling process as directive rather than prescriptive, as is explained further in the following quote:

> Rather than relying on a design process of random variations as often associated with parametric processes of design, controlled decision-making can led to clear performance orientated results. The resulting design operations are a hybrid between intuitive physical interventions

2.16
Post competition, PEG engaged further parametric modelling techniques to translate the digital model into a fabricated hachure model. This model shows the proposed topography as a factor of forces, representing the way water would flow, collect and disperse in this dynamic landscape.

and 'variable' manipulation, and are therefore conceived as 'directive' rather than 'prescriptive' in design outcome.[91]

We can see from this discussion that a parametric approach to landscape architecture is not a style, but instead offers a valuable design operation to engage with the forces, characteristics and temporal qualities of a site, directly within a design process. Further, parametric modelling, does not push landscape architecture into an architectural design language or outcome but instead allows the discipline to work with and maintain its core concerns such as systems, ecology and temporal change.

Performative urbanism

The idea of 'directive' rather than the 'prescriptive' characteristics of parametric modelling are explored further in the following discussion of two master's-level design studios that focused on performative approaches to urbanism. Extreme-weather events such as storm surge and hurricanes, combined with longer term consequences of rising sea levels has revealed the vulnerability of many cities along the east coast of the United States. Beginning with the catastrophic impact of Hurricane Katrina on New Orleans in 2005, design studios have offered important avenues for landscape architecture to explore a more resilient urbanism. Unencumbered by short-term political agendas, the design studio offers a speculative space to explore alternative futures for communities who are directly impacted by climate change.

Since 2010, Chris Reed has led the Flux City studio at Harvard's GSD focused on Jamaica Bay, in Queens, New York. The low lying area is a highly urbanised estuary and extensive coast salt marsh system threaded by significant infrastructure such as the JFK airport (one of the world's busiest), bridges, power lines and roads and is subject to storm surge inundation, high water tables, tidal fluctuations, and in the longer-term sea level rise. The Flux City studio challenges students to conceive of the site as 'performative fields' shaped by systems in a constant state of flux, and to invent and describe urban form and adaptive ecologies responsive to these dynamic conditions.[92]

Working with similar concepts, Karen M'Closkey and Keith VanDerSys chose the complex marine system of Watson Bay, which forms part of Biscayne Bay in southern Florida, to develop their design studio brief, Miami Vice in 2014. The studio was run first at the University of Pennsylvania and in the following semester at Harvard's GSD. The Bay features the human-made Watson Island, and a diverse marine system encompassing saltwater mangroves, freshwater wetlands and poor water quality.[93] Similarly to Flux City, the Miami Vice studio emphasise processes of formation, but guided by the two theoretical concepts of 'simulated natures' and 'liminal machines'. Simulated nature frames systems as 'ecological and social formations conceptualized through "invisible" information (data and flows)', while 'liminal machines' engages with the transitional or 'inbetween' characteristics of overlapping habitats and conditions through the proposal of multifunctional infrastructures.[94]

These conceptual framings, combined with an emphasis on computational design and performance, establish very different frameworks to more conventional landscape architecture studios, which often begin with a comprehensive inventory of the entire site. Guided by a specific research agenda – to develop a resilient urbanism within sites of flux – these studios interrogate the dynamic interface between water, land, infrastructure and urbanism.

The sequencing of workflow is critical to the success of the studios, requiring the careful insertion of skills-based workshops and digital intensives at strategic points. Both studios feature highly structured explorations of systems and associated phenomena, abstracted from the all-encompassing site conditions. These explorations establish a set of rules or parameters to subsequently guide students in their design explorations and their final design proposals.

Over time, as digital technologies become embedded more comprehensively throughout curriculum, the intensity of instruction evident in these studios will lessen. However, during this transitional moment, a computational studio remains challenging for students and staff, requiring a high level of resourcing, matched by a strong commitment from students. Lecturers also face the considerable challenge of introducing digital skills concurrently with the design studio. Marc Aurel Schnabel comments that the 'integration of digital media into the design studio curricula often fails, because the compound acquisition of skills prevents a deep exploration of design and the theoretical aspects involved at the same time'.[95] In the following section, we outline in more detail how the studios were structured to engage with the ecological and social complexities of site, concurrently with providing students with the necessary digital skills.

The performative fields of Flux City

The Flux City studio featured three intensive digital workshops interspersed throughout the 14-week semester. The first digital workshop, coordinated by Zaneta Hong and co-taught with Sergio Lopez-Pineiro was a 1-week intensive. This workshop introduced computational methodologies (using Rhino and Grasshopper) to simulate two definitions of ground-behaviour and formation. Students collected and quantified datasets produced from a single environmental phenomenon that embodies the relationship between air, water, and ground such as tidal fluctuations and inundation, erosion and deposition, pollution and fog. Working across scales ranging from the molecular to larger issues of storm surge and ozone depletion, the behaviours and characteristics of the selected phenomena were investigated and mapped in serial form and at regular intervals to develop 'a matrix of states or instances'.[96] A series documenting the phenomena of fog is presented in Figure 2.17a–b.

Attention then turned to landform typologies and how they affected the performance of the studied phenomena. Using the four geometric conditions of the dune, berm, basin and canal, relationships between the phenomena and form were explored parametrically, through the modification of extrinsic (height, depth) and intrinsic (angle of repose) parameters. Real-time data drawn from websites such as NOAA (National Oceanic and Atmospheric Administration), New York City open source and weather.com furthered a dynamic understanding of phenomena. Students learned to transform data from Excel spreadsheets into Grasshopper definitions, which represented the dynamic behaviour of the chosen phenomena. These explorations were animated (using After Effects) to present real-time representations of the systems interacting with landforms, which offered an understanding of 'performance variability'.[97] Systems disruptions were then introduced into the parametric model, with outcomes documented along with their diagrammatic descriptions, datasets and programmatic functions, into a matrix of ground formations (Figure 2.17c).

Zaneta Hong, a studio instructor concludes of the workshop module:

With the resulting animations, diagrams, and drawings, students gained insight into how computational models of dynamic systems could yield instrumental behaviors and formations, and how landscape architects utilise those products to generate various design responses. This design methodology examined how assemblages of processes, materials, and technologies, simulated through computational media, revealed conditions of ground, which could subsequently be organised by process rather than appearance.[98]

Students move from this digital workshop into the semester-long Flux City studio, which since 2013, has been co-ordinated by Chris Reed and David Mah. The studio is structured into the two phases of Flux Fields and Neighbourhoods. In Flux Fields, students engaged with the larger site systems beginning with the identification of flux ecologies that establish 'the conceptual, performative, physical and temporal bases for the project'.[99] Building on the techniques developed during the workshop, students interrogated the relationship between dynamic processes, physical landform and infrastructures, including the identification of a catalogue of physical and 'operational' parameters that can 'seed dynamics and succession'.[100] A site visit completed this phase.

A second digital workshop focused on landform, which introduced techniques such as physical and 3D digital modelling, plans and sections for translating ecological infrastructures onto the site. The catalogue of ecological parameters developed earlier provided the rules to guide the design of transport, water and energy infrastructure and public facilities on to the proposed landform.

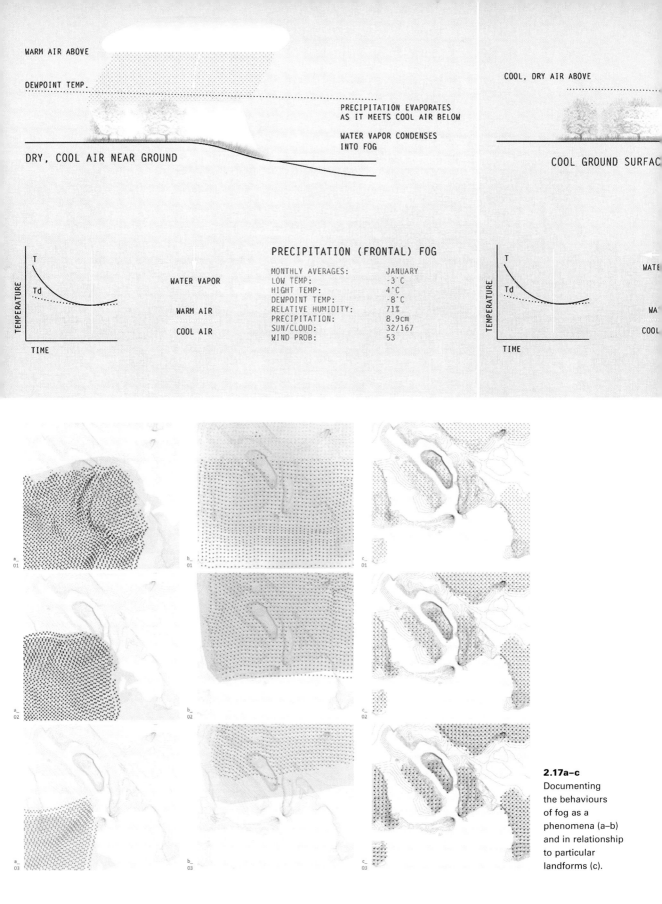

WARM AIR ABOVE

DEWPOINT TEMP.

PRECIPITATION EVAPORATES
AS IT MEETS COOL AIR BELOW

WATER VAPOR CONDENSES
INTO FOG

DRY, COOL AIR NEAR GROUND

COOL, DRY AIR ABOVE

COOL GROUND SURFAC

TEMPERATURE

T

Td

TIME

WATER VAPOR

WARM AIR

COOL AIR

PRECIPITATION (FRONTAL) FOG

MONTHLY AVERAGES: JANUARY
LOW TEMP: -3°C
HIGHT TEMP: 4°C
DEWPOINT TEMP: -8°C
RELATIVE HUMIDITY: 71%
PRECIPITATION: 8.9cm
SUN/CLOUD: 32/167
WIND PROB: 53

TEMPERATURE

T

Td

TIME

WATE

WA

COOL

a_
01

b_
01

c_
01

a_
02

b_
02

c_
02

a_
03

b_
03

c_
03

2.17a–c
Documenting
the behaviours
of fog as a
phenomena (a–b)
and in relationship
to particular
landforms (c).

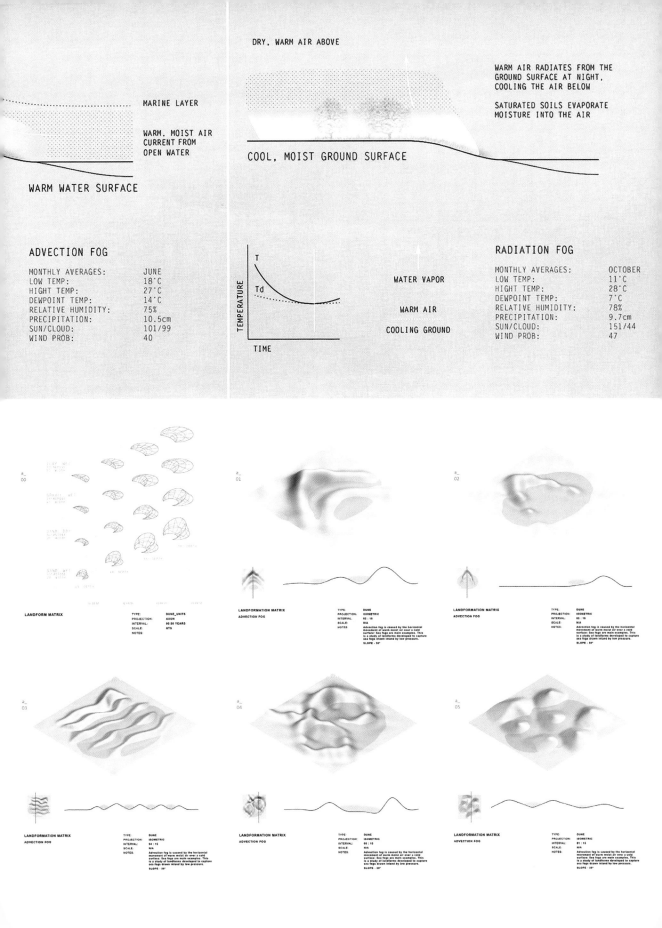

DRY, WARM AIR ABOVE

WARM AIR RADIATES FROM THE
GROUND SURFACE AT NIGHT,
COOLING THE AIR BELOW

SATURATED SOILS EVAPORATE
MOISTURE INTO THE AIR

MARINE LAYER

WARM, MOIST AIR
CURRENT FROM
OPEN WATER

COOL, MOIST GROUND SURFACE

WARM WATER SURFACE

ADVECTION FOG

MONTHLY AVERAGES:	JUNE
LOW TEMP:	18°C
HIGHT TEMP:	27°C
DEWPOINT TEMP:	14°C
RELATIVE HUMIDITY:	75%
PRECIPITATION:	10.5cm
SUN/CLOUD:	101/99
WIND PROB:	40

T

Td

TEMPERATURE

TIME

WATER VAPOR

WARM AIR

COOLING GROUND

RADIATION FOG

MONTHLY AVERAGES:	OCTOBER
LOW TEMP:	11°C
HIGHT TEMP:	28°C
DEWPOINT TEMP:	7°C
RELATIVE HUMIDITY:	78%
PRECIPITATION:	9.7cm
SUN/CLOUD:	151/44
WIND PROB:	47

a_
00

a_
01

a_
02

a_
03

a_
04

a_
05

LANDFORM MATRIX

TYPE:	DUNE_UNITS
PROJECTION:	AXON
INTERVAL:	00:50 YEARS
SCALE:	NTS
NOTES:	

LANDFORMATION MATRIX
ADVECTION FOG

TYPE:	DUNE
PROJECTION:	ISOMETRIC
INTERVAL:	00 : 15
SCALE:	N/A
NOTES:	Advection fog is caused by the horizontal movement of warm moist air over a cold surface: Sea fogs are main examples. This is a study of landforms developed to capture sea fogs drawn inland by low pressure.

SLOPE - 30°

LANDFORMATION MATRIX
ADVECTION FOG

TYPE:	DUNE
PROJECTION:	ISOMETRIC
INTERVAL:	00 : 15
SCALE:	N/A
NOTES:	Advection fog is caused by the horizontal movement of warm moist air over a cold surface: Sea fogs are main examples. This is a study of landforms developed to capture sea fogs drawn inland by low pressure.

SLOPE - 30°

LANDFORMATION MATRIX
ADVECTION FOG

TYPE:	DUNE
PROJECTION:	ISOMETRIC
INTERVAL:	00 : 15
SCALE:	N/A
NOTES:	Advection fog is caused by the horizontal movement of warm moist air over a cold surface: Sea fogs are main examples. This is a study of landforms developed to capture sea fogs drawn inland by low pressure.

SLOPE - 30°

LANDFORMATION MATRIX
ADVECTION FOG

TYPE:	DUNE
PROJECTION:	ISOMETRIC
INTERVAL:	00 : 15
SCALE:	N/A
NOTES:	Advection fog is caused by the horizontal movement of warm moist air over a cold surface: Sea fogs are main examples. This is a study of landforms developed to capture sea fogs drawn inland by low pressure.

SLOPE - 30°

LANDFORMATION MATRIX
ADVECTION FOG

TYPE:	DUNE
PROJECTION:	ISOMETRIC
INTERVAL:	01 : 15
SCALE:	N/A
NOTES:	Advection fog is caused by the horizontal movement of warm moist air over a cold surface: Sea fogs are main examples. This is a study of landforms developed to capture sea fogs drawn inland by low pressure.

SLOPE - 30°

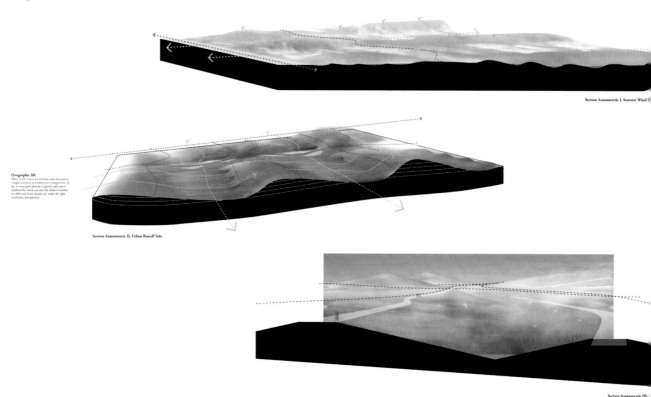

Section Axonometric I, Summer Wind

Orographic lift
When an air mass is forced from a low elevation to a higher elevation as it moves over rising terrain. As the air mass gains altitude it quickly cools down adiabatically, which can raise the relative humidity to 100% and create clouds and, under the right conditions, precipitation.

Section Axonometric II, Urban Runoff Side

Section Axonometric III,

In the Neighborhoods phase, students began with a Relational Urbanism digital workshop run by Eduardo Rico and Enriqueta Llabras-Valls. Relational urban models are parametric 'digital design interfaces' that use parameters (mathematical and intuitive) and the representation of infrastructural and environmental variables to 'generate three dimensional massing of urban environments'.[101] The Relational urbanism work of Rico and Llabras-Valls has evolved over a number years, explored in design studios at the Berlage Institute, the AA, through Rico's work at Arup London, and most recently through the Relational Urbanism cluster at the Bartlett School of Architecture, University College, London. Relational urban models are conceived for use early in the design process, intended to replace the static master plan with a reflexive model that allows designers, decision makers and the community to discuss and test different distributions, spatial protocols and parameters.

Working with Grasshopper, Rhino and Excel, students applied parametric modelling in an exploration of housing and urban block variations, guided by metrics of development standards, to establish a catalogue of type. Now equipped with a suite of rules, types and parameters, students are then challenged to work at the scale of a neighbourhood to develop infrastructure, housing and topography responsive to the dynamic site conditions. Emphasis is placed on refining the intersections and interfaces between the building components, ecological systems and proposed infrastructure. David Mah comments that this final synthesis of ideas is initially overwhelming for many students.[102] However, it is at this stage that they

2.18
Diagram of the phenomena Orographic lift which under the correct conditions can create clouds and produce rain.

2.19
The *Orographic Hills* scheme by Peichen Hao and Ken Chongsuwat. A phased construction of topographic berms, each with a prescribed role.

Performative systems

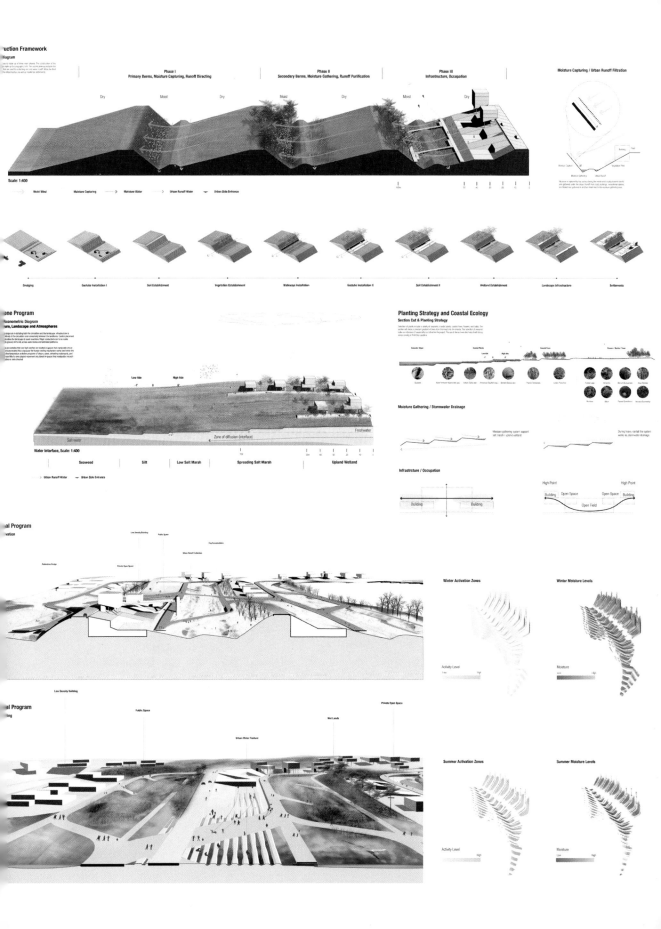

2.20
Rendered perspective of the
Orographic Hills scheme
showing the relationship
between housing, topography
and infrastructure.

2.21
The topographic berms
encourage the development
of particular climatic and
ecologic conditions.

2.22
Laser cut model of the
scheme.

begin to appreciate the complexity and conclusions that have been developed over the course of the studio, which can now be applied in a more holistic manner.

The comprehensiveness of the final design outcomes is reflected in the *Orographic Hills* scheme by Peichen Hao and Ken Chongsuwat which began with an initial exploration of fog. The proposal emerged as a phased construction of topographic berms, each with a prescribed role, as presented in Figure 2.19. The primary berm offers protection from the dynamic and unpredictable water's edge, followed by a secondary berm that collects rain and water runoff, while a third establishes configurations of infrastructure and residential settlements. These design decisions are guided by the typological parametric studies and an understanding of the dynamic effects and behaviours of forms and systems. Rather than react to site conditions, the design consciously creates them. The topographic form develops particular climatic and ecologic conditions conceived to encourage moisture gathering (to establish conditions of fog), harvest water runoff and to be responsive to unpredictable flood conditions. Circulation runs seamlessly and continously throughout the undulating topography, uninterrupted by fluctuating water levels.

Liminal machines

The Miami Vice studio shares similar characteristics to the Flux City studio, structured as three explorations conceived to uncover knowledge of forces, flows and material behaviours which can then be applied in a design intervention. The studio adopted parametric modelling and simulation as methods for understanding patterns of processes that give rise to particular performances and effects. A series of media tutorials focused on Rhino Terrain, Grasshopper, GIS, Maya Particle Flow and Paneling Tools are interspersed throughout the studio.

In the 'Functional/Material Loop' exploration students identified a feedback or system, which is interrogated in relationship to 'production' and 'exchange'. Focus then shifted in the 'Pattern of Processes' exercise to explore patterns established by the natural forces identified in the functional/material loops. These exercises were site-less and scale-less, focused on organisation and qualitative characteristics emerging from forces, flows, transformations and adaptations. Working with time-based parametric models (using Rhino and Grasshopper), students established vector fields 'with attractors (points or curves) as influences which produce changes in direction and intensity'.[103] The subsequent patterns were analysed to produce a visual inventory documenting forces such as tidal and air movement and processes of erosion, sedimentation and deposition.

The final phase 'Simulating Sites' returned to the physical site, to explore these flows and transformations using the software Maya, Ecotect and ANSYS Fluent. Using a range of intensities and directional changes within vectors, students speculated on the characteristics of material change. A focus on forces eliminated

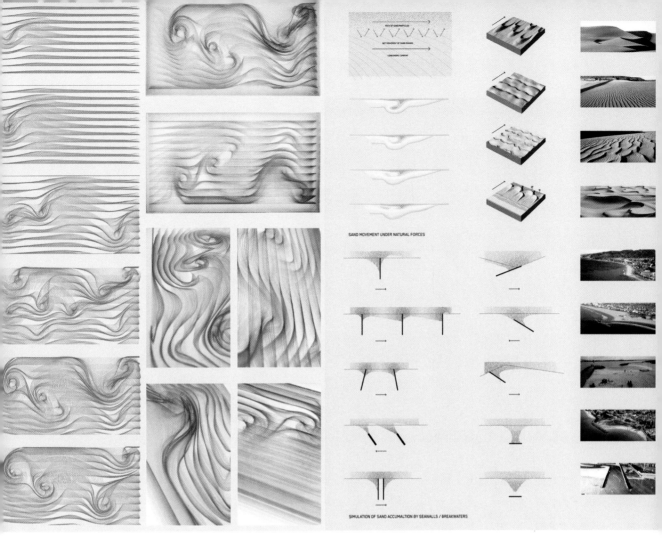

SAND MOVEMENT UNDER NATURAL FORCES

SIMULATION OF SAND ACCUMALTION BY SEAWALLS / BREAKWATERS

2.23
Explorations of flow dynamics and eddy formations (left); understanding of the forces which guide sand movement and depletion (right)

simple opposition framings of land/water, instead revealing transitional and incremental processes. This analysis highlighted potential sites of intervention where existing conditions could be amplified or reduced, with the ambition of finding design opportunities at the interface of land and water.[104]

Lastly, students proposed a working method based in geometry (informed by the earlier explorations) that could be manipulated, either through an operation of transformation or layered together to guide the form and language of the design. The accumulative value of these explorations is evident in Jing Guo's project, which began with the interrogation of flows and eddy formations through drawings, which were later transformed into a series of laser-cut plexi models. This work evolved into an inquiry into the dynamics of the water's edge with a focus on sand movement (Figure 2.23). Computational fluid dynamic (CFD) modelling as shown in Figure 2.24, simulated tidal and air flow which exposed excesses and deficiencies within the system and highlighted areas of sand loss and accumulation.

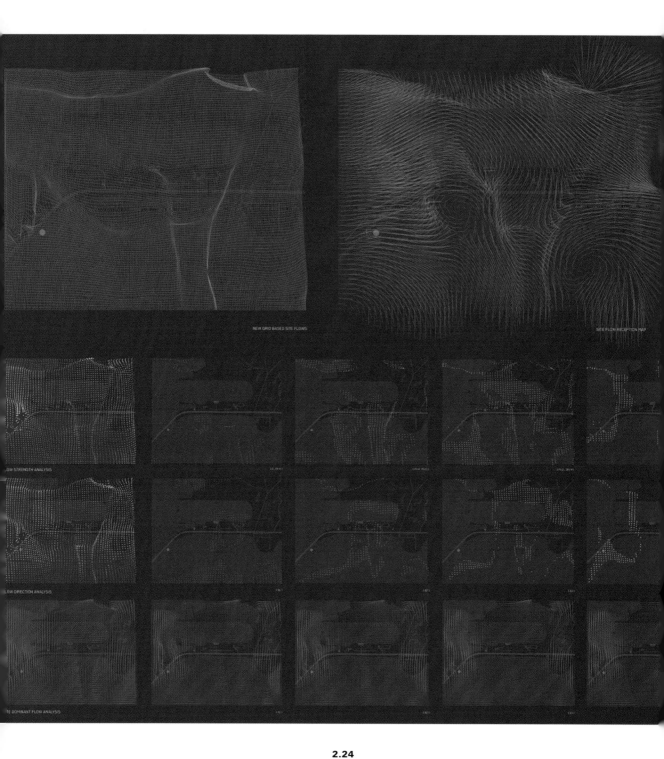

2.24
Documentation of the computational fluid dynamics (CFD)
modelling which highlighted areas of sand loss and accumulation.

Performative systems

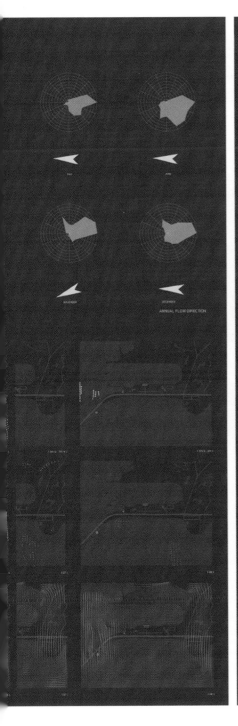

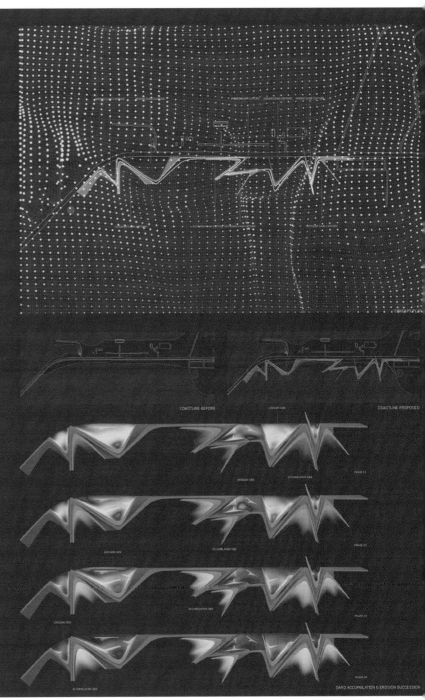

Building on these inquiries, Guo conceived an infrastructural system presented in Figure 2.25 that maintained sand and offered a more viable ecological and economic alternative to importing sand from other cities. Three infrastructure conditions were proposed: a hard structure limestone seawall, a more flexible timber fence and a mesh to stabilise sand and vegetation. These structures carefully sited according to the rules determined from CFD modelling, develop a more socially and ecologically diverse habitat, intermingling sand and water, as well as offering three different sandy field conditions that can be used for beach volleyball and sand surfing.

In a further example, Yongjun Jo and Kyung-Kuhn Lee engaged with the unpredictable context of sea level rise, which could increase by as much as 1.8 metres in Miami by the end of the century. Working at the interface of the island and sea, the scheme introduced a horizontal dyke as a responsive and dynamic buffer zone to mediate wave surge and create new habitats. Earlier explorations of energy attractors and dissipaters informed strategies for the incremental placement of the proposed wetlands. Interrogation of mangrove systems as both patterns (a

2.25
A resilient infrastructural strategy for the coast.

SITE PLAN N   10M

DRY VEGETATION ZONES

2.26
Programmatic interface
for three infrastructural
conditions: deposit, erosion
and stabilisation.

structure of interlocking roots modelled in Figure 2.27b) and system (including the ability to stabilise, clean water and dissipate flows of energy), informed the design of an expanding infrastructure.

The horizontal dyke begins as a thin flexible infrastructure made from palm carbon fibres, floating and moving on the wave surface. Over time, through the addition of plants and mixed material from a 'Tree Bridge', the infrastructure increases in thickness as layers of plant fibre containers, sediment and plant roots decompose to form a rich saltwater marsh (Figure 2.27b–c). This intervention extends the existing urban waterfront area, provides new circulation movements and offers a far more responsive infrastructure than the more commonly applied vertical sea walls.

Pedagogically, the Flux City and Miami Vice studios demand a high level of engaged critical thinking, requiring students to constantly redefine and reframe problems. Students explore research questions rather than respond to a more prescribed brief or programmatically driven outcome. No longer guided by sequential design processes such as site analysis, programmatic and functional explorations

sh Garden_ Hybrid Surface of Natural and Artificial Material

...like starts as thin and flexible infrastructure. However, it is not just shallow and ...surface. Matured plants and mixed materials from the Tree Bridge will form lay-...surfaces, and as time passes, decomposed palm fiber container will be stuck to ...arne and form thick ground. As sea level rises, this artificial ground will expand ...get thicker, form rich salt water marsh.

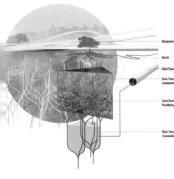

Mangroves

Marsh

Main Structure & Irrigation Tube : *Carbon Fiber*

Basic Structure : *Carbon Fiber & Container : Palm...*
Containing Pit Soil & Purifying The Rain Water

Lime Stone
Purifying The Rain Water

Basic Structure : *Carbon Fiber*
Containing Fresh Water

Artificial Land : *Carbon Fiber + Plants*
Making Land & Dike

Responsive Surface : *Carbon Fiber*

Deck
Basic Structure : *Carbon Fiber*
Preventing Erosion & Containing
The Artificial Land Making Habitats

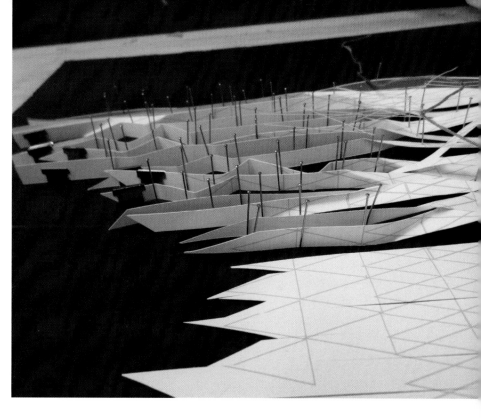

2.27a–c
A horizontal infrastructure by Yongjun Jo and Kyung-Kuhn Lee.

and concept development, computational techniques are used to work concurrently across information, processes and form, requiring students to continually draw conclusions from their investigations. Site analysis is re-conceived from passive information into the very material of design, transformed within parametric modelling into an interrogation of dynamic processes under constant formation.

Parametric possibilities

In the final section of this chapter, we continue the discussion of parametric modelling with a reflection on how it might be applied within landscape planning. Parametric design increasingly informs larger-scale urban design and planning projects; exemplified by Zaha Hadid's monumental visions for the Kartal-Pendik Masterplan in Istanbul. These approaches are often criticised as 'big' architecture, simply the application of parametric architectural techniques on a larger urban scale. Eduardo Rico comments that these schemes often present 'a purely morpho-typological approach to design', where urban form is approached predominantly through the spatial qualities and the aesthetics of urban ensemble and composition.[105]

There are however alternative approaches to large-scale parametric modelling which place emphasis on research driven design methodologies rather than form. For many years, MVRDV have drawn on data-based parametric studies, interactive software and design tools to test the performance of urbanism. MVRDV have been influential in the development of open source design tools such as the (Green) City

Calculator that allow designers, the public, planners and developments to compare, test and optimise design and planning decisions through interaction with constraints and parameters made apparent through design parameters.[106] These tools promote a new collaborative and participatory form of urbanism. The Citymaker tool for instance promotes a bottom-up approach to urban design, allowing inhabitants to generate new urban areas based on their values and needs.[107]

For landscape architecture, we suggest that parametric modelling offers enormous potential to extend the current practices and methodologies of landscape planning into more research-driven approaches that can also engage with design. As we discussed in the Introduction, there is intent to integrate more design and creativity into planning approaches, as reflected by the concept of Geodesign. However, as we suggested earlier, the challenge of inserting design into Geodesign involves far more than adding 'sketching capability' or considering multidisciplinary perspectives, instead requiring generative techniques which can work across data, information, form and systems.

Considered against landscape planning methodologies such as the McHargian overlay method and more recently Steinitz's Framework for Geodesign 2012 (formerly known as a Framework for Landscape Planning), the contribution of parametric modelling becomes clear. The Steinitz Framework for instance is premised on *separate* models of decision, impact, change, evaluation, process and representation.[108] Processes are cycled through and repeated, with the various options compared to establish the optimal outcome. While these processes may involve the use of GIS data, they do not necessarily harness computational power or engage with real-time data.

In contrast, parametric modelling, links 'three dimensional and evidence-based analysis in such a way that design can be dynamically controlled while the outcomes of the various indicators are updated in real time'.[109] These models are simultaneously generative and analytical, presenting an approach for landscape planning that maintains a 'dynamic interaction between design input and evidence-based variables'.[110] Parametric modelling advances McHarg's ambition of 'fitness and fitting – the selection of a fit environment and the adaptation of that environment, and of the organism, to accommodate a better fitting'.[111] McHarg's analytical techniques were intrinsically linked to the technology of his time, first spatial analysis and in later years, ecological data sourced from remote sensing.

Writing in 1984, McHarg highlighted the computer's capability in demonstrating how 'solutions vary with the value systems of the problem solver', influenced by the 'quite different value systems representing developers, conservationists, agricultural preservationists, historic building preservationists, and others'.[112] McHarg's views align with Rico and Llabres-Valls' aspirations expressed 30 years later, to establish a 'dynamic interaction between design input and evidence-based variables'.[113] However, unlike McHarg who relied on 2D plans, computational design offers reflexive models where designers, decision makers and the community can discuss and test different distributions, spatial protocols, and parameters, with changes updated in real time.

It is therefore our speculation that a computational approach encompassing parametric modelling and simulation offers valuable techniques for working across design, planning, GIS and real-time data, with many of the design examples included in this chapter offering demonstration of this.

The transition of planning processes into the realm of the computational also aligns with the evolution of Esri's software, such as the acquisition of CityEngine. This program emerged from the PhD research work of Pascal Mueller, conducted at the ETH Computer Vision Lab. In 2008, Swiss company Procedural Inc. released the first commercial version, with Esri acquiring the software in 2011.[114] Fully integrated with ARC GIS, CityEngine contributes a rules-based tool (parametric) allowing fast development of 3D models, which can test zoning in 3D, model parameters such as heat, shadows and views and develop rule-based reports.[115] Currently Esri's marketing of CityEngine emphasises the software as a visualisation tool, to 'create realistic content' and 'build flexible scenarios faster', rather than as a tool for more generational modelling.[116] However it is important that landscape architects work with the powerful computational capability of CityEngine, rather than limiting its use to the passive 'visualising' of 2D GIS data into 'realistic' 3D views.

Through his teaching and research, Tom Morgan aims to expand the use of CityEngine into more critical investigations of the real world. He challenges the normative uses of parametric modelling which he argues focuses too much on accurate modelling, the simulation of systems or the pursuit of controlled repro-ducible geometries/structures.[117]

System stories

In 2014, Morgan ran the Tideland Studio at RMIT, Melbourne with architecture students. The studio framework was influenced by 'systems-stories', a concept proposed by writer, academic and practitioner Mitchell Whitelaw, who works across culture and new media art. In his consideration of software arts, Whitelaw suggests their value lies in their capacity to model (as distinct from simulate) complex processes that allow for the interrogation of the real world. Rather than reproduce conventional forms or processes, these new models operate for thinking rather than results, offering 'narrative simulations' that frame a discussion in an unexpected or unanticipated manner.[118]

Morgan challenged his students to 'hack' (to refine a program through scripting) the CityEngine software and access open data sources to produce crafted and critical digital models that would amplify the confronting and unfamiliar characteristics of urban form. Applying this theoretical framing, students used open source datasets of Melbourne, Google Street View, census data, and finer-grained data including building footprints and cadastre information from local government areas to develop their models. Most of the architecture students were already familiar with readable scripting processes, which were further developed in a series of scripting workshops (using the language Python). Their difficulties however were not in working with code, but in comprehending the processes and terminologies of urbanism.

Morgan's approach provides a valuable reminder of the value of the parametric model in allowing designers to see things differently. He is not interested in parametric models as 'declarative tools', but instead considers their value lies in the ability 'to present new models (or new criticisms) that aren't simple reproductions of conventional forms or processes'.[119] Further, Morgan is interested in the capacity of the model to establish 'parallel or subversive narrative threads' highlighting the potential to embed an emotional connection through 'a particular character or inhabitant; ideally one that sits outside of the expected, normative client/tenant'.[120] This aspect also references the role of gaming in constructing narratives in space. Morgan comments that 'in general, students are better equipped (or at least, primed) to understand parametric or "unit operations"... due to their exposure to games and gaming conventions', which is premised on ideas of the fragment and contingent rather than a totalising narrative.[121]

Wen Yap's scheme *Sereneland* leveraged the scalar potential of CityEngine software to develop urban typologies responsive to local street and site conditions, and map long-term change at the scale of the suburb. This investigation 'exposed edges and gradients of activity that were otherwise invisible', provoking Wen to develop a set of architectonic forms positioned at the interface between the existing and proposed (Figure 2.28a–b). Maintaining the scale of the suburb, she used CityEngine to manipulate form, merging exaggerated and fantasy forms of inhabited opalescent Australian fauna (kangaroos) and travertine pyramids, with functional indexes of the suburb such as aerials and picket fences. The deliberate insertion of fantasy form operates as a strategy of hyper-exaggeration, magnifying

2.28
Strategic hyper-exaggeration exposes difference in repetitive form (a & b) while mapping census data highlights 'invisible' economic disparity (c).

differences and change within the repetitive suburban urban form. This exploration comments Morgan highlights the underlying contingencies (and inanities) of urban zoning', revealing how small decisions may be amplified and long-term processes curated.[122] Wen's model therefore offers a critique of the formal consequences of planning strategies and guidelines, which often remain hidden within textual documents.

In contrast Arjuan Benson's proposal *Opt In City* developed a model of the middle and outer western suburbs of Melbourne constructed from census data. Arj was interested in the inherent biases of selecting datasets to construct models, with his ensuring model assessed according to values of lot suitability explored through the two polities of libertarian and communitarian. The resultant mapping was cycled back into the model, inspiring the development of a series of iconographic structures generated from the mapped values of freedom, wealth, education and pollution. These new mappings, one of which is shown in Figure 2.28c, reveal the disparities and adjacencies that are common, yet invisible, within urban fabric.

Beyond the political or subversive, Morgan's studio further highlights the value of designers investing in scripting to maintain a critical and innovative engagement with software. Similarly Rico comments on the need for designers to remain vigilant in their engagement, commenting that in many cases software 'end up designing for you'.[123] Daniel Davis states that in the United States the majority of architects are dependent on software provided by Autodesk, with the company playing a major influence in the disciplines development.[124] For landscape architects, Esri has a similar influence, comprising over 40 per cent of the global GIS market. Esri products have become problematically associated with particular method-ologies of application, disseminated and marketed in various publications, seminars and events. It is important that academics and designers continue to extend and explore software capability beyond marketing messages, which are driven primarily by market share, not necessarily innovation.

2.29a–e
Analytical mappings of alpine
conditions developed using
GIS data and parametric
models (a–d). Alpine
infrastructure designed
in response to these
conditions (e).

As Morgan highlights software such as CityEngine have considerable flexibility and computational power, with the program able to work with extremely large datasets and vast amounts of geometry (in the order of 10 to 20 million polygons).[125] One of the aspirations of this book is to provide students and designers with enough motivation to invest in scripting knowledge to enable the hacking of proprietary software to match their particular design agendas or explorations. It is in the conceptual and procedural space of scripting that the designer can continue to push innovative ideas and explorations, working beyond the predetermined rules and associations presented within the proprietary software.

Responsive infrastructure

In the final example of this chapter, we shift the discussion of parametric modelling from an urban context into the spectacular regional context of the Austrian Alps to explore its value in developing environmentally responsive infrastructure. We return to the design practice of LAAC, who we first introduced in Chapter 1 in relation to their innovative design for *Eduard-Wallnöfer-Platz (Landhausplatz)*. LAAC's research-driven approach to infrastructure shifts the role of designer from minimising the impact of infrastructure within the visually sensitive alpine landscapes to developing design approaches that responds to specific behaviours and qualities of this environment. Their schemes, often conceived in partnership with the industrial sector, are driven by explorations of the specific forces, morphologies and sublime qualities of the alpine landscape, set against the background of climate change (Figure 2.29). Working with Rhino and Grasshopper, LAAC proposed an abstract

design language best described as 'forms of forces', which inspired a suite of infrastructure including the design of avalanche barriers, viewing platforms, inter-pretation centres and energy infrastructure.[126]

LAAC has also collaborated with Leitner – an alpine infrastructure company, to examine the potential of solar energy in the alpine environment (given the reluctance to use visually dominant wind turbines). Working with GIS data, parametric models were used to interrogate the spatial, topographic, ecological and climatic relationships of this dynamic environment. These included the relationship between geological surfaces and plant ecology to understand the dynamic flows of seasonal change, growth and erosion patterns. Analysis was expanded through the consideration of landscape perception, aesthetics and landform morphology, in acknowledgement that that any infrastructural insertion into this iconic landform will form a dominant feature.

The designers tested these ideas across a range of parameters. For instance LAAC applied the environmental modelling software Ecotect (which is discussed in more detail in Chapter 3) with site-specific data to interrogate the mean daily solar application on the mountain faces, while the implication of wind dynamics was explored through a customised Grasshopper definition. A scaling typology based on the rules of maximising solar radiation, avoiding prescribed visual conditions and establishing particular territories emerged, which was then applied in determining the form and siting of the solar panels. The panels shown in Figure 2.30 developed as hexagon shapes to maximise the south-east and west solar aspect. The siting of these panels was tested for their visual appearance on the mountains in both summer and winter as documented in Figure 2.31.

2.30
A scaling typology for solar panels which emerged from the GIS driven explorations.

Together, Morgan's Tideland studio based in the suburbia of Melbourne and LAAC's multifaceted infrastructural investigations of the Austrian Alps demonstrate the possibilities of working with GIS data and parametric modelling at a planning scale in generative and creative ways. VanDerSys observes that 'landscape architecture has invested too much in the restrictions of information rather than the generative possibilities of that information'.[127] The approaches of Morgan and LAAC highlight how data and information, when combined with parametric modelling and driven by research questions, can be used to inform speculative investigations that bridge the conceptual divides between analysis, planning and design.

When we consider these approaches against ASPECT Studios and Snøhetta's parametrically driven infrastructure designs discussed in Chapter 1, we can identify two distinctive approaches to parametric modelling. The infrastructural examples of ASPECT Studio and Snøhetta required the designers to work across very precise parameters such as maximum slopes, dispersal of vibrations, the consideration of precise viewing points and the balance of cut and fill – and these particular parameters were transformed into focused design generators, which we describe as 'modelling through constraint'. In comparison, the parametric modelling discussed in this chapter demonstrates a more speculative approach where the interrogation of behaviours, conditions, systems and phenomena provide the parameters or rules to guide design development. Rather than react to site conditions, the designer consciously creates them.

Conclusion

In this chapter we have clarified attributes of parametric modelling and its potential to landscape architecture. This has been explored against the theoretical background of performance, which frames parametric modelling as a speculative research process where form emerges through the interrogation of information, and performance. The featured projects highlight the particular questions that drive landscape architects in their approaches to parametric modelling, which we argue is reflective of a landscape understanding of topology – one in constant formation, shaped dynamically by forces and processes. Consequently, landscape architects

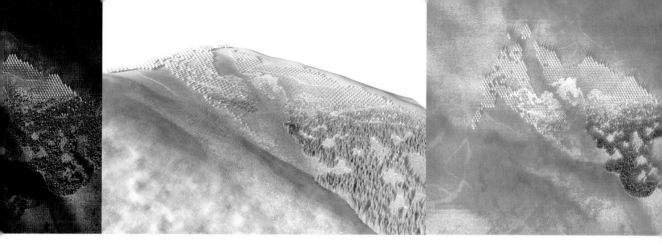

2.31
Testing the siting of the solar panels in summer and winter.

model behaviours and relationships of systems, phenomena and form and seek to establish a set of rules to apply within further design approaches. Rather than predictive, the modelling is directive, situated between analysis and formation. Whereas architects in their topological investigations of surface seek to integrate *spatial* differences within a continuous yet heterogeneous surface, landscape architects are examining relationships between form and systems, looking for changes in the behaviours, concentrations and intensities of systems and phenomena.

The emphasis on the relationship between form and system establishes a point of distinction in how landscape architects engage with parametric modelling, reflective of the inability to definitively control and influence form, systems and phenomena. As we discussed in relationship to *Phase Shifts Park*, the modification of external climatic conditions can only be understood as a factor of graduation rather than absolutes. This places the designer in a very different philosophical and technical position to that presented by architecture where systems are often closed, and by consequence more predictable and controllable. Instead the landscape architect must intervene in systems that have their own agency and characteristics, requiring different types of design strategies and tactics. This challenge will be explored in more detail in the following chapter.

This discussion has also highlighted the new design logic inherent in the modelling process, reflective of a different relationship between designer, information and process. The ability to conceive and maintain the parametric model through the identification of influential parameters, combined with ongoing critical reflection, has ramifications for pedagogy and practice. It also demonstrates the imperative for landscape architects to engage with scripting, which fortunately a new generation of students are increasingly interested in. However it is equally important that this skill is not developed in isolation, but is instead grounded firmly in design practice.

And finally, parametric modelling offers enormous potential to extend the methodologies of landscape planning, moving from a scientific empirical process into a practice of research and speculation, bridging the long-standing divide between planning and design. This opportunity is extended further still by the incorporation of simulation, prototyping and real-time data into design and planning processes, which we will turn to in Chapter 3.

3 Simulating systems

For landscape architects, exploring the dynamic and often invisible forces and systems that shape landscape through digital tools or prototyping has immense potential. Environmental and civil engineering have a long tradition of testing design performance through physical modelling (such as wind tunnels or hydrological models) or digital simulations. Increasingly accessible software capable of modelling the fluid dynamics of wind, water, tides, heat, humidity and pollution present new opportunities for embedding temporality and change into design processes. This chapter explores how these digital tools, combined with access to real-time site data, are expanding landscape architecture's design and research practice to achieve increased performance capability and novel design outcome.

Increasingly, clients are demanding evidence of design performance. For example, in 2011 New York City Department of Parks & Recreation in collaboration with the Design Trust for Public Space released *High Performance Landscape Guidelines: 21st Century Parks for NYC*. As Deborah Marton the former Director of the Design Trust comments, this type of document reflects a major shift in the conception of open space, 'from park as end-product to park as work in progress'.[1] This repositioning emphasises the multifaceted role of the park in the city, providing recreation and relaxation, in addition to contributing to storm water capture, addressing water and air quality, increasing biodiversity, lowering heat island effect and improving the general liveability of the city

Simulations and real-time data offers landscape architecture techniques for introducing an evidence-based metric into design processes, heightening the performative ambitions of spaces and providing quantitative and qualitative arguments for the value of parks, gardens and green infrastructure. *Cities Alive: Rethinking Green Infrastructure* published by Arup in 2014 uses social, environmental

3.1
The Supertrees, *Gardens by the Bay*, Singapore.

and economic benefits to argue for green infrastructure.[2] Tom Armour, Global Leader Landscape Architecture at Arup, highlights the significance of metrics in the current economic context, stating 'we need to get the value out of landscape' by demonstrating its potential in lowering pollution and air temperature levels, reducing carbon and contributing to healthier cities.[3] Similarly, Stephanie Carlisle environmental researcher and designer at Kieran Timberlake, comments that 'if we want to have projects built we have to be able to argue about what they are and what they do'.[4]

Of course models do not represent reality and always provide an incomplete understanding of systems. Therefore designers must remain critical in their application of simulations, not defaulting unquestioningly to simulation results. As Rob Holmes states of simulations 'sometimes they are very useful and other times they are worrisomely misleading or unpredictably wrong, with the skill lying in the negotiation between and evaluation of those two possibilities'.[5] There is no question however of the value of digital simulations in extending a designer's understanding of the performance of designed systems and spaces, especially for engaging with 'factors and forces that remain outside humans' perceptible limits'.[6]

Modelling tools are increasingly available to practice and students. The popular environmental modelling software, Ecotect emerged in the 1990s from the work of Australian researcher Dr Andrew Marsh who initially conceived the software as a teaching tool. In 2008 Ecotect was purchased by Autodesk and is widely used as a performance and analytical tool for simulating shading, solar access, lighting, acoustic and thermal conditions. The use of computational fluid dynamics (CFD) modelling software such Aquaveo SMS and ANSYS Fluent (used in the design of *Phase Shifts Park* discussed in Chapter 2) are also becoming more common in landscape architecture.

The application of these modelling techniques, however, provokes the question of what landscape architects are qualified to interpret in reviewing the resulting models, given that most landscape architects lack the specialised knowledge of the engineer or environmental scientist. As this chapter documents, approaches vary and are unfolding. Director of Technology at OLIN Studio Christian Hanley comments that while he is not qualified to interpret the detailed data generated by simulation programs, digital modelling offers an understanding of how a design intervention may be affected by conditions such as wind or solar access.[7] Keith VanDerSys adopts a more generative approach, using modelling to reveal shifts in the magnitude and speed of systems that are 'representative of processes that have material consequences'.[8] Influenced by ecologist Gregory Bateson, simulations aid VanDerSys to uncover 'a difference that makes a difference', identifying conditions, behaviours and forces of greatest degree of change in which to intervene.[9]

The insertion of simulations and associated metrics into design processes have been accompanied by theoretical frameworks that reconceive of the city within a biological metaphor defined by metabolic flows of energy, information and matter.[10] This move from static space, (exemplified in the figure–ground diagram), to an urbanism of connectivity is featured in the AD *System City: Infrastructure and the Space of Flows* published in 2013. Leading design practices discuss their application of environmental systems modelling to urbanism.[11] Designers from Skidmore, Owings & Merrill for example highlight the value of these approaches, stating:

> As other sciences like sociology and economics continue to develop computational modelling paradigms, the abilities to leverage knowledge embedded in models across discipline boundaries promises to enrich all of those engaged. Metabolic flows and transactions are at the heart of all of these types of models. Through the use of these technologies we stand to gain a much better understanding of the metabolic patterns of cities, a stronger theoretical foundation regarding the fundamental nature of cities, and a greater ability to intervene.[12]

Similarly Foster + Partners' Applied Research and Development group conclude that while the computer cannot replace the 'human experience of the idiosyncrasies that make urban living inspiring' it does 'provide us with an increasingly sophisticated foil for testing ever-more elaborate hypotheses about what makes cities work'.[13]

More specifically within landscape architecture, recent symposiums and forthcoming publications reflect a growing interest in the potential of simulation and prototyping. In March 2015, PennDesign hosted the 2-day research symposium Simulating Natures, which explored how contemporary forms of media influence an understanding and formation of landscapes with a focus on computationally enabled imaging and models. Bringing together engineers, scientists, landscape architects, artists and architects, the symposium focused on three aspects of computational techniques and associated technologies; namely their value in perceiving a fluid conceptualisation of environment and systems; their capacity to analyse and simulate the behaviour of living systems and their value in making data tangible through human–machine interfaces or through real-time translations.[14] Bradley Cantrell and Justine Holzman's book *Responsive Landscape: Strategies for responsive technologies in landscape architecture* (2016) builds on these questions, showcasing interactive and responsive projects that respond to environmental phenomena and systems.[15] Their book highlights how iterative prototyping and feedback processes offer valuable operational techniques for understanding and responding to the outside world, in addition to showcasing the value of technological advancements such as autonomous robotics sensing and distributed intelligence to design.

Beginning with a focus on Singapore's *Gardens by the Bay* and PARKKIM's design for Danginri *Thermal City* in Seoul, this chapter focuses on the application of simulation modelling and real-time data in landscape architecture practice, teaching and research. These projects highlight the opportunity that simulation provides for designers to respond to specific and dynamic climatic conditions towards the development of optimum growing environments and external spaces of higher thermal comfort, while engaging efficiently with energy resources.

Modelling systems

Singapore's *Gardens by the Bay* emerged from an international design competition for a 54-hectare public garden. In 2006 the Bay south competition was won by the multidisciplinary collaboration of Grant Associates (landscape architects), Wilkinson Eyre Architects and the engineering firms of Atelier One (structural) and Atelier Ten (environmental). The predominantly UK-based design team had previous experience in the design of London's Kew Gardens Alpine House. The project's success relied on the establishment of a successful growing environment for a range of plants within Singapore's cloudy environment of subdued light and high humidity levels. The consortiums' scheme was ambitious, proposing 'a highly sophisticated and integrated three-dimensional network of horticulture, art, engineering and architecture'.[16]

The design of the two feature biomes conservatories, shown in Figure 3.2, was particularly challenging. At close to 20,000m square, and up to 58 metres in height, the conservatories are some of the largest in the world. The challenge within the Singapore context was to adequately ventilate, cool and dehumidify the equatorial environment, while meeting horticultural lighting requirements and limiting the carbon footprint.[17] For 95 per cent of the year, Singapore's equatorial

3.2a
View of the 54 hectares public garden with the two conservatories featured on the left.

tropical climate maintains temperatures between 24 and 32 Celsius with humidity measuring between 17 and 21g/kg.[18] The Cool Moist (cloud mountain) Dome, designed for species from the mountainous tropical regions, requires mild air temperature night and day combined with an almost saturation level of humidity, while The Cool Dry (flower) dome replicates the Mediterranean springtime of mild dry days and cool nights.

Advanced environmental testing was critical to developing a carbon-neutral design that also achieves the necessary day lighting requirements. A combination of proprietary software such as Ecotect and Radiance and bespoke software generated by Atelier Ten, facilitated the evaluation and comparison of various proposals.[19] Daylight simulation techniques assessed the availability and quantity of daylight for the inhabited volume for each hour of a typical year.[20] A dynamic shading structure, responsive to the changing solar environment, emerged as the solution for achieving the desired growing environment. Internal light levels with and without shades were modelled for a complete reference year. The final scheme comprises 419 individually controlled external shades, featuring 'an intelligent self-learning algorithm' that adjusts shades in response to the sun paths, the geometry of the internal spaces and the external cladding.[21]

3.2b
Diagram from the competition submission showing the environmental system which is fueled by green waste and a bio-mass boiler.

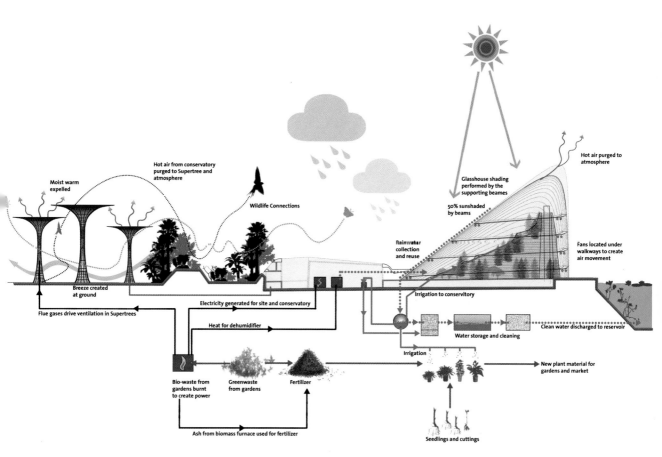

Hot air from conservatory purged to Supertree and atmosphere

Moist warm expelled

Hot air purged to atmosphere

Glasshouse shading performed by the supporting beames

Wildlife Connections

50% sunshaded by beams

Rainwater collection and reuse

Fans located under walkways to create air movement

Breeze created at ground

Irrigation to conservatory

Electricity generated for site and conservatory

Flue gases drive ventilation in Supertrees

Heat for dehumidifier

Clean water discharged to reservoir

Water storage and cleaning

Irrigation

Bio-waste from gardens burnt to create power

Greenwaste from gardens

Fertilizer

New plant material for gardens and market

Ash from biomass furnace used for fertilizer

Seedlings and cuttings

Energy efficiency

A carbon-neutral energy system to power the conservatories presented a further challenge. Initially solar was assumed as the energy source, however the cloudy nature of Singapore reduces its efficiency. Discussions with the National Parks Board of Singapore revealed that the city regularly prunes several million trees, generating extensive green waste largely incinerated or sent to landfill.[22] Plans altered to include a bio-mass boiler fuelled by the city and garden's horticultural waste. Steam from the boiler feeds a turbine to generate electricity. Remaining ash is used as fertiliser, while surplus energy is fed back into the grid.

The iconic Supertrees perform an essential role in this complex energy system (Figure 3.2b) which was conceived as a larger symbiotic relationship that included the conservatories and gardens, through an exchange of energy, air, water, nutrients and water cycles. These spectacular tree-like structures are multifunctional 'environmental engines' designed to disperse hot gases generated by the biomass boiler and the desiccant process, generate energy through photovoltaic solar panels and provide shade for the public areas below as well as extensive valuable habitat for birds and insects.

The Gold Cluster of Supertrees, which is located near the entrance, conceals the major chimney from the energy centre's boiler, discharging non-toxic flue gases high above any occupied areas. The steam turbine powers the electric chillers, producing chilled water to cool the domes. Adopting principles of thermal stratification, chilled water runs through pipes within the floor slabs, while the rising warm air is vented out at higher levels or is captured to harvest heat. Computational fluid dynamic modelling allowed the engineers to analyse and optimise this airflow and accurately predict outcomes.[23]

Any waste heat is used to regenerate the liquid desiccant, necessary to dehumidify the air for the Flower Dome (the cool-dry biome). Conventional cooling of humid air requires an energy-intensive process; chilled water removes water vapour through condensation, followed by reheating to the desired temperature.[24] In contrast this system uses liquid desiccants to remove water vapour from the air through a chemical process; leaving the air temperature similar but drier. Used in conjunction with conventional cooling systems, this technology requires less energy, while the desiccant is recycled through treatment from waste heat from the biomass boiler.[25] The Silver Cluster of Supertrees, masks the hot moist air discharge from the regeneration unit of the liquid desiccant dehumidification system.

This complex environmental system (Figure 3.3) encompassing the entire garden facilitates a number of 'virtuous cycles' involving either the reuse of resources or the maximisation of their use.[26] The Supertrees however were designed as far more than environmental infrastructure. Their inspiration, states landscape architect Andrew Grant, are the monumental karri forests of Western Australia (which feature a sky walkway) and the 1997 anime film Princess Mononoke depicting a young warrior's encounter with forest gods and those wishing to destroy the forest resources and beauty. Rising 50 metres to match the monumental scale

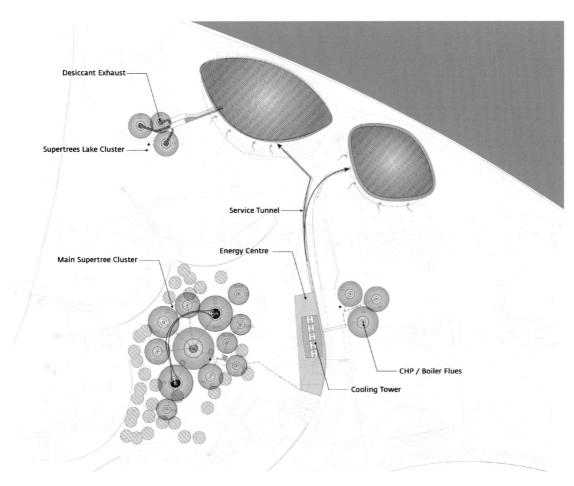

Desiccant Exhaust

Supertrees Lake Cluster

Service Tunnel

Main Supertree Cluster

Energy Centre

CHP / Boiler Flues

Cooling Tower

3.3a–b
Diagrams explaining the
infrastructural relationship
between the Supertrees,
the conservatories and the
environmental system.

grant associates

Simulating systems

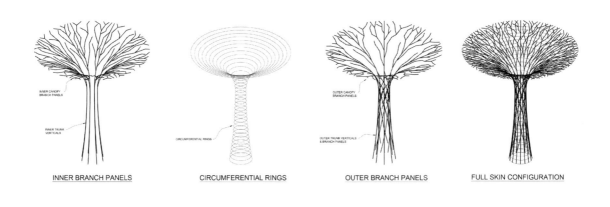

INNER BRANCH PANELS   CIRCUMFERENTIAL RINGS   OUTER BRANCH PANELS   FULL SKIN CONFIGURATION

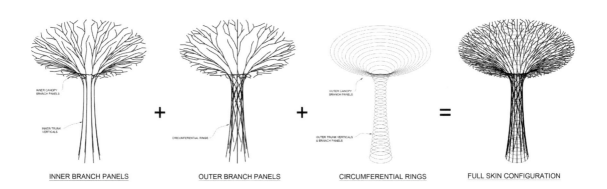

INNER BRANCH PANELS   +   OUTER BRANCH PANELS   +   CIRCUMFERENTIAL RINGS   =   FULL SKIN CONFIGURATION

3.4a–b

The structural geometries of the Supertrees which were explored parametrically and conceived as doubly curved anticlastic forms (a). The largest configuration of Supertrees in the Lion Grove Plaza which features an aerial walkway, bar and viewing platform suspended 20m above the ground (b).

3.5a–b

Screenshots from using Ecotect software to test the siting of the Supertrees in relationship to sun paths and their shading potential for public areas in plan (a) and perspective (b).

of the conservatories, the structures were conceived as a magical 'other worldliness of space', including a unique night-time experience.[27] The largest configuration forming the Supertree Grove are particularly immense, supporting a 135m long aerial walkway (Figure 3.4b) suspended over 20 metres above the gardens, with the tallest structure featuring a bar and viewing gallery.

The competition entry featured an atmospheric fly-through developed with 3D animation technology by the firm Squint/Opera. Grant comments that this animation was influential in 'defining the spirit' of the Supertrees.[28] The designers were challenged to translate this mystical imagery depicted in the competition film into structures; while maintaining their structural strength, experiential qualities and performance as environmental infrastructure.

The landscape architects worked closely with structural engineers Atelier One (led by Neil Thomas), who had considerable experience in light-weight structures such as the design of travelling stage sets. The team also called on the engineering expertise of the University of Bath. First versions, stated Grant were very 'clunky' which 'looked like bits of the Eiffel tower'.[29] Slowly the form evolved through a process of testing structural form and exploring environmental efficiency through physical and sectional analysis and 3D studies. Two key decisions influenced the final form; that the structural integrity would develop through a central concrete core, and that the diameter of the canopy would equal the height of the Supertree.

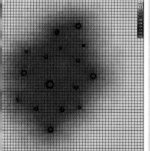
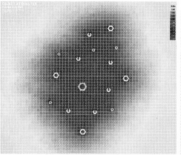
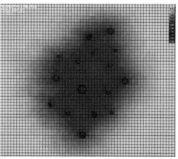
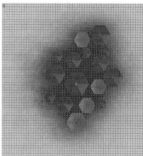

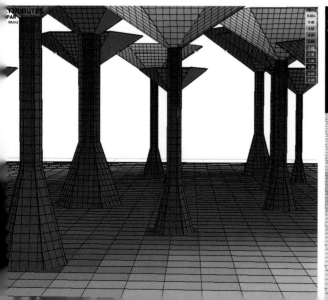
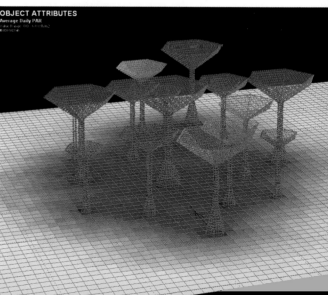

grant associates

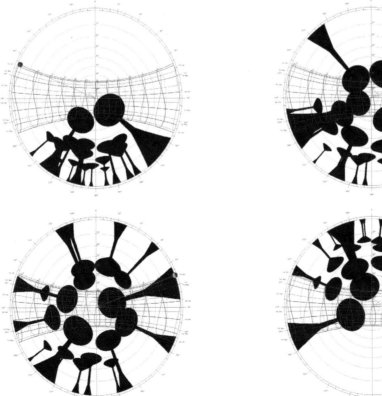

The geometries of the structures were established parametrically, developed as two repetitious modules that 'overlap each other, and reinforce each other but give the appearance of being random'.[30] The form emerged as 'doubly curved anticlastic surfaces, using form to create stiffness'.[31] Planting panels were designed to attach either directly to the concrete core, or to the steel skin covering the core. This novel typology challenged Singapore's existing building codes, raising questions for authorities and engineers on how to classify them. Should they be considered buildings or bridges? Figure 3.4a documents the development of this form. Testing the overshadowing of the trees was an important stage of design development. Some of these testing are documented in Figures 3.5 and 3.6.

Officially opened in 2012, *Gardens by the Bay* has been awarded numerous international design awards in recognition of the quality of the public space, architecture and gardens and the innovative response to climate change adaption, sustainability and technology. The Supertrees have developed iconic status, quickly adopted as a symbol of Singapore. Grant Associates continues to explore relationships between environmental systems, technology and resources. This is demonstrated (in conjunction with Wilkinson Eyre Architects, Atelier One and Atelier Ten) in their competition entry for the UK pavilion planned for the 2015 Milan Expo. The future of food forms their inspiration, developed through an exploration of the integral relationship between the sea and land. Their design comprises a seawater greenhouse, which features a desalination process driven by natural processes.

During the course of the research for this book, it became evident that many landscape architects and designers were unaware of the infrastructural capability of the Supertrees. Anecdotally, our decision to feature the Supertrees on the cover of the book received mixed reactions, with some people questioning whether they were too object focused and thereby not 'landscape' enough. This response, combined with reactions to the climatic devices designed for *Phase Shifts Park* discussed in Chapter 2, exposes a tension concerning the use of obvert technologies within landscape.

This attitude is reflective of larger anxieties regarding the application of technology as a dystopian replacement to nature. Why replicate nature when you can simply plant a tree, and further isn't technology the primary cause of environmental issues in the first place? This argument is not without merit. For example Dutch artist Daan Rosegarrde's *Smog Free Project* uses patented ion technology to make the 'largest air purifier in the world' to create the cleanest park in Beijing.[32] The project is accompanied by the marketing idea of creating souvenir smog rings from the particles captured from the air, with each ring representing the cleansing of $1000m^3$ of polluted air. Much emphasis is placed on the development of a 'smog-free movement' promoted through exhibitions and public events. Nowhere in the extensive promotional material however is there mention of the energy requirements and energy source necessary for the purification process. This raises questions over whether the energy source remains brown coal, which creates the irony of the purifier both cleaning and contributing to air pollution.

3.6a–b
A 3D printed model of a Supertree and a photosynthetically active radiation (PAR) study indicating the different levels of direct sunlight falling on the vegetated faces of the Supertrees and the surrounding surfaces.

But beyond this question of energy, the *Smog Free Project* also presents a very limited response to the broader question of pollution and the performative role of open space in the Chinese City. It is in this realm that landscape architects with their wider understanding of ecological and social infrastructure and systems, have a greater role to play, as demonstrated in the *Gardens by the Bay* and *Phase Shifts Park*. Landscape architects are in an ideal position to guide the use of technology, working with it to enhance the ecological performance and experience of the park.

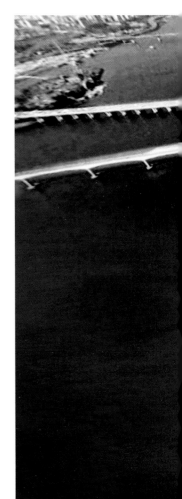

온돌형 통석(T40)

발전소의 온배수를 활용한 온열 파이프(Ø20)

3.7
The heating system references the ondol, a traditional Korean technique for heating architecture.

In the case of *Gardens by the Bay*, technology was central to developing an environmentally responsive system that also provides exceptional recreational and aesthetic experiences. Andrew Grant stresses that the Supertrees should not be viewed as a replacement to nature or 'elements' to be reproduced in other locations. Instead, he highlights their origins in a very specific design context, emphasising their value in reconceiving infrastructure to operate intelligently to address environmental issues and limited energy resources.

Thermal comfort

The reconceptualisation of infrastructures and external spaces of cities is becoming increasingly urgent as we begin to experience the reality of climate change. With 2015 considered the hottest year on record, the implication of climate change on the liveability of our cities is becoming increasingly apparent, especially in Asia and Australia. A 2015 report identifies that Australia will be 'hit harder than the rest of the world', with temperatures predicted to rise by 5 degrees by 2090.[33] These effects are already being felt. Melbourne's 2014 record-breaking 4-day January heatwave is estimated to have contributed to 167 excess deaths[34] and cost an estimated loss of revenue of AU$37 million from businesses in the Melbourne metropolitan area.[35] This event, which is expected to be a frequent summer experience, has necessitated the design of urban heat refuges for the young and the elderly.

The design of open space for thermal comfort is emerging as a pressing issue in many Asian cities. There is no standard thermal comfort index for external spaces, with comfort relative to different geographic conditions. However there are agreed criteria that influence comfort indexes for perceived temperature; namely the relationship between air temperature, air velocity, air humidity, clothing, activity of the person and radiant temperature (solar and infrared radiation), all factors that can now be simulated within design.[36] As an example German climate engineers Transsolar are currently developing new design tools based on human biometerological data, driven by their experience in designing major sporting events in difficult climatic conditions such as for the World Cup 2022 Qatar.[37] Transsolar engineer Christian Frenzel highlights the value of comfort modelling in identifying

3.8a–b
Thermal City proposed a climate conscious park on the site of Korea's first thermal power station. A new power station is located under the park, with hot excess water from the power station circulating through stone surfaces to provide heated seating in winter.

the potential to improve occupant comfort, with CFD software producing '3D recommendations in order to generate micro-scale comfort locations in a macro-scale context'.[38]

Likewise, Korean designers PARKKIM adopt thermal comfort levels as a major design driver in their 2013 competition entry for the Danginri underground Combined Heat Plant, the site of Korea's first thermal power station. In a world first, the old power station constructed in the 1930s will be replaced by an underground combined cycle power plant (requiring a space equivalent to five football pitches) with a cultural complex encompassing sport and performance facilities, eco-park and library planned above.[39] The complex is envisaged as a new landmark for Mapo-gu, Seoul, located next to the Han River.

PARKKIM's scheme *Thermal City* aims to create and control temperatures within the open space, observing that Seoul's challenging winters and summer seasons are becoming more extreme and longer, noticeably shortening the more comfortable spring and autumn seasons.[40] Topographic valleys, shown in Figure 3.8a, inspired by the once frequent sand dunes of the Han River, are aligned to maximise cool summer air flows and, combined with vegetation, provide barriers to the winter winds. In a major design innovation, excess heated water from the underground power station runs through pipes located under stone surfaces within the park (Figure 3.8), before expelling into the river as cool water. This feature has two functions; to address the ecological damage of pumping hot water directly in the river (a common practice in power stations); and to provide warm seating and microclimates within the park in winter. This technique references the use of ondol (or gudeul) found within traditional Korean architecture where heat from wood smoke is applied under a thick masonry floor to heat sleeping and living areas.

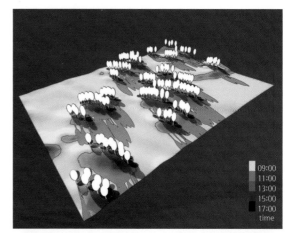

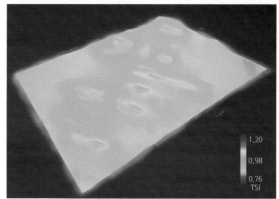

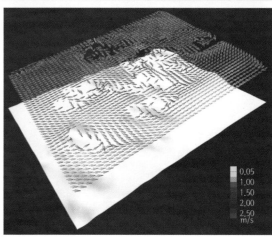

3.9
View of the proposed
park showing the terraced
landscape and the wind
turbines used to generate
energy.

3.10a–c
Initial climatic testing of the
proposed topographic form
and the location of planting
using Ecotect software.

3.11a–d
Arup's simulations testing
thermal comfort indexes
for Seoul in December
(top) and June (bottom).
The left images represent
site conditions prior to the
PARKKIM's scheme.

The park also produces its own energy through a solar canopy over the car park and wind turbines (Figure 3.9) located throughout the park.

During their design process, PARKKIM used the environmental simulating software Ecotect to test the effectiveness of their topographic form and siting of vegetation to improve cooling and shade, shown in Figure 3.10. In this process, PARKKIM engaged Arup for detailed analysis of thermal comfort performance, applying a Thermal Sensation Index equation which had emerged from research in Japan and Tel Aviv.[41] This index establishes a reading of 4 out of 7 as most comfortable with 3 to 5 as acceptable levels of comfort. Arup's simulation was used to test PARKKIM's design for June 2–5 p.m. (summer) and December 2–5 p.m. (winter) comparing site conditions before and after design implementation. As shown in Figure 3.11, during summer months the design extends areas of comfort from those located in the shadow of buildings into the central open space. In winter, the simulation result showed, while the mounds are beneficial during summer, the valley created between landforms could expedite wind velocity and worsen the thermal comfort partially: in response, PARKKIM strategically placed the heated stone seatings on the south-eastern slopes to warm the colder areas.

Gardens by the Bay, *Thermal City* and *Phase Shifts Park* (discussed in Chapter 2), all demonstrate the value of embedding simulation modelling within design. Simulation facilitates the testing of performance during the design process, as well

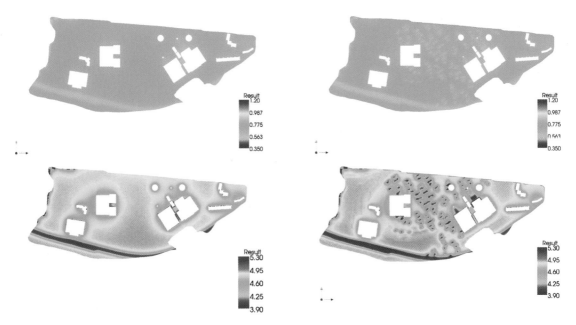

as providing evidence-based metrics to support design decisions such as quantifying energy and resource consumption and achieving thermal comfort levels. These innovative outcomes prove that a focus on performance does not diminish creativity and innovation, nor does simulation alone generate design. Instead it is argued by academics such as Elizabeth K. Meyer and Karen M'Closkey that the current emphasis on sustainable design guidelines complete with 'typical' design concepts is more likely to produce formulaic responses that diminish 'expression and experience'.[42] Meyer's 2008 manifesto *Sustaining Beauty: The Performance of Appearance: A Manifesto in Three Parts* for example criticises landscape architects for deferring from the challenge of design, in favour of the implementation of management guidelines.[43]

The value of simulations within design processes is further enhanced by the rapidly increasing ability for the designer to access real-time site data, the focus of the following section.

Real-time data

The concept of datascapes has intrigued many designers, most notably the Dutch designers MVRDV. Their 1999 publication *Metacity/Datatown* proposed a new development methodology premised on data-supported 'extreme scenarios', provocatively presenting city form derived entirely from data, without context, topography or ideology.[44] In the two decades since, interest in data has expanded exponentially, fuelled by the twenty-first-century phenomena of Big Data, where data is continuously generated and increasingly accessible. Big Data challenges the very production of knowledge, capable of revealing new patterns and relationships without guidance by a prior hypothesis. Consequently a 'new data analytics' where knowledge is generated directly from data has emerged, replacing earlier conceptualisations where theory is tested through the analysis of relevant data.[45] The sheer scale and pace of data production however relies on a critical engagement, or as Chris Leckie describes it 'the identification of high value problems'.[46] The challenge with Big Data, states Leckie, is transforming it into 'a little bit of knowledge', which requires the extensive filtering of events to find relevant issues or problems.[47] This filtering requires human intelligence, combining the identification of patterns in the data (through the computer) with the contextualisation of the data in relationship to problems.

As discussed earlier in this chapter, it is critical to recognise disciplinary limitations in interpreting data. That said, it can be predicted that data analytics, like coding, will form a major part of future generations' education embedded in school and university curriculum. As Nathan Eagle and Kate Greene state in their 2014 book *Reality Mining: Using Big Data to Engineer a Better World*, 'the era of Big Data is here and it isn't going to be over anytime soon'.[48] While acknowledging the importance of addressing privacy, individual liberties and security, Eagle and Greene believe 'that within a conscientious context of data collection, it's possible to use Big Data to engineer better systems and potentially a better world'.[49]

The data lab

The establishment of specialised data or media labs have accompanied this data expansion. Linking governments, institutions, private organisations and citizens, these labs pose new questions for engaging data, cities and society. Medialab-Prado formed in 2000 as part of Madrid City Council's Department of Arts, Sports, Tourism offers an early model.[50] Conceived as 'a citizen laboratory', the lab performs as a multidisciplinary hub supporting the development of collaborative and experimental cultural projects emerging from digital networks.[51] Future Everything, established in Manchester in 1995, explores how 'technological, creative and societal innovation' inspires change.[52] *Open Data Cities*, the lab's longest-running project (2009) was instrumental in establishing the *Open Data Cities* movement. This project proposed the open sharing of data from the Greater Manchester Region, encouraging citizen access to government workings (and democracy) and supporting developers and businesses in designing new applications from the data. Conceived as 'innovation ecology', the project encourages collaborations 'where the ability to aggregate and disseminate information through the Internet by individuals is a key enabling technology'.[53]

San Francisco (datasf.org) and London (data.london.gov.uk) were among the first urban authorities to publicly release large datasets concerning the urban environment. Cities throughout the world have since followed, encouraging public participation and more accountable governance. Designers can freely access datasets describing the economic, political, social and environmental workings of our cities. *Open Data Cities* is now considered an emerging body of practice with direct economic benefit, with research suggesting it contributes up to £6.5 billion to the UK economy.[54]

SENSEable City Laboratory at Massachusetts Institute of Technology offers a further model, exploring the potential of sensors and hand-held electronic devices to understand and transform the city.[55] Under the direction of Carlo Ratti, researchers develop projects ranging in scale from the regional to the individual. The *Hubcab* project (2014) for instance uses smart technologies to understand how taxicab services operate, proposing a more socially and environmentally accountable transportation systems.[56] *One Country, Two Lungs* (2014) places a miniature network of sensors on a team of 'human probes' who travel between Shenzhen and Hong Kong mapping the 'atmospheric boundaries' of particulate matter (PM 10), carbon monoxide (CO) and nitrogen dioxide (NO_2).[57] Conceived as an alternative to fixed ground monitoring of air pollution, the project develops a more accurate reading of human exposure, offering information relevant to public health research.

Generating data

Data opportunities extend beyond the use of third party sources to designers generating their own site data through portable technologies ranging from smart phones, digital cameras, 3D terrestrial laser scanners, hand-held Global Navigation Satellite Systems, in addition to small unmanned aerial vehicles (UAV) such as quadcopters and small drones. For a site-specific discipline such as landscape architecture this development fundamentally challenges the way site information is gathered and recorded. Jörg Rekittke and Yazid Ninsalam comment on the future of site information, stating:

> It will be handheld, respectively mobile and light, broadly affordable, and will allow digital landscape capture in the form of 3D data progressively in high precision, high density, and geo-referenced manner.[58]

Christophe Girot from the ETH Zurich highlights the possibilities afforded by sensor-based data collection which can record and measure intangible characteristics of space such as humidity, lux, radiation, temperature and pressure. These phenomena, argue Girot, offer alternative modes for conceiving sites beyond the standard GIS data techniques that privilege surface-based data and the visuality of site analysis.[59] Real-time data contributes accuracy lacking within 2D site mapping, significantly extending the capability of the designer. Antoine Picon comments further:

> mapping and monitoring become inseparable, just like the understanding of what lies beneath the eye of the observer and what is not yet there. Mapping understood as the exploration of scenarios of evolution rather than as the production of static representations enables the blending of these two categories.[60]

3.12a-c
ETH Zurich: using drones fitted with sensors to record atmospheric data such as humidity, temperature and air quality. The data can be translated into point clouds such as the voxel rendering of humidity shown in (c).

Since 2010 the postgraduate Master of Advanced Studies in Landscape Architecture (MAS LA) at ETH, directed by Pia Fricker, has focused on the integration of the latest information technologies within large-scale landscape projects. Students are encouraged to create their own data and provoke 'curiosity about the intangible'.[61] The MAS LA module Field Oriented Programming led by researcher James Melsom challenges 'the conceptual depth' of traditional modes of site analysis to measure and simulate ambient and micro climatic site attributes.[62] UAV drones (shown in Figures 3.12a–b) generate sets of data horizons (a term borrowed from aeronautical engineering that emphasis a vertical dimension) to establish 3D spatial scans.[63] The drones, fitted with microcontrollers and sensors to record humidity, dew point, air quality and temperature, are flown in layers (or horizons) to record the 'volumetric dynamics' of the site.[64]

Data from sensors, airborne and terrestrial laser scanners is presented within a 3D point cloud (shown in Figure 12c). A point cloud establishes data points within a geo-referenced, spatial coordinate system. Spatial data can also be accessed from 2D sources to construct a point cloud. In a process known as photogrammetry, a dense series of 2D images from digital cameras can be converted into 3D point clouds. Various software including GIS and modelling programs (for example Rhinoceros and Bentley Pointools V8i) can be used to transform point clouds into topographic maps, spatial models and mesh surfaces.

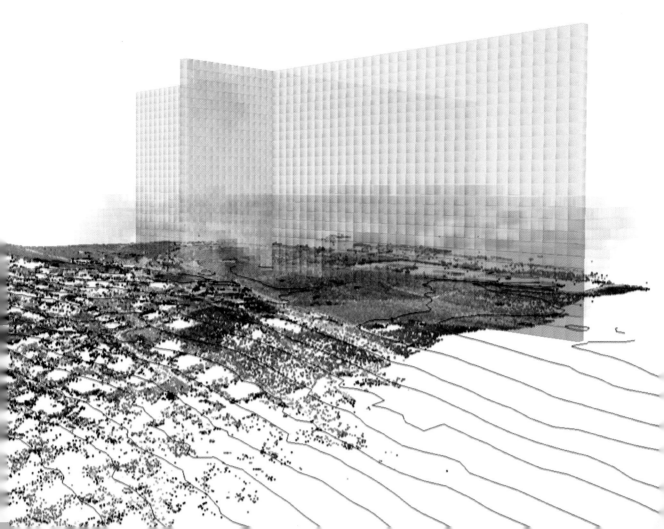

Transferring across programs is becoming increasingly efficient, with plug-ins such as gHowl (Grasshopper) allowing a simpler exchange of information. Smoother cross-translation platforms are encouraging a more fluid feedback between analysis and design, allowing designers to move analytical data into GIS, where it can be sampled, sorted and sifted and isolated, then translated back into a design model, where it can be further tested with simulation and the results fed back into design iterations. VanDerSys comments that earlier applications, tended to maintain activities within discrete 'rooms', requiring the replication of simulation within design models, rather than a more direct application.[65] This interoperability continues to improve through the constant evolution of plug-ins and software, offering faster and simpler workflows between data, simulation and design processes.

Girot's investigation into data-driven techniques owes much to his critique of existing tools and practices, unable to deal with large 'unwieldy' 3D datasets that can be 'difficult to convert into meaningful workable formats'. He argues that 'a renewed approach to landscape through such modelling can provide a stronger, well-informed basis for design'.[66] To this end, researcher Ervine Lin programmed a suite of custom tools enabling ETH students and researchers to manipulate, reconstitute and edit point clouds within Rhinoceros.

The value of these approaches is well demonstrated by Atelier Girot's design for the *Sigirino Alptransit Depot*, which is a 'landscape by product of the largest infrastructure project in Swiss history'.[67] Over 3.7 million cubic metres of material was excavated from the Ceneri Base Tunnel to form the *Sigirino Alptransit Depot*, a highly visible piece of 'artificial nature'.[68] Forming the largest artificial mound in Switzerland, the design team were challenged to mechanically stabilise this excavation material and to facilitate plant growth on inorganic substrata. Detailed point cloud models offered the designers a valuable technique for engaging the mound with the surrounding landscape.

3.13
Flight pattern of the fixed-wing UAV and photo-capture locations used in the development of a geo-referenced point cloud model.

3.14a–b
The 3.5 million m³ Sigirino Depot embedded in the 3D geo-referenced point cloud model of the valley and below the Panorama of the Sigirino Depot from the village Mezzovico, Ticino, Switzerland (a).
Visualisation of the final stage of the Sigirino Depot (b).

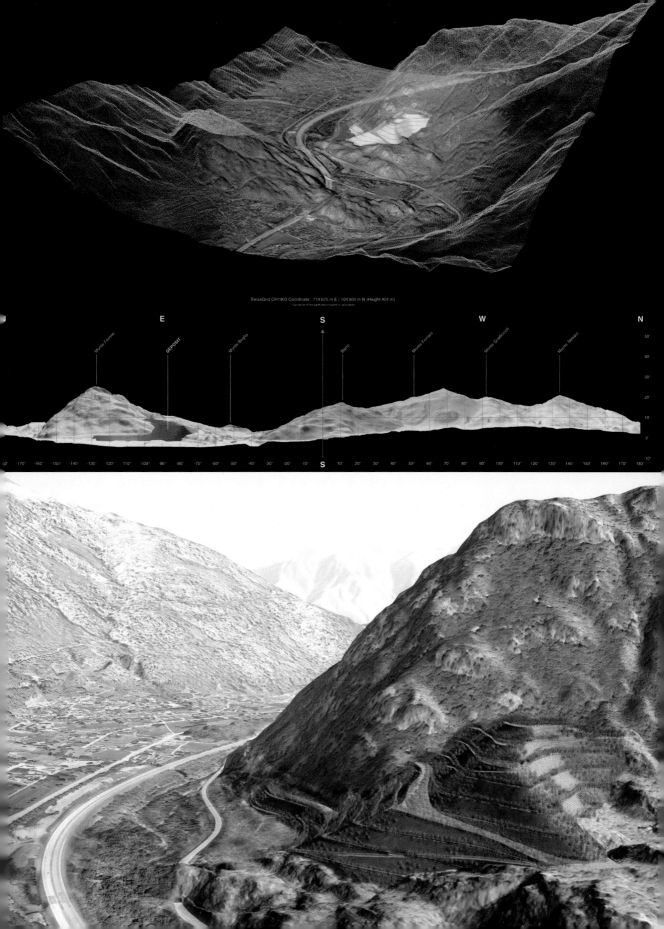

SwissGrid CH1903 Coordinate   714'675 m E / 104'800 m N (Height 404 m)
* curvature of the earth not included in calculation

E   S   W   N

Monte Fermo   DEPOSIT   Monte Boglia   Barro   Monte Ferraro   Monte Graeficosti   Monte Tamaro

50°

30°

10°

0°

-10°

-180° -170° -160° -150° -140° -130° -120° -110° -100° -90° -80° -70° -60° -50° -40° -30° -20° -10° S 10° 20° 30° 40° 50° 60° 70° 80° 90° 100° 110° 120° 130° 140° 150° 160° 170° 180°

Working in collaboration with the LVML (Landscape Visualisation and Modelling Laboratory) of the ETH Zurich, the designers used geo-referenced point cloud technology produced by a terrestrial laser scanner (Figure 3.13). These accurate models allowed them to test and verify design iterations, offering detailed understanding of how this monumental landform would perform in relationship to drainage, planting and visual impact. The incremental creation of point clouds was used by engineers to alter the distribution of material throughout the project's evolution, and adjust the final implementation on site (Figure 3.14). These models were also valuable in presenting the project to the Swiss Confederation for final approval.

3D models of site are beginning to replace the 2D survey plan as the starting point for site analysis. This significant representational revision observes Brian Osborn, fundamentally extends the type and accuracy of information considered within site analysis, transforming the traditional site survey into a strategy of site surveillance.[69] The site is observed 'as an ongoing act of keeping watch' departing from the 'perceived fixity in conditions' offered by the survey which is 'often done only once'.[70] This dynamic analysis, when combined with parametric modelling encourages design responses that encompass true variable field conditions. To explore the potential further, Osborn introduced the subject Surveillance Practices into the University of Virginia's landscape program in 2014, to examine how Big data might change the spatial practices of landscape architects.[71] Working across analogue and digital, students developed techniques for recording site data for the abandoned Milton airport, including making their own sensors such as the soil moisture sensor (shown in Figure 3.15).

Explorations from this subject highlighted the new possibilities for recording the dynamic behaviours of systems, which have so far been overlooked in landscape architecture. For example Jenna Harris's project *Drawing the [O]rganic [Soil] layer*, explored processes of carbon storage and exchange, recognising the significance of the natural decaying of organic carbon in releasing carbon dioxide into the atmosphere.[72] Her surveillance practice interrogated the relationship between plant litter, top soil decomposition and the rate of top soil formation.[73] Four techniques were developed for recording data; a detritus meter for testing plant material; a surface temperature gun, a decomposition tester for recording environmental conditions and soil colour testing for understanding soil conditions. The mapping of this data highlights the manipulability and relationship of parameters that influence the renewable resource of soil such as decomposition, plant type, soil type and surface temperature.

Monitoring performance

Cheap and easy to use, sensors not only record site phenomena and processes but also enable the performance monitoring of constructed designs. Ibuttons ($20–50) shown in Figure 3.15 are small durable computer chips with an internal battery that can be mounted discretely in soil or on paving to log periodic humidity and

3.15a–b
A soil moisture sensor made with Arduino (a). An ibutton (b).

3.16
Diagram interpreting the behaviour of heat recorded in a suburban carpark in Melbourne using ibuttons.

temperature. The graph shown in Figure 3.16, developed from ibutton recordings documents the fluctuating heat conditions in a suburban car park in Melbourne. This continuous data recorded peak temperatures but even more importantly for designers, highlights the ability of materials and spaces to cool down quickly, offering more rigorous understanding of the performative characteristics of heat, materials and spatial contexts. This accuracy is an important contribution to landscape architecture, which has often been guided by 'rule of thumb' principles that may not hold true in more complex contemporary contexts. For example this exploration of heat revealed that temperatures under trees were cooler during peak daytime temperatures but then retained heat for longer through the afternoon and evening.

This ability to accurately record and understand the performance of landscape systems, aided by data gathering technologies, is leading to the establishment of applied landscape research labs. The University of Toronto's GRIT (Green Roof Innovation Testing Laboratory) and Burnley Living Roofs project at the University of Melbourne both emerged in response to the limitation of standards guiding the green roof industry. In 2010, Professor Liat Margolis established GRIT Lab on the roof of the John H. Daniels Faculty of Architecture, Landscape, and Design[74] (Figure 3.17). The Lab's interdisciplinary focus differs from other green roof studies, which typically isolate biological, hydrological and thermal functions according to their respective science and engineering fields of study.[75] Instead, GRIT Lab focuses on the interrelations and co-benefits between plant growth (cover and diversity), growing media composition and water inputs (rainfall and irrigation) to better understand which variables are most critical for water retention and reduction (to improve urban water management), thermal cooling (to reduce ambient temperature and

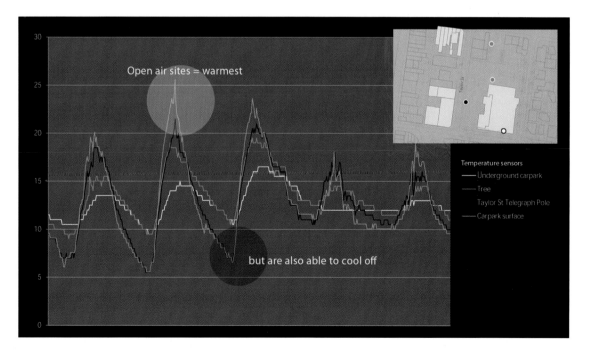

associated energy consumption for cooling during the summer), and habitat value (e.g. pollinators, insects). To properly understand the full complexity of green roof performance, GRIT Lab brings together faculty and student researchers from the Landscape and Architecture, Engineering and Biology programs, as well as members of the green building industry and the municipality.[76]

The green roof experimental design establishes four testing variables (Figure 3.19). Two planting types – a pre-vegetated Sedum mat and a mix of 16 grass and forb species are tested within two different planting substrate types – FLL compliant (free-draining low organic and high mineral content) and a high organic content (compost) blend that is intended to support vascular plants.[77] Two depths of the planting substrate (10 cm and 15 cm) offers a further variable, while the beds are also tested against three irrigation schedules – no irrigation, timer activated, soil moisture sensor activated.[78] Each of the 33 beds, present a different combination of these variables, and also reflect common green roof products, assemblies and maintenance practices in the Toronto region and beyond.

The modules are equipped with eight sensors including a rain gauge tipping bucket to measure discharge flow rates, soil moisture sensor, infrared radiometer to record surface temperature, and five thermal sensors set along a vertical axis to measure cooling (Figure 3.18). Data from the sensors, recorded at 5-minute intervals is then analysed: first in relation to plant growth (surveyed bi-weekly manually)[79] and second in relation to data from an on-site weather station, which

3.17
The testing modules of the GRIT Lab constructed on the roof of the John H. Daniels Faculty of Architecture, Landscape, and Design at The University of Toronto.

3.18
The layout of the testing modules which features eight sensors.

3.19
Variations of the test plots which offer different combinations of growing media, planting, irrigation schedules and media depth.

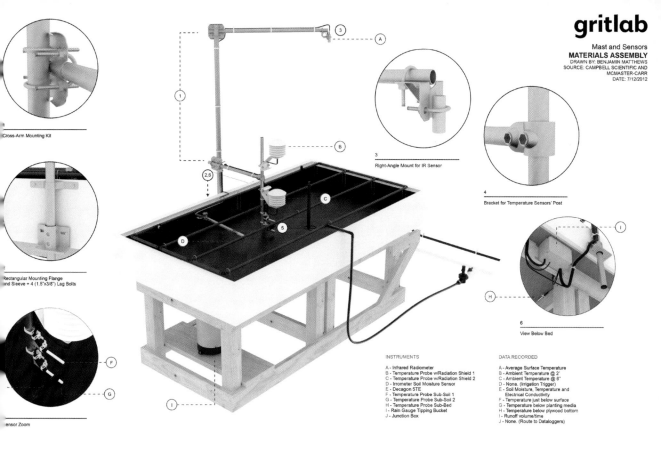

gritlab

Mast and Sensors
MATERIALS ASSEMBLY
DRAWN BY: BENJAMIN MATTHEWS
SOURCE: CAMPBELL SCIENTIFIC AND
MCMASTER-CARR
DATE: 7/12/2012

Cross-Arm Mounting Kit

Rectangular Mounting Flange
and Sleeve + 4 (1.5"x3/8") Lag Bolts

Sensor Zoom

3
Right-Angle Mount for IR Sensor

4
Bracket for Temperature Sensors' Post

6
View Below Bed

INSTRUMENTS

A - Infrared Radiometer
B - Temperature Probe w/Radiation Shield 1
C - Temperature Probe w/Radiation Shield 2
D - Irrometer Soil Moisture Sensor
E - Decagon 5TE
F - Temperature Probe Sub-Soil 1
G - Temperature Probe Sub-Soil 2
H - Temperature Probe Sub-Bed
I - Rain Gauge Tipping Bucket
J - Junction Box

DATA RECORDED

A - Average Surface Temperature
B - Ambient Temperature @ 2'
C - Ambient Temperature @ 6"
D - None. (Irrigation Trigger)
E - Soil Moisture, Temperature and
    Electrical Conductivity
F - Temperature just below surface
G - Temperature below planting media
H - Temperature below plywood bottom
I - Runoff volume/time
J - None. (Route to Dataloggers)

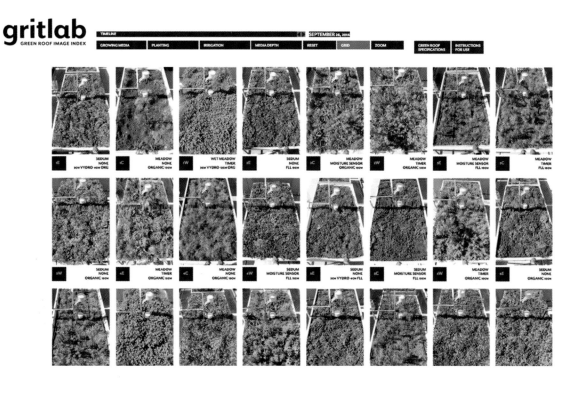

gritlab
GREEN ROOF IMAGE INDEX

Simulating systems

records solar radiation, precipitation, humidity, and wind speed and direction. This allows for comparison between individual beds as well as with local climatic conditions.

One of the primary challenges of integrating real-time data acquisition is the need to troubleshoot and calibrate sensors. This is because the sensors that are currently available on the market are designed for different contexts, or applications. For instance, the soil moisture sensor was designed for natural mineral soils, found in agricultural applications. At the GRIT Lab, this sensor is embedded within the planting substrate, which differs greatly in composition and structure from agricultural soils. After having monitored the soil-moisture measurement readings for several weeks, it became clear that calibrating the sensor according to the specific composition of the planting substrates is essential for accurate water balance analysis.[80]

By correlating weather data, irrigation schedules, soil moisture, and runoff rates, the research team is able to evaluate materials and maintenance in relation to hydrological performance. Finally, the hydrological analysis at the GRIT Lab is not limited to the specific planting substrates that are currently being tested. In fact, the statistical modelling is based on understanding the composition and structure of the two different substrate types in relation to weather patterns and irrigation schedules, which can then be applied to a variety of planting substrates on existing green roofs around Toronto through core sampling and soil analysis, etc.

The research work at the GRIT Lab is intended to inform the 2009 City of Toronto Green Roof Construction Standard and potentially improve the current construction practices to optimise the performance of green roofs. In 2013 GRIT Lab received the ASLA Professional Award of Excellence in Research.[81]

The Burnley Living Roofs project is the first research facility to interrogate the particularities of designing and maintaining green roofs in Australia. Three different roof types were designed in collaboration with landscape architects from HASSELL. A demonstration roof operates as an exhibition and teaching space; featuring seating and gathering areas located among irrigated and non-irrigated planting zones which vary in soil depth. A research roof provides a testing ground for design experiments such as investigating the insulation properties of green roof profiles, while the biodiversity roof featuring insect, bird and reptile habitats indigenous to Melbourne explores the influence of different materiality and substrate on biodiversity. These projects are monitored for performance and fed back into the development of standards appropriate to the particularities of the Melbourne context.

Unobtrusive data gathering capability also means research agendas can easily extend to in-situ sites, away from the laboratory. Luis Fraguada, researcher at IAAC, Barcelona, and James Melsom's research at ETH adapts the sensors used on the UAV drones to public transport infrastructure (such as trams) to capture data corresponding with human usage patterns. Temperature, humidity, light levels and air quality data can verify and contribute to climate simulation models, as well as producing publicly available data of value to designers.[82]

Smart systems

The potential of real-time data extends beyond the recording of information or performance to the development of smart or intelligent design systems. Smart systems have their origins in the Internet of Things (IoT), defined as 'making a computer sense information without the aid of human intervention', thereby reconceiving the Internet as a 'network of interconnected objects'.[83] Facilitated by wireless networks, objects use data to interact with the physical world, thereby developing a 'smart environment'.[84] In 2013, there were approximately 9 billion interconnected devices, with this expected to increase to 24 billion by 2020.[85] These devices provide analytics and applications, ranging from visions for an entire smart city through to smart building management of heating, ventilation, air-conditioning and energy usage.

In June 2014, IBM in conjunction with the Lodha Group, announced the construction of smart city infrastructure for the new Indian city of Palava. Premised on efficiency and participation, IBM aims to use 'advanced data driven systems to integrate information from all city operations into a single system to improve efficiency and deliver an enhanced quality of life for residents'.[86] Anthony Townsend in his 2013 book *Smart Cities: Big Data, Civic Hackers and the Quest for a New Utopia* highlights how smart systems alter the way designers engage with urbanism, necessitating the need to 'draw on informatics and urbanism simultaneously'.[87] However he also warns of defaulting to smart technology to solve problems, to the detriment of more fundamental societal, economic and political changes.

Within landscape architecture, the design of 'smart' infrastructures, systems and open space responsive to fluctuating and unpredictable environmental condi-tions has enormous potential, especially in the era of climate change. Through real-time sensors and control mechanism, infrastructure can respond to cloud-based control systems such as weather reports offering cost-saving measures, resource management and in some cases the diversion of disasters in extreme-weather events. These systems are easily and cheaply constructed, using components from companies such as ioBridge (founded in 2008) or Arduino (established in 2005) that provide solutions to connect 'things' to the Internet.

The North American engineering firm Geosyntec Consultants for examples develops water infrastructure systems such as retention systems, rainwater harvesting systems and roof irrigation linked directly through the cloud to the National Oceanic and Atmospheric Association forecast.[88] These water systems can respond to predicted changes in conditions – emptying before extreme-weather events or not irrigating when rain is predicted.[89] Engineer Mark Quigley considers this the beginning of 'high performance green infrastructure' shifting from sub-optimal passive systems' to 'making decisions in real time to achieve specific environmental goals'.[90]

Smart infrastructure is essential to HASSELL's design for the *Medibank Building* in Docklands, Melbourne, considered a benchmark for green infrastructure in Australian cities. The design of a 'green' headquarters forms a central part of

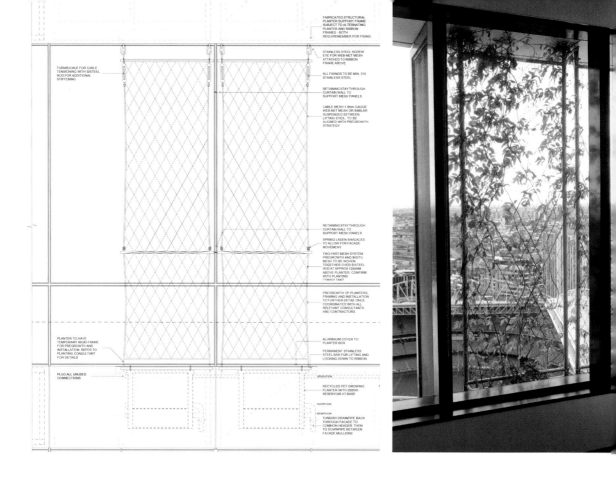

The figure contains the following labels:

FABRICATED STRUCTURAL
PLANTER SUPPORT FRAME
SUBJECT TO ALTERNATING
PLANTER AND RIBBON
FRAMES - BOTH
REQUIREMEMBER FOR FIXING

STAINLESS STEEL SCREW
EYE FOR WEB-NET MESH
ATTACHED TO RIBBON
FRAME ABOVE

TURNBUCKLE FOR CABLE
TENSIONING WITH SISTEEL
ROD FOR ADDITIONAL
STIFFENING

ALL FIXINGS TO BE MIN .316
STAINLESS STEEL

RETAINING STAY THROUGH
CURTAIN WALL TO
SUPPORT MESH PANELS

CABLE MESH 1.5mm GAUGE
WEB-NET MESH OR SIMILAR
SUSPENDED BETWEEN
LIFTING EYES. TO BE
ALIGNED WITH PREGROWTH
STRATEGY

RETAINING STAY THROUGH
CURTAIN WALL TO
SUPPORT MESH PANELS

SPRING LADEN SHACKLES
TO ALLOW FOR FAÇADE
MOVEMENT

TWO PART MESH SYSTEM
PREGROWTH AND INSITU
MESH TO BE WOVEN
TOGETHER OVER SISTEEL
ROD AT APPROX 1200MM
ABOVE PLANTER. CONFIRM
WITH PLANTING
CONSULTANT

PREGROWTH OF PLANTERS,
FRAMING AND INSTALLATION
TO FURTHER DETAIL ONCE
COORDINATED WITH ALL
RELEVANT CONSULTANTS
AND CONTRACTORS

PLANTER TO HAVE
TEMPORARY RIGID FRAME
FOR PREGROWTH AND
INSTALLATION. REFER TO
PLANTING CONSULTANT
FOR DETAILS

ALUMINIUM COVER TO
PLANTER BOX

PERMANENT STAINLESS
STEEL BAR FOR LIFTING AND
LOCKING DOWN TO RIBBON

PLUG ALL UNUSED
CONNECTIONS

IRRIGATION

RECYCLED PET GROWING
PLANTER WITH 200mm
RESERVOIR AT BASE

OVERFLOW

RESERVOIR

TUNDISH DRAINPIPE BACK
THROUGH FAÇADE TO
COMMON HEADER, THEN
TO DOWNPIPE BETWEEN
FAÇADE MULLINS

Medibank's repositioning from a standard health insurance business into a more aspirational vision where well-being and prevention are highlighted. The project is one of the largest green façade projects in Australia, building on research from The Burnley Living Roofs project discussed earlier, and the extensive research and development of Fytogreen Australia, a specialist in roof garden, vertical gardens and green façade construction.[91] The design features two 20 metre vertical green walls, roof gardens as well as 520 planter boxes of climbers (Figure 3.20) which form a living façade over 18 levels.

Managing Director of Fytogreen Geoff Heard highlights the challenges of living façades, which far exceed the demands of roof gardens or green walls. Each façade orientation experiences different environmental conditions while access for ongoing maintenance is limited. Smart irrigation systems are critical to their success. This design is irrigated from the 250,000 litres of water, which is collected and recycled through the building. A Galcon system provides an 'online' cloud-based irrigation management application which delivers real-time data information on dynamic flow management, irrigation logs, and water consumption reports, as well as system failure warnings sent to contractors' email and smart phones.[92] This information can be further supplemented with sensor input recording factors such as temperature, wind, soil and rain.

A 'predictive' management strategy informed by real-time weather station

3.20a–c
Medibank Private Headquarter, Melbourne: the challenging growing conditions of the living façades required the plants to be pre-grown off site in their planter boxes (for up to 6 months), before being slotted into their façade position.

input could further extend the capability of the system. However Heard is wary of this technology in regard to green façades. Unlike green infrastructure and parks located on the ground, there is little buffer for planting on built structure if data proves inaccurate.[93] He also identifies limitations in the existing irrigation systems to link effectively into cloud-based data.

The concept of smart systems is not limited to constructed projects, as demonstrated by the United States Forest Service establishment of 'smart forests'.[94] Data collected from web cams, humidity and temperature sensors, combined with instruments for solar radiation, wind vanes and rain gauges offer scientists real-time information to inform their management strategies for the changing climate. Until recently, Forest Service scientists had little data on urban forests, with most information gathered from wilderness areas. The Forest Service is increasingly including more urban sites (such as Alley Pond Park in Queens) into their sensored system to gain a more comprehensive understanding of the impact of climate change on urban ecology.

So far this chapter has introduced two ways in which designers engage with the simulation of systems; firstly embedding digital simulation directly within design processes and secondly using real-time data and sensors to develop new analytical understandings of site, to research the performance of space and systems and to develop smart or intelligent design systems. In the following section, we introduce

the use of physical and digital prototyping within design processes as further
techniques for understanding relationships between form, effect, data and systems.

Design as a laboratory

A prototype is defined as a sample or a model used to test an idea or process
that offers knowledge. The terminology is rarely used with landscape architecture,
more commonly associated with engineering, industrial design, architecture and
electronics. Engineering has a long history of using scaled-down physical models to
explore the fluid dynamic of wind and water or in the study of material movement.
But as Enriqueta Llabres-Valls and Eduardo Rico highlight, it is important to
consider dimensional analysis when applying knowledge from scaled-down prototypes. Dimensional analysis concerns the achievement of 'similitude' between the
prototype and the real condition, establishing a comparable ratio, either 'geometrical
(scaling down), kinematic (similar shape of flow lines) or dynamic (where ratios
between forces and pressures are similar)'.[95]

In a pre-digital era, it was not unusual for engineers to produce large-scale
physical models to understand dynamic water flow valuable in the management of
extensive catchments. For instance the US Army Corps of Engineers constructed
physical models of Mississippi River (1949–73) and Chesapeake Bay (1978) to
inform management strategies.[96] Digital simulation has replaced many aspects of
the physical model. However, for landscape architecture, the ability to understand
materiality in relationship to flow is significant, and remains difficult to simulate

3.21a
Construction of the hydraulic
model for the Bowtie River
Prototype.

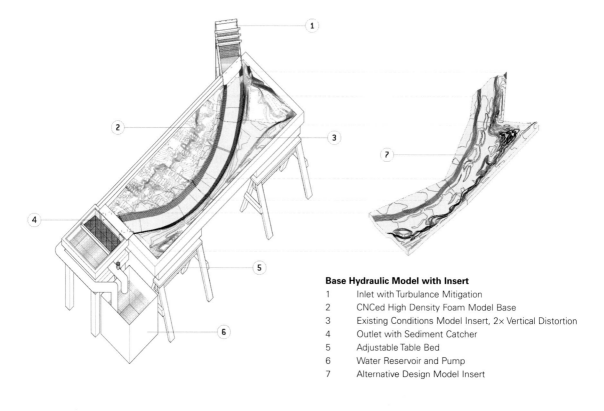

Base Hydraulic Model with Insert

1   Inlet with Turbulance Mitigation
2   CNCed High Density Foam Model Base
3   Existing Conditions Model Insert, 2× Vertical Distortion
4   Outlet with Sediment Catcher
5   Adjustable Table Bed
6   Water Reservoir and Pump
7   Alternative Design Model Insert

digitally. While parametric modelling and the virtual simulation of systems offers understandings of the relationship between form and systems, these models provide limited engagement with the specific materiality of landscape. A physical prototype engaging both fluid and medium therefore remains a valuable interrogation of dynamic processes such as sedimentation, revealing 'dependencies of different elements' in dynamic environments.[97]

The Landscape Morphologies Lab (LML) at the University of Southern California (USC) utilises a combination of robotics, physical and virtual modelling to examine relationships between landscape morphology, infrastructure and performance.[98] Established in 2011 under the leadership of Alexander Robinson, the LML collaborates with government agencies such as Los Angeles Bureau of Engineering and the Army Corps of Engineers and the USC Landscape Architecture Program and School of Engineering to develop infrastructural outcomes that combine design with efficiency.

The Los Angeles River is a major site of investigation. In collaboration with the City of Los Angeles's LA River Project and graduate landscape architecture studios, the LML constructed a physical hydraulic model of a section known as the Bowtie Parcel. This concrete section of the river is currently under review, thereby providing an excellent opportunity to test alternative design proposals. Working with the physical model and running water (Figure 3.21), successive design studios test the performance of new morphological forms presented as 3.5 metre foam inserts. The dynamic hydraulic tests are visually documented, recording processes of sand sedimentation and deposition, scouring and water flow.

A focus on the Owens Lake Dust Control Project introduces robotics to the exploration of materiality and flows. Since the 1920s, Owens Lake, situated in Lone

3.21b
Testing new inserts in the hydraulic model. The use of coloured dyes aid the comprehension of water flow.

Pine, California has been depleted by the Los Angeles Aqueduct, creating over 100 square miles of salt bed and frequent dust storms. In 2008 the Los Angeles Department of Water and Power proposed a 'moat and row' technique of berms, fences and ditches to control the dust.[99] This waterless method was never implemented, with concerns raised over habitat destruction and visual impact. However, Robinson also highlights reaction to the extreme 'operational efficiency' of the scheme as a further issue, with evidence of the public and some agencies arguing for a more 'creative' response.[100]

The LML developed a multimedia system comprising a robotic sand modeller, a 3D scanner, projection capability and a custom software interface for exploring alternative dust mitigation techniques (Figure 3.22). The project aims to 'create a common ground where designers, engineers, and the public can dynamically engage in the multiple concerns inherent to the lake'.[101] An interactive Landscape Prototyping Machine will be exhibited at a visitor centre in Lone Pine (next to Owens Lake). This exhibition will allow users to 'tune' aspects of proposed landscapes to their preference such as selecting dust control surface treatment and adjusting water levels.

LML's application of robotics in the exploration of dust mitigation remains experimental, with its application yet to be tested at the scale of the site. However, it demonstrates important prototyping techniques for engaging with material processes. While limited in empirical measurement, these techniques generate qualitative information concerning behavioural relationships between site materiality, form and the fluid dynamics of air and water. Robinson comments further:

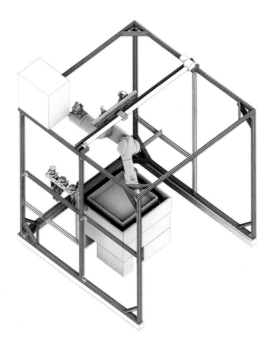

3.22a–b
The Rapid Prototyping Machine with 6 –axis robotic arm, vacuum box, sand box, tool changer, projector and laser 3d scanner (a). Custom end arm tools for the robotic arm for subraction and calibration (b).

3.23a–b
Algorithmic Toolpaths: The tool paths are generated by custom algorithms which are projected onto the sand prior to implementation. The resultant topographic form is scanned and input into custom analysis software where the form can be analysed for performance.

Feedback systems, such as modelling and analysis tools, are paired with designer-based generative processes to create a condition that further empowers the unparalleled cognitive-design ability of effective designers and other individuals to discover good solutions. These tools and methods promise to allow landscape architects to gain further agency and expertise in the design of infrastructures, high-performance living systems, and almost any twenty-first century landscape.[102]

Digital prototyping however does not require expensive robotic equipment or complex programming knowledge. Plug-ins such as Grasshopper's Firefly, developed in 2010, offer accessible techniques for linking real-time feedback between hardware devices such as the Arduino microcontroller or mobile phones, and the Internet to drive 3D geometry within a parametric model.[103] The developers Andrew O. Payne and Jason Kelly Johnson explain further:

> Firefly's toolset gives the designer the ability to quickly test how well a design will perform when confronted with different real-world environmental conditions, saving on physical prototyping costs and times. It also opens up the possibility to control digital prototypes using a range of real time data – creating 'live models' whose parameters can be iteratively tested until a desired set of outcomes are achieved.[104]

The North American based Dredge Research Collaborative utilises these technologies in their prototyping explorations. This multidisciplinary group investigates human sediment handling practices through design studios, research and events.[105] In January 2014, the DredgeFest Louisiana symposium brought together government, academics, practitioners, students, theorists and the public to interrogate the control of the Mississippi River. Workshops featured prototyping techniques, utilising Grasshopper, Firefly and Arduino.

The Adaptive Devices workshop, devised by Bradley Cantrell, David Merlin and Justine Holzman, explored the design potential of sedimentary technologies to control navigation, floods and the manipulation of sedimentation. Participants focused on 'the landscape-making potential' of dredgers, silt fences and turbidity curtains explored through prototyping devices, together with physical modelling. Similarly Alexander Robinson and Richard Hindle's Hybrid Landscape workshop combined physical (sand modelling) and digital modelling tools to develop morphological alternatives for the 'bay bottom terracing' of Louisiana's Vermillion Bay.[106] These alternatives were then evaluated according to landscape performance metrics.

Next we focus on three studios, which embed systems prototyping into their design processes, effectively shifting the conceptualisation of the design studio into the design laboratory. Importantly, these examples introduce a design process which commences with the prototyping of a dynamic system (physical, digital or combined) which is then hacked or modified during the course of the design process. This differs from earlier examples such as *Gardens by the Bay* (which modelled a closed system) or PARKKIM's *Thermal City* which tested design outcome against more singular phenomena such as heat or wind.

Synthetic ecologies

For over a decade, Bradley Cantrell has used design studios and practice to explore the potential of 'sensing, automation and robotics in the conceptualisation of ecologies'.[107] Acknowledging that ecological systems do not reach a climax, Cantrell proposes the idea of 'synthetic ecologies' utilising real-time sensing of site phenomena to develop adaptive management strategies.[108] 'This view of ecological systems, through the lens of responsive technologies', states Cantrell 'posits that the designer is responsible for the creation and implementation of processes that curate, manage, and sculpt landscape systems'.[109]

This philosophy underpins the 2013 design studio Synthetic Urban Ecology taught by Bradley Cantrell and Justine Holzman at the Louisiana State University. Focusing on West Oakland and the Port of Oakland, the studio used a combination of virtual and physical prototypes to interrogate the 'relationship between urbanity, industry, ecological fitness, habitat, and infrastructure'.[110]

For Cantrell and Holzman, the prototype model is not simply a representation of system. Instead it has dual functions: to deconstruct the site processes to provide

3.24
Diagraming Stoke's law to understand the relationship between humidity, particulate removal and velocity.

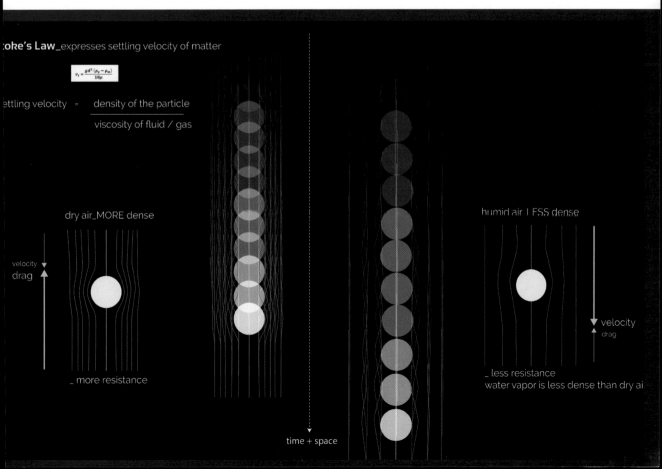

:oke's Law_expresses settling velocity of matter

$$v_t = \frac{gd^2\,(\rho_p - \rho_m)}{18\mu}$$

ettling velocity = $\dfrac{\text{density of the particle}}{\text{viscosity of fluid / gas}}$

dry air_MORE dense

velocity
drag

_ more resistance

humid air_LESS dense

velocity
drag

_ less resistance
water vapor is less dense than dry ai

time + space

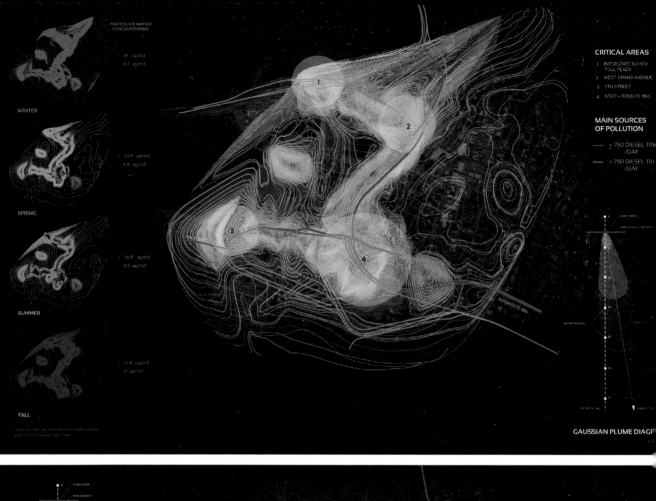

PARTICULATE MATTER
CONCENTRATIONS

8.1 ug/m3
11.7 ug/m3

WINTER

35.9 ug/m3
6.8 ug/m3

SPRING

56.8 ug/m3
6.5 ug/m3

SUMMER

75.8 ug/m3
9 ug/m3

FALL

CRITICAL AREAS

1   INTERSTATE 80 HOV
     TOLL PLAZA
2   WEST GRAND AVENUE
3   7TH STREET
4   SOUTH BEND OF 880

MAIN SOURCES
OF POLLUTION

> 750 DIESEL TRU
/DAY

< 750 DIESEL TRU
/DAY

GAUSSIAN PLUME DIAGF

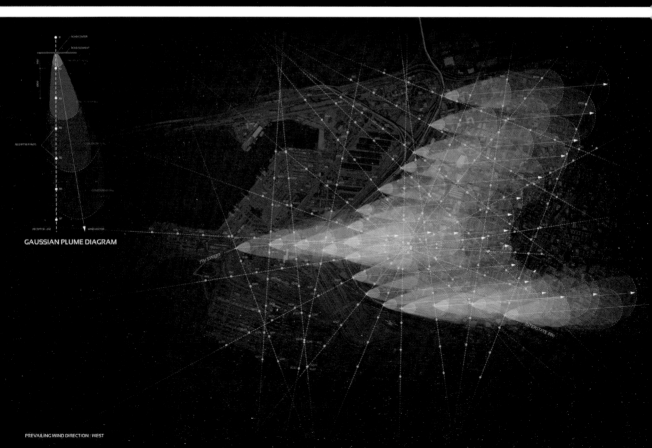

GAUSSIAN PLUME DIAGRAM

PREVAILING WIND DIRECTION : WEST

3.25a–b
Documentation of the wind conditions and
air pollution dispersal in West Oakland.

3.26a–b
Design Strategies for *Metabolic Forest* by
Silvia Cox and Prentiss Darden.

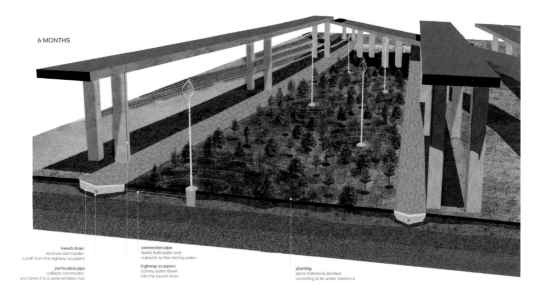

6 MONTHS

french drain
receives stormwater
runoff from the highway scuppers

connection pipe
feeds both water and
nutrients to the misting poles

perforated pipe
collects stormwater
and takes it to a sedimentation box

highway scuppers
convey water down
into the french drain

planting
plant material is planted
according to its water tolerance

FOREST TYPOLOGY 1 - IMPLEMENTATION

HIGH WATER TOLERANCE
ferns and mosses

fungi:
- Glomus intraradices
- Pisolithus tinctorius

MID WATER TOLERANCE

LOW WATER TOLERANCE

TYPOLOGY 2
PRODUCTION FOREST

TYPOLOGY 1
ABSORPTION FOREST

PRODUCTION FOREST

ABSORPTION FOREST

SELECTED TREE SPECIES

a datum or baseline to measure change, compare and understand iterations; and to operate as a 'malleable and hackable' model to test 'site proposals, data acquisition/ construction, and performative tweaks' in a series of speculations and inquiry.[111]

This approach is demonstrated in the scheme *Metabolic Forest* by Silvia Cox and Prentiss Darden which focused on the health issues of particulate matter found within diesel emission. A digital prototype model interrogated the processes of air pollution, testing multiple factors including wind speed and traffic idling, calculating particulate matter concentrations and mapping their levels across the year.[112] This digital prototype was constructed according to Stoke's law (Figures 3.24), a mathematical equation describing the settling velocities of small particle in a fluid. The resultant model identified 'rules for manipulation that respond to the overall performance of the ecology's capacities' allowing for the conceptualisation of a site-specific ecological fitness.[113] The model offered a framework (derived from vegetative, soil and atmospheric performance) for conceiving a range of conditions that would support specific growth patterns or suggest new trajectories for species to colonise as the ecosystems evolved. These conditions were also matched with specific cultural and social performance criteria to create a set of complementary or counter protocols to suggest new forms of ecological and cultural crossover.

In phase two, students assumed the role of 'curator of processes', to propose an adaptive management strategy.[114] Cantrell and Holzman adopt the term 'catalytic resistance' as a tactical description for engaging with 'ecosystem's adaptive and generative capabilities' as distinct from designing a defined system. This target of resistance, states Cantrell, operates 'to sculpt and inflect' allowing for the 'small adjustments to effectively manipulate the overall structure of the network over time'.[115]

For example the *Metabolic Forest* scheme (Figure 3.26) as the name suggests, developed an urban forest system shaped by the ambitions to capture and metabolise air pollution and to provide biomass as an economic resource (to be used for biofuels, fibre and timber), aligned with the port's reconceptualisation as an ecoport.[116] The staged implementation, begins with a tactical strategy for decreasing pollution around residential and recreational areas, through sensored misting devices which emit a fine mist when emissions are high. This mist leads to less dense air, encouraging particulate matter to fall more easily to the ground, before being metabolised by mycorrhizal fungi in the soil. A strategic network of misting devices establishes an adaptive urban forest conceived within the two processes of absorption and biomass production.

The design is positioned as 'a synthesis of technological and natural components', considered 'part hardware and software'.[117] The forests are intrinsically linked to areas of high pollution, growing in areas where mist is emitted in response to high pollution level. The urban forest network also contributes to a greater public understanding of the largely invisible phenomena of pollution through LEDs embedded in the misting device to display daily pollution levels.

The strategy is both tactical and performative, generated by an understanding of pollution gained through the digital prototype, with this knowledge then applied within the specific social, economic and ecological context of urbanism. As demonstrated in these outcomes, the interrogation of ecological systems through prototyping does not, by default, direct designers to an overtly 'naturalistic' design response. Instead the modelling exploration makes apparent the often invisible forces and processes that impact on the formation and performance of landscapes. This is demonstrated further in the following example where CFD modelling forms an important tool for engaging wind and water in the conceptualisation of a design intervention for a community art program on the Delaware River.

Simulated natures

In 2014, the Department of Landscape Architecture at the University of Pennsylvania ran the Simulated Natures seminar as part of their Digital Media curriculum sequence. Developed by Keith VanDerSys, the seminar interrogated the temporal and relational qualities of landscape through computational tools including computational flow dynamics (Aquaveo SMS, ANSYS Fluent and Ecotect), geospatial analysis (GIS) and parametric software (Grasshopper). These tools, state VanDerSys, form the basis for engaging with the 'invisible' information (data and flows) that shape ecological and social formations, offering an engagement with 'the forces and factors outside humans' perceptible limits'.[118]

3.27a–b
Exploration of form & forces using the Paneling Tool.

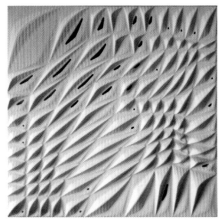
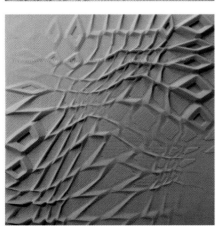

The seminar operated as a mini studio (3 hours a week) with the first half structured as a series of exercises to introduce students to digital techniques and to develop their understandings of the relationships between data, processes and effect. Students began with a topographic exploration developed with the Grasshopper plug-in Paneling Tools (which supports the modelling of panelling patterns). The resultant landforms (Figure 3.27) were then interrogated for its effects on drainage to reveal patterns of dispersal. These exercises build on knowledge developed in previous grading classes, but with emphasis on the relationship between landform and water behaviours. VanDerSys encouraged students to look for shifts in time and speed of water flow, moments that 'are representative of processes that have material consequences' such as erosion and collection.[119]

In the next phase, a more precise engagement with temporality and quantity was introduced to the CFD simulations through the use of real-time data from the NOAA (National Oceanic and Atmospheric Administration) website. Models were run as a time sequence, requiring students to consider the implications of data sampling. For example at what interval should tidal flux be examined, every 10 minutes for 20 hours or over longer intervals? Output values from these simulations were then exported into Grasshopper where they were transformed into

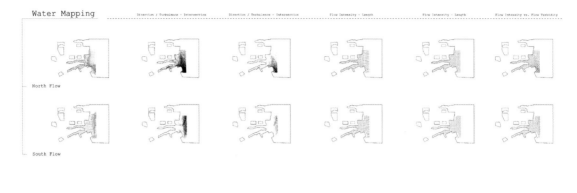

Water Mapping

Direction / Turbulence - Intersection   Direction / Turbulence - Intersection   Flow Intensity - Length   Flow Intensity - Length   Flow Intensity vs. Flow Turbidity

North Flow

South Flow

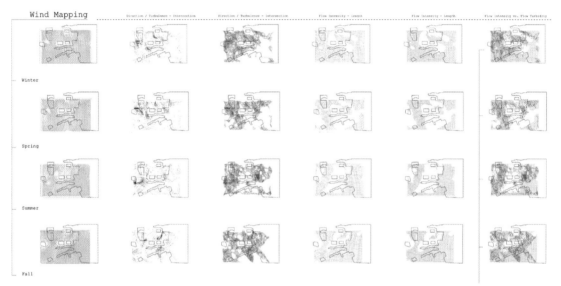

Wind Mapping

Direction / Turbulence - Intersection   Direction / Turbulence - Intersection   Flow Intensity - Length   Flow Intensity - Length   Flow Intensity vs. Flow Turbidity

Winter

Spring

Summer

Fall

visual representations of vectors, forces and quantity. These were also animated to simulate flow in real time. Learning how to import and export data across software platforms (for example as organised lists of comma separated values) formed an important objective.

In the final exercise, students returned to the initial panel exercise, this time to apply an 'effect' to develop landform. Unlike the first exercise where the form was largely arbitrary, the now uncovered behaviour of water (force and flow) becomes the generator for topography, the result of a generative analytical process.

In the second half of the semester, students applied this new knowledge in the development of an intervention for old piers (inaccessible due to structural issues) along the Delaware River. Rather than renovating the pier, the Delaware Waterfront Corporation is exploring the idea of art as an activator. Students were asked to reconsider the concept of landscape art and intervention, challenged to develop something temporary that could also provoke awareness about the Delaware River redevelopment and/or environmental issues.

3.28
Documenting the intensities and turbulences of wind and water in the *Gliding Networked Flows* project.

3.29
Kite flying simulations.

3.30a–b
Determining the seasonal anchor points for the kites.

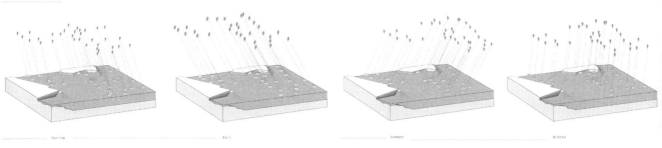

Spring   Fall   Summer   Winter

Anchor Points
Seasonal Cropped Zone
Spring
Summer
Fall
Winter

Seasonal Patterns for Anchor locations
Spring   Summer

Fall   Winter

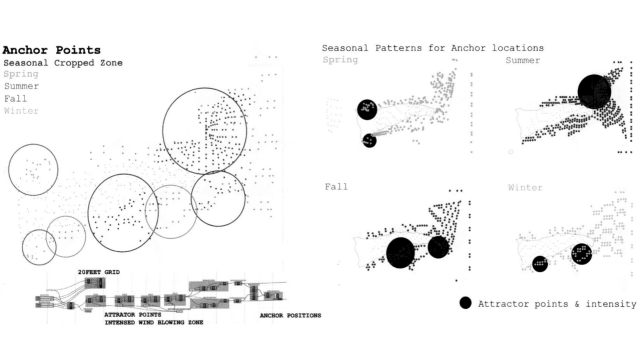

● Attractor points & intensity

20FEET GRID

ATTRATOR POINTS
INTENSED WIND BLOWING ZONE   ANCHOR POSITIONS

Kite flying&swimming simulations
Kite Trajectory
Constant Anchor Points ●

Spring   Summer

Fall   Winter

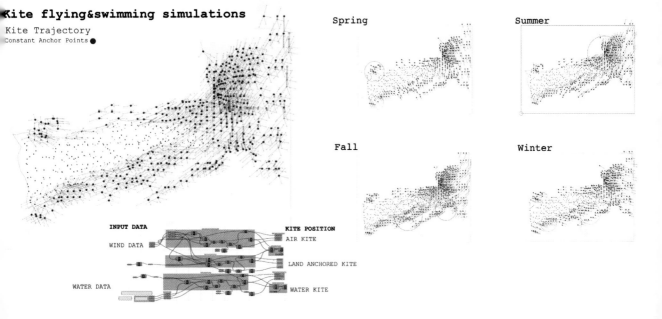

INPUT DATA   KITE POSITION
     AIR KITE
WIND DATA

     LAND ANCHORED KITE

WATER DATA   WATER KITE

With a focus on wind and water movements, teams of four explored these invisible conditions and their relationships to each other through simulations and imagination, exposing moments of greatest flux and forces which could be heightened or registered through devices.

The scheme *Gliding Networked Flows* by Chris Arth, Leeju Kang and Elise McCurley proposes a series of kites that register the amount of drag and force within the water landscape. Their site simulations, shown in Figure 3.28, identified the most intense areas of conflicting wind and water direction, considered across the full seasonal range of the year. These points of intensities and attractors informed the seasonal anchor points for the kites. The amount of anchor drag is dependent on the relationship between the tidal conditions and wind patterns, which registers in two ways: by the flocking behaviours of the kites and through colour change of the kites. Arduino movement sensors capturing water fluctuation trigger the projection of colour onto the kite's reflective surface.

The *Windy Islets* scheme by Drew Grandjean, Shunkuang Su and Qing Zhang used hydrodynamic simulations (explored with Aquaveo SMS) to document patterns of high and low water movement, which also identified where areas of less flow accumulate pollutants of nitrates and phosphates.

Their design response features a series of floating wetlands constructed from PVC material and planting suitable for pollution remediation. These are sited in areas of low water movement. Given that plant roots in water quickly exhaust the available oxygen supply, the wetlands each include a wind turbine that drives a bubbler. Importantly, this bubbler produces an apron of air around each island, providing extra oxygen for the plants. The wind turbine, which also features an LED light on its tip, leans towards areas of higher intensity aerodynamic flow, thereby operating as a wind index on the water surface.

These designs demonstrate how the '"invisible" information of microscopic and macrocosmic forces' can inspire a design intervention reflective of the topological properties of landscape.[120] Computational tools, such as CFD modelling

3.32
Testing the hydrodynamic
flow of water and pollutants.

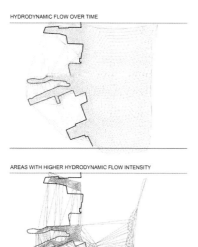

HYDRODYNAMIC FLOW OVER TIME

AREAS WITH HIGHER HYDRODYNAMIC FLOW INTENSITY

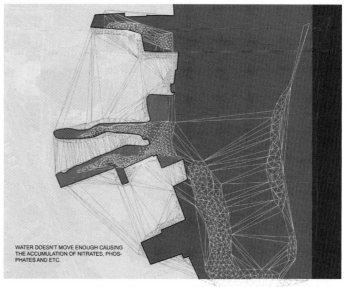

POLLUTED AREA

WATER DOESN'T MOVE ENOUGH CAUSING
THE ACCUMULATION OF NITRATES, PHOS-
PHATES AND ETC.

FLOATING WETLAND PLACEMENT

Point Grids

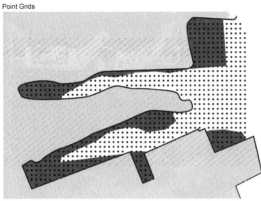

Selected Spots

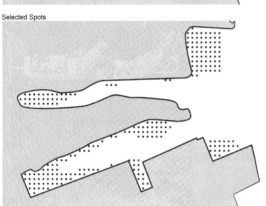

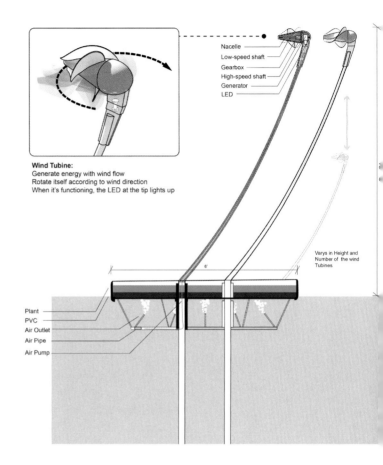

Wind Tubine:
Generate energy with wind flow
Rotate itself according to wind direction
When it's functioning, the LED at the tip lights up

Nacelle
Low-speed shaft
Gearbox
High-speed shaft
Generator
LED

Varys in Height and
Number of the wind
Tubines

6'

Plant
PVC
Air Outlet
Air Pipe
Air Pump

FLOATING WETLAND

Cause of different kinds of plants were planted on floating wetland,
the flower appear various color during seasonal change

PVC Material

Matrix & Root hair

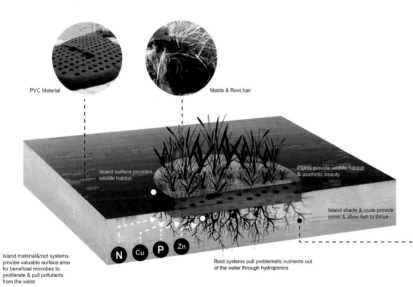

Island surface provides
wildlife habitat

Plants provide wildlife habitat
& aesthetic beauty

Island shade & roots provide
cover & allow fish to thrive

Island material&root systems
provide valuable surface area
for beneficial microbes to
proliferate & pull pollutants
from the water

Root systems pull problematic nutrients out
of the water through hydroponics

N Cu P Zn

Pontederia cordata
Jul-Aug

Canna flaccida
Aug-Oct

Iris virginica
Apr-May

Lobelia cardinalis
Oct-Jun

Crinum americanum
Jun-Nov

Hibiscus moscheutos
Jun-Sep

Oxygen: Plants require oxygen for respiration to carry out their functions of water and nutrient uptake. In soil adequate oxygen is usually available, but plant roots growing in water will quickly exhaust the supply of dissolved oxygen and can be damaged or killed unless additional air is provided. A common method of supplying oxygen is to **bubble air** through the solution.

Simulating systems

3.33
The floating wetlands
featured in the *Windy Islets*
proposal by Drew Grandjean,
Shunkuang Su and Qing
Zhang.

combined with access to real-time data, expose what VanderSys describes as 'the conditions of consequence'.[121] Used in conjunction with the designer's imagination, the simulations contribute to the generation of designs responsive to the effects of the dynamic systems.

In the final example, we significantly shift scale to explore how a combination of digital and physical prototyping can be applied at a regional scale in the interrogation of the controversial large-scale mining and extraction processes in Alberta, Canada.

Proxy modelling

The Relational Modelling practice of Enriqueta Llabres-Valls and Eduardo Rico was briefly introduced in Chapter 2. Llabres-Valls and Rico are particularly interested in the representational challenges of working with spaces in constant flux, exploring relationships and interfaces between 'mathematically defined relationships within a digital model' and the 'materially formed proxy models'.[122] Their 2014 studio focused on the mining and extraction processes in the Athabasca Tar Sands Area in Alberta, Canada (Figure 3.34) which offered a valuable platform to explore these ideas. This studio formed part of the Master of Urban Design, Relational Urban Design Cluster (RU18) at the Bartlett Architecture School, University College London.

This controversial mining process leads to the generation of extensive sedimentation within tailing ponds of a scale similar to the natural formations of the sand braided rivers channels found to the north of the mining areas. Currently, less than 2 per cent of the waste tailing ponds has been rehabilitated.[123] Orthodox techniques for engaging with this landscape, post mining, observe Llabres-Valls and Rico, involves either 'a naturalistic postrationalisation (devolving the landscape to nature) or a romantic one (describing it as industrial heritage)'.[124] Their studio, run in conjunction with Zachary Fluker, explored the alternative approach of considering the formation of landscape concurrently with the production process.[125]

The studio's innovation lies in conceiving an interface linking three models: a mathematical model engaging ecological, social and economic factors; a proxy model exploring the physical and ecological simulation of landform patterns as they change over time and a digital model offering analysis on the emerging behaviours and conditions evident in the proxy model. Together these different modelling and prototyping techniques encompass top-down and bottom-up influences, and offer the designer important knowledge for intervening in this complex ecological, economic and industrial process.

The mathematical model worked across ecological, social and economic factors to establish relationships and behaviours of these systems within a database. Importantly this data encompassed both site-based factors such as ecology and external influences like fluctuating oil prices to develop a system reflective of indeterminacy and change, linked to broader global and national influences. The model facilitated the testing of systemic flexibility, calculating quantity of change when one

Fort Mckay

Syncrude Oil Industry Area

Fort McMurray

or more variables alter.[126] The ecological data for this model was supplemented by the analysis of the physical and digital model, discussed later in this section.

The proxy model presents a very different type of time-based model to that of the mathematical, instead focusing on the patterns and processes of formation. In the case of the Athabasca Tar Sands Area, a scaled-down model of the Gilbert delta (characterised by large bodies of water, with little wave movement) was developed as the proxy model. This large physical model shown in Figure 3.35 simulated the tailing discharging process of sand mining. Sediment and water were dropped into a corner of a tank with water flowing towards another corner. Over time the process established layers of sedimentation spreading within a fan-delta shape. These processes were recorded using a Kinect sensor or video camera.

Once a level of complexity was achieved, the proxy model provided the vehicle to test interventions and acquire knowledge of material behaviour. These included testing saturation levels, introducing artificial built channels to direct water to areas of mine extraction and exploring different forms of dams and obstacles. Figure 3.36 documents the different processes applied as the students worked across physical and digital models.

Importantly, the Kinect sensor and the video camera allowed the changes emerging in the proxy model to be translated into a digital model. Beginning with a physical (proxy) model, the video recording of the processes was translated into a bit map, from which a Grasshopper definition captured the contour lines and

3.35
The proxy model comprised of a computer, a Kinect scanner or camera, a simulation tank, a sand container, a water pump and a fish tank.

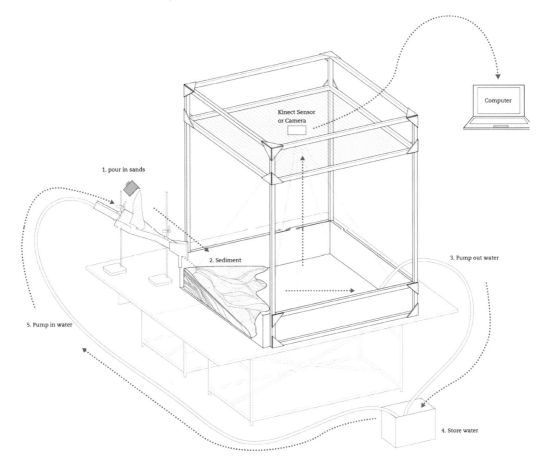

Kinect Sensor
or Camera

Computer

1. pour in sands

2. Sediment

3. Pump out water

5. Pump in water

4. Store water

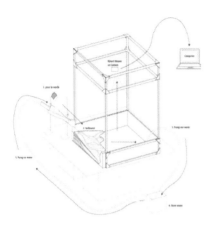

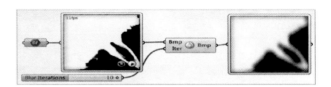

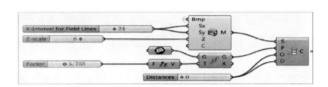

1. Testing different materials and
water processes through the
proxy model.

2. The video recording
of the proxy model is
translated (using bitmap and
Grasshopper) into a digital
topographic surface.

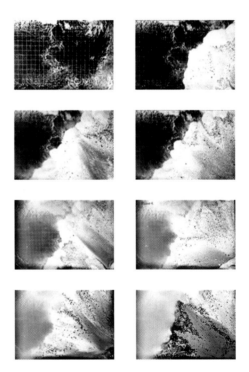

Simulating systems

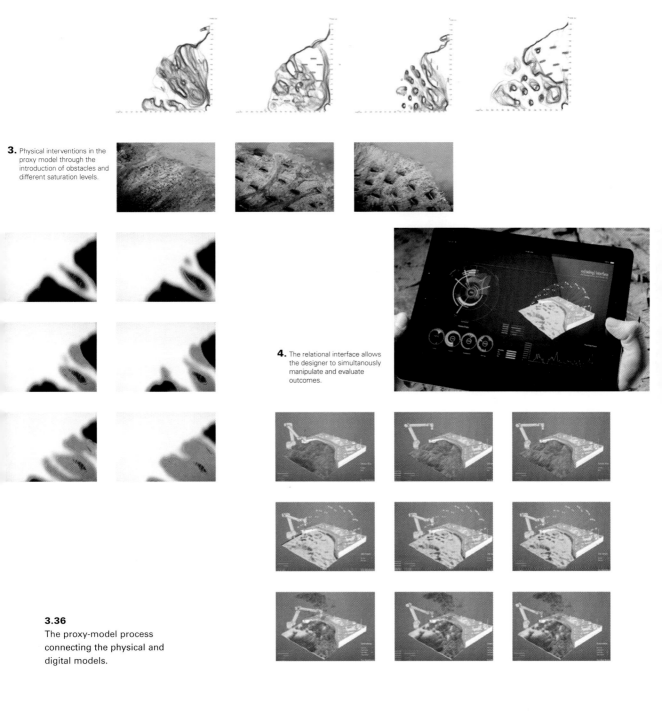

3. Physical interventions in the proxy model through the introduction of obstacles and different saturation levels.

4. The relational interface allows the designer to simultaneously manipulate and evaluate outcomes.

3.36
The proxy-model process connecting the physical and digital models.

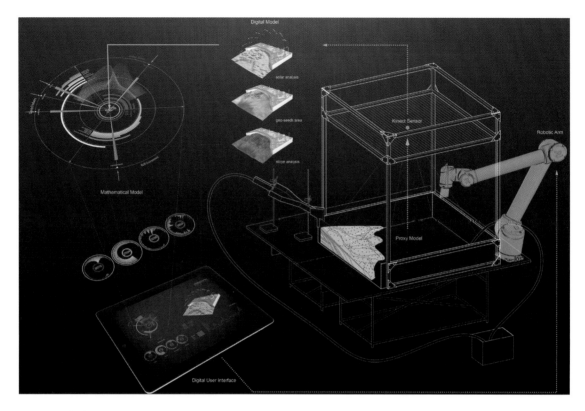

Digital Model

solar analysis

geo-seeds area

slope analysis

Mathematical Model

Kinect Sensor

Robotic Arm

Proxy Model

Digital User Interface

vectors, which were then translated into a topographic surface comprising meshes and contours.

The resultant digital model can then be analysed, offering further knowledge about emerging behaviours and conditions forming in the proxy model. Analysis of slope, wind, surface water flow and solar analysis can be fed back into the mathematical model, helping to calibrate its data against these more specific site conditions.

All three models link to a digital interface, which simultaneously allows the designer to manipulate and evaluate outcomes. As shown in Figure 3.37, this digital interface controls a robotic arm that manipulates the physical model, the results of which are analysed and fed back into the mathematical–ecological model.

This studio offers an exciting glimpse of a design future, where a landscape system can be prototyped and then analysed (using a real-time feedback loop) according to ecological, social and economic performance. This mix of physical and digital prototyping, which engages top-down and bottom-up influence, shifts the design of landscape systems beyond broad speculation, into a relational model reflective of systemic methodology and the material processes of the site.

When asked to describe her future vision for design and landscape architecture, Claire Fellman, Director of Snøhetta's New York office, identified the ability to design more directly within dynamic systems, harnessing GIS data, Grasshopper and simulations so that design 'really becomes about landscape performance and ecological systems'.[127] The three design studios just described present design

3.37
The digital interface connecting the mathematical, proxy and digital models.

processes that are close to matching Fellman's vision. Rather than 2D site plans, these models or prototypes of systems provide the apparatus for design, constructing a continuous feedback loop, that interrogates relationship and behaviours between the biological and synthetic. Within these techniques, the system remains dynamic, fluid and ever present.

Conclusion

Landscape architecture is often described as the art of time. Until recently the discipline lacked techniques that could integrate and speculate on change directly within design processes. Simulation, physical and digital prototyping, combined with access to real-time data, offer landscape architecture new operative techniques for conceiving and testing the dynamic behaviours and relationship of systems and phenomena.

This chapter has identified two approaches for intergrating these techniques within design processes: first, applying digital simulation of systems directly within design processes to test performance; and, second, a more fundamental reconceptualisation of design processes which position the physical and/or digital prototyping of systems as the starting point, in which to hack, test and explore design interventions. Real-time data is central to both of these approaches, offering iterative feedback to designers.

Technology such as sensors offer further prospects to engage with change within the constructed design, offering opportunity to design 'intelligence' responsive to fluctuating and dynamic environmental and social conditions, in addition to measuring and monitoring performance post construction to customise longer-term management strategies. In a further advancement, real-time data combined with portable technologies for gathering data such sensors, laser scans and photogrammetry reframe site analysis from a 'visual' understanding of site conditions to a more comprehensive engagement with intangible phenomena and invisible forces such as heat, pollution, wind and water.

Performance underpins all of these techniques, however, as demonstrated in the design examples, this focus does not reduce the designer's ability to produce innovative and novel outcomes. This increased role for metrics and data raises questions over what knowledge best equips future landscape architects to maximise these new tools of simulation and prototyping. Many landscape architects interviewed for this book highlighted the need for the discipline to move away from more general rule-of-thumb knowledge gained from areas such as horticulture to instead realign with more comprehensive knowledge of systems, ecology and environmental sciences.

We continue the discussion on prototyping in the following chapter, with a focus on new digital-inspired techniques for fabrication and construction.

4 Materiality and fabrication

Economies of scale and limited budgets often limit the opportunities for bespoke design in landscape architecture. Furniture, engineering infrastructure, paving and lighting are frequently specified from design catalogues, rather than specifically designed and constructed for a project. Advancements in digital fabrication and construction processes however provide new opportunities for exploring materiality and construction techniques, thereby broadening the scope of landscape design practice to feature a stronger commitment to 'making'.

Digital fabrication describes the use of computer-controlled machines as tools to make parts or components during the construction process. Considered a 'sub-category' of Computer-Aided Design (CAD) and Computer-Aided Manufacturing (CAM), digital fabrication has been applied for over 50 years in engineering and industrial design in the manufacturing of products ranging from airplanes and cars to consumer goods.[1]

Within architecture, digital modelling techniques – such as Computer Numerical Control (CNC) milling – have been experimented with since the early 1970s. However, a more committed investment in new fabrication techniques became necessary as the design of complex forms and surfaces began to challenge conventional construction techniques. Gehry Partners and Gehry Technologies have contributed significantly to the advancement of digital fabrication. The design and construction of the Walt Disney Concert Hall in 1989, conceived as the 'first comprehensive use of CAD/CAM'[2] in architecture, signalled an important step in the evolution of architectural manufacturing and construction. As Branko Kolarevic explains

4.1
Construction of the Supertrees, *Gardens by the Bay*, Singapore.

as constructability becomes a direct function of computability, the question is no longer whether a particular form is buildable, but what new instruments of practice are needed to take advantage of the opportunities opened up by the digital modes of production.[3]

With its intriguing complex curve structure, the Concert Hall project tested the limits of materiality and constructability by working between digital and physical models developed with CAD/CAM fabrication methods at various stages in the process. Originally conceived as a stone building, these explorations included generating full-scale physical prototypes of the exterior stone walls from digital templates and the milling of the stone surface to test the curvilinear shapes and material breaking points. When it was later decided to construct the building using metal, CAD/CAM processes were employed to solve the sheet components. And in a further ground-breaking development, contractors worked 'out of the same computer model without shop drawings, fabricating their components directly from the computer model'.[4]

Architects now regularly explore a range of fabrication techniques as part of their design and construction processes, with CNC cutting (2D fabrication) one of the most commonly applied. Other techniques include subtraction fabrication where a volume of material is removed from a solid using multi-axis milling, additive fabrication where a material is developed through an incremental layering of material, and formative fabrication where material is reshaped using mechanical forces such as heat and steam. These new techniques are accompanied by a renewed interest in materiality, uncovering new composite materials and working with familiar materials such as concrete and wood in innovative ways, and exploring the mutability of materials where properties change according to conditions. This extends into an investigation of 'biomimicry technology' where designers look to biological precedents for inspiration.[5]

This focus on materiality, fabrication and manufacturing processes has led to what Kolarevic describes as a new emphasis on material-first design processes, re-establishing architecture as a fundamentally material practice.[6] This technology-inspired direction states Kolarevic produces new architectural forms that are 'affecting in novel ways our perceptions of surface, form, and space through carefully crafted effects'.[7]

Fabrication techniques therefore offer landscape architecture far more than an efficient construction process, fundamentally shifting concepts of design generation. Nick Dunn observes that 'this process has facilitated a greater fluidity between design generation, development, and fabrication, than traditional approaches which necessitated a more cumulative, staged process'.[8] Within a digital fabrication process, material testing and prototyping assume an important part of the design process. Further, the ability to make components or objects directly from digital design information, states Dunn, is a major transformative

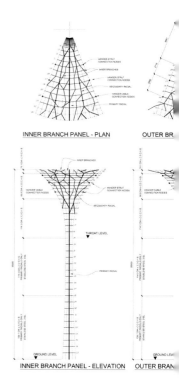

INNER BRANCH PANEL - PLAN   OUTER BR

INNER BRANCH PANEL - ELEVATION   OUTER BRAN

moment for design disciplines,[9] and is captured in the commonly used term 'From File to Fabrication'.

This process is demonstrated in the manufacturing of the steel work for the Supertrees featured in the *Gardens by the Bay* discussed in Chapter 3. The Supertrees were fabricated by Singapore company TTJ Design and Engineering, who applied Tekla BIM software in the development of the general drawings and the connections.

The canopy presented a particularly complex geometry (Figure 4.2a), requiring the detailing of interlocking branches as a delicate network of steel tubes, enclosed by a stainless steel cable for structural support. Working with the designers and BIM software (which provided immediate updating of any changes), each tree took just 6 weeks to model, with the engineers claiming that standard CAD modelling would have taken three times longer.[10] Once the general drawings were agreed upon, the software was used to develop shop drawing, which indicated joint design and the position of steel bolts. The fabrication factory worked to these shop drawings, along with 3D models that helped the fabricators to visualise the structure. These structures were preassembled in the factory to check and paint, before being sent to the site for their final assembly, as shown in Figure 4.2b.

Characteristics of landscape architecture such as scale and unpredictable site conditions can make it more challenging to engage with fabrication. For example the flowing surfaces of LAAC's *Landhausplatz* introduced in Chapter 1 were fabricated in situ. The final geometry of the scheme could not be established until the removal

4.2a–b
Structural drawings detailing the steel work used in the construction of the Supertrees (a). View of the fabricated steel work being attached to the concrete core of the Supertrees (b).

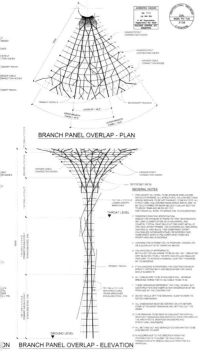

of all the existing paving from the site, which occurred late in the documentation process.[11] Consequently the use of precast concrete would have extended the construction schedule. Instead the smooth topographic surface was constructed from concrete panels fabricated on site using a B7 concrete mix. A timber template set out with surveyor precision, shown in Figure 4.3a–b, was used to define the precise geometries. The surface was constructed over a layer of foam glass gravel which was covered in a 15–20 cm of quick-setting concrete which was then grooved and polished.[12] A mix of black, yellow and white granite chips was mixed into the concrete to develop a more dynamic finish to the surface, as shown in Figure 4.3c.

Despite these challenges, there are many aspects of digital fabrication that are of significant value to landscape architecture. This chapter explores this potential, beginning with the construction of the large-scale infrastructural projects, such as the *Victorian Desalination Plant* and *Max Lab IV* projects, introduced in Chapter 1. Both schemes were conceived and designed using parametric models. As we will explain in more detail, the construction phase can be considered a 'paperless process' with the digital models offering the data necessary to directly inform the construction machinery.

Towards a paperless construction process

Undoubtedly one of the greatest advantages of working with digital terrain models in landscape architecture reveals itself in the delivery of projects that involve a significant proportion of earthworks. Economic and environmental considerations increasingly require the balancing of cut-and-fill volumes while simultaneously demanding high-quality design outcomes. Precision, productivity and effective site management and coordination prove to be vital in delivering complex topographic landform within increasingly tighter time-frames. This heightens the need for landscape architects to operate in 3D terrain models informed, as Peter Petschek

4.3a–c
In-situ concrete construction of *Landhausplatz*.

suggests by 'new developments in surveying and visualization' that 'affect how we receive data and visualize terrain in Landscape Architecture'.[13]

ASPECT Studios' design for the *Victorian Desalination Plant*, as well as Snøhetta's proposal for *Max Lab IV* would not have been achievable through conventional design and construction processes, instead relying on precise digital terrain models as well as new construction technologies. Developments in the construction industry have focused on introducing more time – and subsequently – cost-efficient technology which has its origins in the large earth moving practices associated with the mining industry. Whereas conventional earthwork construction relied on time-consuming processes that involved staking out the terrain on site to mark reference heights for the proposed landforms, bulldozers are now able to directly embed 3D design models into the machine's system, reducing the need for paper-based documentation. Peter Petschek suggests that these stakeless grading processes could achieve cost savings of up to 15–20 per cent.[14]

For example, the overall scope and complexity of the Desalination project provided enormous challenges for all stakeholders involved in the project's design and construction. In addition, the project was extremely fast paced, a factor of financial constraints and the project's political significance. The expanded role for the landscape architects was also achieved with financial efficiency gained by working with the digital model. First, the major topographic forms emerge from the need to maintain the huge amount of fill generated from the excavation on site. Second, the iterative design generation process facilitated by 3D modelling was time efficient with far more exploration and iterations than in other more orthodox design processes. According to ASPECT Studios, these iterations were produced in less than 20 per cent of the time required using more conventional representation techniques. Third, this speed in working with landform translated right through to the construction process. The landscape digital model was fed into the consolidated engineering model, which was then send to surveyors in Brisbane to convert the files into formats, readable by the bulldozers.

Materiality and fabrication

Stakeless grading

Effectively, the incorporation of satellite positioning and 3D digital models into earthwork construction processes recasts the entire design and construction procedure into a monumental example of 'file to fabrication'. Simple machine-controlled systems provide small monitors to visually reference and navigate between existing and proposed terrain, more advanced systems control the positioning of the blade via GPS and robotic total stations located on-site. Increasingly important in large-scale infrastructural and landscape projects with significant earthworks are GPS-directed machines, which enable the machine operator to reference their location on the site plan in real time while simultaneously controlling cut-and-fill volumes to the highest level of accuracy.

Bulldozers used in the Desalination project were fully automated without the assistance of grade foremen, meaning that no manual input was required to control the blade's position and machine location on-site. Simultaneously, the dozers recorded the new profile, subsequently allowing the surveyor to check the proposed landform against the existing profile without referring to 2D plans. Although 2D drawings were initially produced by the engineers to check the design, the new technologies provided a far more reliable control systems. Melvyn Leong from the engineering firm Thiess in charge of constructing the Desalination project notes 'nobody looks at drawings anymore'.[15]

The *Max Lab IV* project was constructed using similar technologies. Working with PEAB, one of the leading construction and engineering companies in Scandinavia, enabled Snøhetta to utilise the latest technology and to program their terrain data directly into the bulldozers. The real-time GPS positioning also allowed the adoption of a more effective in-situ construction process instead of temporarily storing excavated soil for later application. Thus, cut-and-fill procedures occurred in one-move operations meaning the waved landscape could be constructed simultaneously to the excavation of the building foundation.

Due to this process, almost 60 per cent of landscape was completed only 4 months after commencing the construction, allowing the design and construction team to achieve the design within the tight time-frame. More importantly, this digital design and construction practice proved to be the biggest cost-saver on the project, effectively allowing the landscape architects to 'buy' acknowledgement from clients, who before the project did not pay much attention to landscape values.

Strong competition and demands for ever increasing productivity drives further developments in construction technology. In 2015, Japan's largest manufacturer of heavy construction equipment, Komatsu, announced its newest investment in technology that will mark the next step towards fully automated construction processes.[16] Driven by Japan's declining population, leading to labour and skill shortage in the surveying and construction industries, Komatsu has started to reposition its business focus from heavy to soft machinery, investing in new drone technology. The drones will focus on site surveying using sensors and cameras to produce high-precision 3D point cloud data, thereby shortening the

4.4a–b
The *Victorian Desalination Plant* posed challenges to coordinate the complex site and the construction process.

surveying process from multiple days to a few hours. This data can be overlayed with proposed terrain models directly into the dozer's computer. Ultimately, the drones should be able to control the entire grading process including navigating blade position, profile checks and machine movement, giving rise to unmanned construction machines. Komatsu predicts that the first drones and fully automated dozers will be in use on construction sites for the 2020 Olympic Games in Tokyo.

Similar to the influence of fabrication technologies on the architectural profession, these advancements in earthwork construction should expand both the client and the landscape architect's ambitions for the design potential of landform. While these construction techniques are presently associated with large-scale infrastructural projects, their future application will extend into smaller site works as technology continues to become more affordable and accessible.

In the following discussion we move from large-scale landform to a more detailed focus on the materiality and fabrication of landscape components and systems.

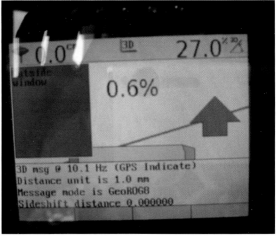

Material behaviour

Landscape architects are increasingly interested in a 'material-first' design practice where the consideration of material behaviour and fabrication techniques are given more prominence at the beginning of design processes.[17] Of particular interest is the design of infrastructural components such as geo-textiles and geo-cells that control runoff, sedimentation and erosion processes and have conventionally been associated with engineering.

A focus on performance combined with parametric modelling and fabrication technologies expands the scope of landscape architecture design to encompass the materiality of surface, the fabrication of systems and the innovative uses of stone, concrete and timber. As the following three examples will demonstrate, these design processes emphasise the testing of material behaviour and performance through a mix of physical and digital prototyping. They also highlight how fabrication technologies alter the relationships between the designer and contractor and offer more efficient manufacturing techniques that encourage customised approaches to design detailing.

4.5a–d
Grading process and earth work construction for the *MaxLab IV* project: (a) GPS controlled bulldozer, (b) real-time control of profile levels, (c) during construction August 2011, (d) completed landforms February 2012.

Fabricating surface

In his 2013 seminar subject Surface FX, Brian Osborn interrogated the potential of CAD/CAM techniques in the design and fabrication of landscape surfaces. The seminar, which formed part of the Landscape Architecture program at the University of Virginia, focused on 'the dynamic boundary between the ground and human inhabitation' as expressed in erosion control systems, drainage structures, paving and retaining walls. These surfaces state Osborn 'have the unique capacity to simultaneously influence biologic process and sensory experience (effect + affect)'.[18]

Importantly, the seminar emphasises material behaviour rather than material properties (with the later placing emphasis on questions of durability and strength). Instead a focus on behaviour encourages the exploration of the 'tendencies of material' in relationship to dynamic environmental conditions and processes including the consideration of 'emergent happenings' such as transmission, erosion and failure.[19] Chris Woods's project *LAG* demonstrates how an exploration of material behaviour considered against temperature fluctuation can inspire novel form making. Working with concrete, Woods examined how the thermal mass of concrete responded to temperature change, with these principles applied in the design and fabrication of a concrete seat.

The design intent was not to produce a homogeneous condition but to instead manipulate the thermal mass to create varied conditions through temperature. Beginning with a solid form, Wood subtracted material to create 'a gradient of voided space'.[20] A one-third-scaled prototype was constructed using high performance ductal concrete and CNC fabrication, as shown in Figure 4.6a. Testing in different conditions recorded through thermal imaging highlighted temperature variance of up to 10 degrees.[21] The final form was fabricated and features a 'slow' and 'fast' end. The fast end responds quickly to changes in temperature, for instance warming quickly on a cool morning, while the more substantial massing of the slow end maintains temperatures for longer. In a further detail, the thermal coefficient of the thin concrete edge was increased through the addition of metal aggregates.

Osborn's ongoing research project *Tech Mat* (Temporary Erosion Control Mat) builds on the agendas of Surface FX to explore the potential of paper in controlling erosion on sloping sites.[22] Beginning with convex and concave shapes, Osborn explored how these geometries influence processes of erosion and deposition over sloping sites. A complex pattern comprising concave and convex forms proved valuable in producing a series of small terraces that balanced and stabilised soil and water movement (Figure 4.8). These explorations provided the principles for a more refined form, which evolved into a folded surface that could be flat-packed for ease of transportation and site installation. Material testing of paper explored its ability to absorb water and to support plant material while slowly degrading. *Tech Mat* prototypes were constructed and tested on an 80 per cent slope with the results incorporated into a larger-scale version, which further evolved through detailed consideration of suitable planting materials (Figure 4.8d).

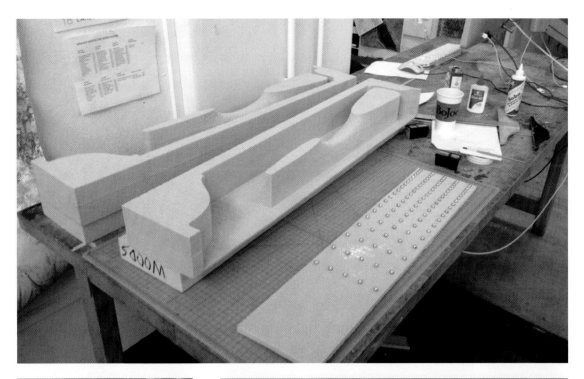

4.6a–c
Foam moulds were used
to cast a scaled prototype,
which was then tested
for performance in varied
temperature conditions using
thermal imaging.

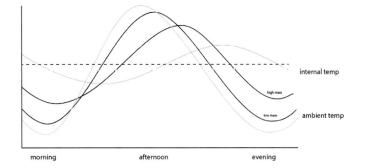

internal temp

high mass

low mass

ambient temp

morning   afternoon   evening

A final prototype emerged as 'a single, highly articulated surface, capable of modulating a range of environmental effects over time'.[23] The structural form of the paper-based geo-textile interacts with the dynamic processes of erosion and deposition to produce terrace structures, while the degradable qualities of the paper encourages the embedded mineral additives and plant seeds to drop into the trapped soil. Over time the plants will replace the eroding structural strength of the paper to stabilise the slopes and slow water runoff, contributing, what Osborn hopes are 'aesthetically satisfying forms and memorable places for human habitation'.[24]

This 'material first' design process produces an innovative response to erosion control which is conventionally solved with minimal consideration of aesthetics, materiality or ecology. Osborn's focus on the materiality and performance of landscape surfaces is equally shared by the design practice of PEG office of landscape + architecture who we first introduced in Chapter 2. As we discussed previously, PEG are interested in the manner in which pattern through geometric repetition or temporal re-occurrence can register, guide and convey site processes.

4.7a–b
The final form of the concrete seat incorporated knowledge gained from testing the material behaviour of concrete and features a 'slow' and 'fast' end.

4.8a–c
Exploration of geometries, structural form and the behavioural qualities of paper informed the development of the *Tech Mat* prototypes.

4.8d
The prototypes were tested for performance, with further refinements guided by a more comprehensive consideration of planting materials.

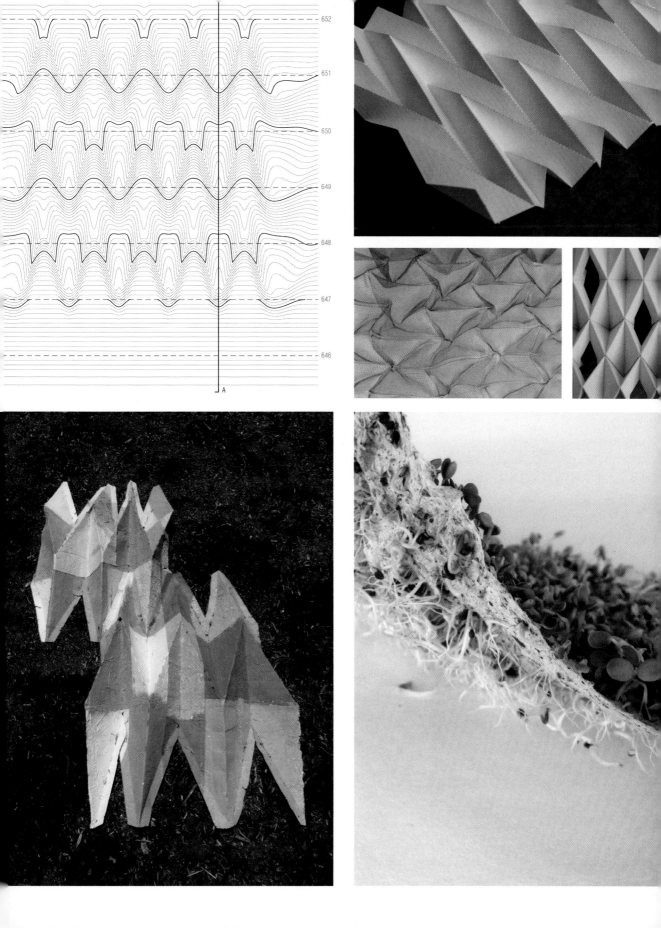

PEG argue that the capacity of geometry to articulate site functions such as water flow or plant growth make pattern a valuable strategy for extending engineering solutions beyond conventional approaches.[25]

PEG has been exploring the potential of these concepts in the development of new approaches for maintaining the extensive number of vacant sites (over 60,000) found across Philadelphia. So far, a Neighbourhood Transformation initiative, which began in 2002 has cleaned over 3000 vacant lots. Adopting a 'greening' strategy', this program removes rubbish, regrades the sites, establishes lawn and trees and reinstates a picket fence around the vacant site's perimeter. PEG is interested in developing an alternative approach which 'achieves the same aesthetics of care but provides more expressive diversity with lower maintenance'.[26]

Not Pattern

Similar to Osborn, PEG explores the potential of customising geo-textiles for constructing new strategies of surface control. In a distinguishing feature, PEG's design response registers the relationship between organic and inorganic material on the ground surface through the application of pattern which they argue is particularly useful in working with the phenomena of vacancy.[27]

This philosophy informs their design concept for the *Not Garden* (and in a further iteration *Not Again*) which offers a contemporary interpretation of the geometric patterns of the historic knot garden. Working with parametric software and laser-cut fabrication, a series of repetitive patterns shown in Figure 4.9a were cut from geo-textile material. This material was then laid onto the regraded surface of the vacant site. Over time, plants grow around the patterns, which as illustrated in Figure 4.9(d), remain legible. PEG has explored this approach with a variety of intricate patterns and planting material ranging from turf to flowering drought tolerant ground cover. As an alternative weed control measure, achieved with

4.9a–d
Geo-textile fabric was laser cut into repeated patterns (a). Patterns continue to register as plants grow around the geo-textile fabric thereby maintaining an 'aesthetic of care' (b–d).

4.10a–d
Documentation of the water flows on site (using parametric modelling) informed the development of new geo-cells prototypes.

minimal maintenance, the registering of the pattern on the lot's surface contributes to an 'aesthetic of care'.[28]

These concepts are further employed in the project *Edaphic Effects* that focuses on issues of water infiltration and the design potential of customised geo-cells. During rain events over 16 billion gallons of raw sewerage currently flows into Philadelphia's rivers and streams. Encouraging on-site water infiltration and retention on the extensive vacant sites forms an important strategy for addressing the issue. PEG's *Incremental Infrastructure* project, funded by a 2011 Boston Society of Architects research grant uses 'customized substrates' and new configurations for geo-cells to propose innovative responses to on-site storm water collection.[29]

Conventionally, geo-cells are geometrically uniform 3D structures filled with plants, soils or gravel that are laid within surfaces to encourage water infiltration. PEG maintained the infiltration characteristics of the cell, while developing alternative shapes that accommodate a greater variety of pattern. These new patterns emerged through parametric modelling shown in Figure 4.10(b), which allowed the designers to explore existing and new water flows. Prototypes were then developed, using petroleum-based plastics (commonly applied in the manufacturing of geo-cells) and compostable corn-based plastics, which are currently limited to use in the packaging industry.[30] These customised geo-cells were then installed on-site to test their effectiveness for drainage, as well as design effect.

The design and fabrication processes shared by Osborn and PEG reveal the expanded scope for design and making in landscape architecture as it begins to explore the potential of digital technologies and fabrication, while simultaneously interrogating material behaviour, biologic process and sensory experience. In the following example we introduce the design practice of Marco Poletto and Claudia Pasquero who are directors of ecoLogicStudio. Their research-driven

Materiality and fabrication

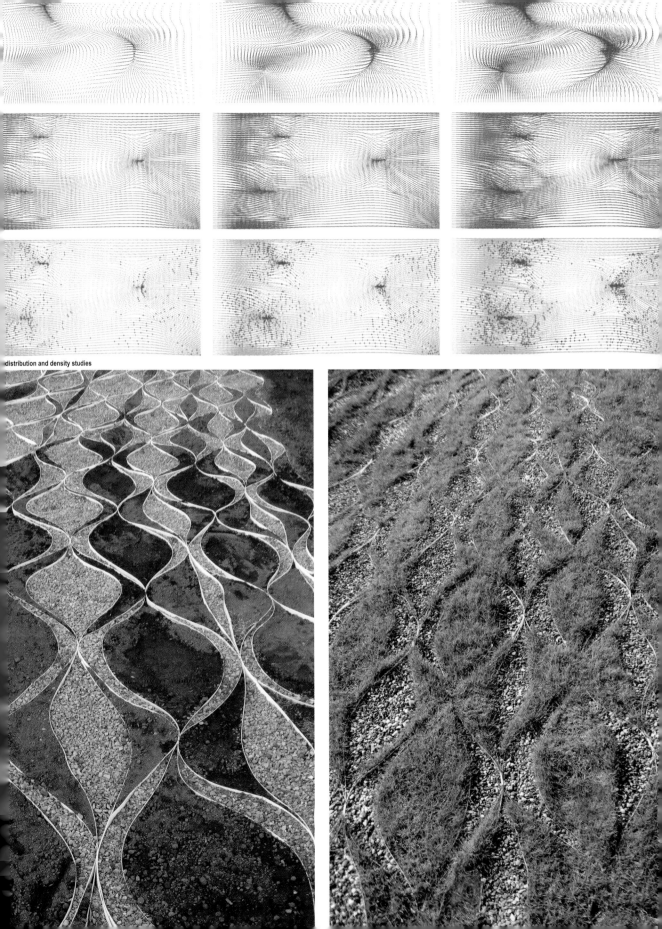

distribution and density studies

practice explores the relationship between computational design and an urbanism inclusive of ecological systems, by incorporating ecological processes into fabrication techniques and prototyping.

Fabricating systems

Aiming to 'embed technology into material organizations that become part of everyday ecological practices',[31] ecoLogicStudio seek to intensify and cultivate biodiversity. Drawing similarities with the research-driven design practice of landscape architect and philosopher Gilles Clément, they state:

> The formalization of the garden becomes for Clément a process of formalised transmission of biological messages or, in our terms, of algorithmic coding; algorithms are for the gardener machines for breeding biodiversity.[32]

Prototyping and fabrication are central to their practice. These models says Poletto are not representational but instead operate as 'machines that compute occupations and patterns within a non-homogeneous surface'.[33] They help to 'solve spatial problems in relationship to urban or environmental forces', with feedback loops 'offering mechanism of self-regulation' allowing an understanding of how systems evolve and change.[34] This design philosophy is evident in ecoLogicStudio's explorations of algae.

Their interest in algae was triggered in 2006 by an encounter with a local botanist in London's Victoria Park where algae was slowly colonising the park's ponds.[35] This formed a catalyst for *ecoMachines*, a prototype that interrogated the highly efficient machine-like qualities of algae. Initial experiments

[AgI] Algae Itinerary
Algvägar

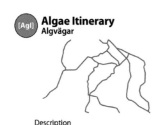

Description
A new network of summer cycling paths and winter X-country sky piste is connecting the algae regional infoPoints; tourists and locals alike will be able to use the network to visit the exhisting algae business and learn how to set up new ones.

Regions [LS], [FL], [WL], [VL], [PT], [RB]

Actors + Agents
⬤⬤⬤⬤⬤ Algae Regional info Point
⬤⬤ Algae farming cycling/ skiing routes
⬤⬤ BioSensing Research
⬤ Food itinerary

Cycles [ecology, food, energy]

[CGh] Crane Greenhouse
Kranar Blir Växthus

Description
Underused ports and coastal areas are ideal hosts for new symbiotic algae and seefood/fish farms; craneslike strcutures holds etfe canopies creating adaptive greenhouses able to support year round production.

Regions [SS], [PT]

Actors + Agents
⬤⬤ Algae farming cycling/ skiing routes
⬤ Food Itinerary
⬤ Biodiesel and biogas production
⬤ Algae, seafood and fish farming
⬤ ecoPharmaceutical prodcution
⬤⬤ BioSensing Research

Cycles [ecology, energy, food, water, microclimate]

[FNt] Farming Network
Odlingsnätverk

Description
The old regional clusters of farms are connected by new high-tech alge farming infrastrcutures, an agri-town hosting production facilities, touristic itineraries, and research centers on industrial algae products

Regions [FL], [WL]

Actors + Agents
⬤ Food Itinerary and production
⬤ Biodiesel production and research
⬤⬤⬤ Farming and building products
⬤ Industrial products production
⬤ ecoPharmaceutical production
⬤⬤ ⬤ bio-photovoltaic and biofuels research

Cycles [energy, food, waste, materials]

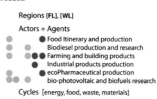

modified architectural components in order to host algae colonies. This 'choreographing of biological systems' within the prototypes highlighted new 'potentials for evolution and interaction, both within the environment and with an excited public'.[36] EcoLogicStudio has subsequently explored hybridities of form and algae systems across a range of scales.

The *Simrishamn Regional Algae farm* (2011), commissioned by the local municipality near the Swedish Baltic Sea, proposed a new economic–urban system for an ageing population.[37] The potential of algae as a source of renewable energy was used to draw local farmers, residents and fisherman into a collaborative plan of action. This master plan was conceived as a participatory interface, mixing top-down investment strategies with bottom-up community involvement.[38] Strategies outlined in Figure 4.11a include filtering gardens, an underwater museum, high-tech algae farming infrastructure, greenhouses and migrotowers. Architectural prototypes were conceived for different sites. The *Hanging Algae Garden* offered an 'interactive public space of cultivation' positioned between the Simrishamn Marine Centre, the Tourist Office and the port. Comprising the seven most common algae species within the region, the public contributed to the garden's cultivation by blowing carbon dioxide into the photo-bioreactor bags. Hand-held magnifying glasses allowed the visitor to observe the micro and macro algae. The *Hanging Algae Garden* was presented as part of an exhibition, featuring a floor map and tourist map documenting the regionally distinctive algae, prototype speculations and an algae-based gourmet lunch finale.

EcoLogicStudio's installation *Hortis Paris* (2013) exhibited at the EDF foundation, Paris as part of the Alive Exhibition, featured a full-scale working model shown in Figure 4.12 of a 'man-made eco-system'. Working with flows of energy (light radiation) and matter (biomass and carbon dioxide), the prototype showcased processes of self-organisation and self-regulation. Visitors participated in the

4.11a–c
A new economic-urban strategy utilising the potentials of algae as a renewable resource. Proposals for an underwater marine science museum which features floating algae farms and filtering gardens which treat sewage water, contribute to organic food production and monitor biological systems.

4.12
The *Hortus Paris* exhibition presented a responsive bio-architectural hybrid which incorporated micro-algal organisms into an interactive and living environment.

farming processes, and were invited to influence the system's growth through an air pump system within the photo bioreactors which modified nutrient content (Figure 4.13). Embedded sensing technologies provided data to a virtual interface accessible by smart phones, encouraging participants across the globe to send tweets to 'nurture the virtual plots'. EcoLogicStudio describe this interaction as 'a computer generated sedimentation process', with the visitors both physical and virtual conceived as cyber gardeners.[39]

Their most recent project *Urban Algae Canopy* shifts their algae explorations from exhibition to urban structure. The canopy forms part of the *Future Food District Project* curated by Carlo Ratti for the Expo Milano 2015.[40] The development of the structure shown in Figure 4.14 continues the themes of technology, biological systems and interaction evident in earlier projects to present a 'bio-digital canopy integrating micro-algal cultures and real-time digital cultivation protocols on a unique architectural system'.[41]

Increased solar access influences algae growth, thereby altering the transparency of the canopy. Similarly to the *Hortis Paris* installation, the visitor interacts with carbon dioxide levels, further manipulating the shading and transparency of the canopy. Pasquero comments: 'In this prototype the boundaries between the material, spatial and technological dimensions have been carefully articulated to achieve efficiency, resilience and beauty.'[42] CNC welding technology creates flexibility within the morphology of the canopy, allowing control over water behaviour and thereby creating a further responsive relationship between water and algae. The canopy is envisaged to produce up to 150kg of biomass daily (60 per cent of which

4.13a–b
Public participation occurred
in two ways: (a) through the
manipulation of the carbon
dioxide levels in the system
or (b) by tweets which
'nuture' the garden.

4.14a–b
The *Urban Algae Canopy*
integrates micro-algal culture
within an external shade
structure, transforming in
transparency according to
changing solar conditions and
biological growth.

are natural vegetal proteins) while releasing oxygen equivalent to that produced by 4 hectares of forest.[43]

Poletto observes that many design projects that claim to be performative are actually produced in a linear and predictable manner. Often, a computational approach leads to an early separation of design from the forces and systems of the external world. In contrast, their design processes rely on physical and digital prototypes, positioning design within 'interrogative open models' that facilitate 'way of thinking about behaviours'.[44] The prototypes operate as material and system explorations that are not necessarily scalable, instead requiring multiple processes to construct new hierarchies and configurations reflective of different scales of interventions.

EcoLogicStudio highlight the contribution of the Valldaura Self-Sufficient Lab (developed by the Institute for Advanced Architecture of Catalonia) in advancing the application of technology guided by ecological principles. The research centre applies knowledge gained from ecological processes and resource management to explore self-sustainable design options that address the challenges of the twenty-first-century city. A 'green fab lab' works with natural resources including minerals, earth and wood in a combination of high technology and ancestral processes, a 'food lab' interrogates food production processes encompassing growth, human consumption and waste management including technologies for large-scale and small-scale production, while the entire Valldaura development operates as a 'energy lab' ensuring efficient management of power and water.[45]

We conclude our discussion of fabrication with a detailed exploration of the innovative design and construction processes necessary in the realisation of the *Diana, Princess of Wales Memorial*. Most landscape architects are familiar with the evocative clay model that formed the starting point for Gustafson Porter's winning scheme. Few are aware of the innovative design and fabrication processes that allowed the hard granite 'necklace' to be manufactured in just 26 weeks.

The making of the *Diana, Princess of Wales Memorial*

At the time of winning the design competition in the summer of 2002, Gustafson Porter knew the major challenge was to identify how to construct the stone memorial, the major component of the design. With 9 months allocated to design, and a year for construction, Gustafson Porter initially employed designers experienced in Rhino. They soon realised this 3D modelling package would not provide the complex information needed for manufacture, so they turned to the automotive car industry, the Ford motor company, for help. This decision was the beginning of a ground-breaking design and fabrication process, which to date has received minimal attention in landscape architecture. What follows is a detailed description of this process, which should be read in conjunction with the diagram shown in

Figure 4.15, which visually documents the innovative construction process and complex workflows.

The first stage of design development involved taking a rubber mould of the clay model (prepared for the competition), which was then used to produce a cast that could be digitally scanned. A highly accurate GOM scanner, commonly used in the automotive and aerospace industry, produced a detailed 3D point cloud of the cast. GOM (Gesellschaft für Optische Messtechnik), established in 1990 specialises in optical measuring products and processes such as 3D digitising, 3D coordinate measurements, deformation measurements and quality control.[46] This was the first time this software had been used for architectural purposes.[47]

SurfDev (Surface Development and Engineering), a design and 3D scanning bureau with expertise in developing accurate freeform shapes for manufacture were then commissioned to further develop the 3D model. The scan was transformed into a surface mesh CAD model (using the Uniserf program) that became known as the jelly mould (a term used in the automotive industry for the basic form of a car prior to detail design). In a parallel process, Gustafson Porter developed sections at 1:100 exploring the human height and scale of the memorial. SurfDev and Neil Porter met weekly, working between the sections and the digital model, with the final digital model emerging after 9 weeks.[48]

The basic profile of the memorial was envisaged as two edges, containing a middle section of textured blocks. Adopting this form, the smooth jelly mould was broken into a 3D puzzle of 549 separate blocks (with a 5mm gap), detailing the shape and location of each stone. The model produced the shape of the stones as they intersected with the ground plane, providing the Arup engineers with enough information to produce an underside stepped foundation and devise the water drainage.

Envisaging the stone textures was a more challenging process, requiring the expertise of Texxus Ltd. Founded in 2002 by industrial designer John Gould, Texxus specialises in the production of textured surfaces. In 1999 Gould noticed that designers had no means of generating the texture they wanted for a product on a screen.[49] Working with software sources from the car industry, John devised techniques for simulating a 3D surface pattern onto a 3D form. Fortunately, Neil Porter had worked with John during his architecture degree. In a chance encounter, Neil Porter's appearance on TV reconnected him with his former employer, and the dilemma of how to texture the stone was solved.

Working with the representation of Princess Diana's life through the metaphor of water, Gould and Porter developed textures of water conditions moving from mountain brook through rapids into gentler waters. Textures, abstracted from photographs, were explored within Photoshop, followed by 3ds Max, where forms were repeated and extruded into depths of up to 50mm.

The individual block configurations developed from the jelly mould formed the base for Texxus to accurately place and align the digital textures. Two types of prototypes were developed concurrently. The first involved working with the Vero

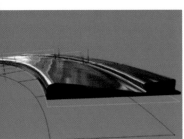

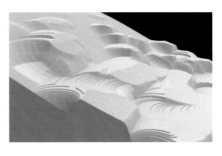

1. Translation of the clay model into a digital jelly mould, followed by a 3D CAD model which was then broken into 549 separate blocks.

3. The milling of the stone was tested through physical and digital protyping to establish the fabrication times and final finishes.

2. Surface textures were abstracted from photos using 3dsMax which were then extruded into digital models and applied to individual blocks.

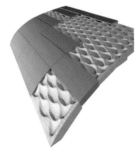

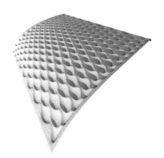

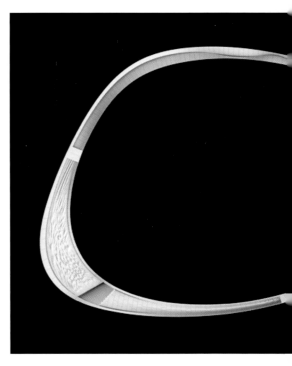

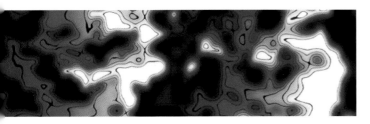

4. Circular saws were first used to remove the bulk of the stone. Manufacturing commenced June 2003.

5. Finer cutting bull and flat bottom tools were applied to produce the detailed stone textures.

6. The stones were assembled on site. The fabrication process was so accurate that the blocks could be laid in sections while the milling process continued. The fountain was officially opened on July 6, 2004.

4.15

The fabrication process for the
Diana, Princess of Wales Memorial.

Software company, a leader in developing and distributing CAD/CAM software for design and manufacturing processes for stone and wood working, metal fabrication, tooling and production engineering. Using software developed only 6 months prior, Vero digitally prototyped the texturing of the stone. This tool path analysis (applied to granite for the first time), allowed for the visualising of the finished block, and importantly, provided an indication of machining time, thereby informing decisions on efficiency and how much detail to include in the textures. For example close inspection of the textured stones reveals small ridges, which aided in faster stone cutting (as distinct from a smooth finish), and also resulted in a less slippery surface.

The second prototype tested the effects of adding water into the memorial. Most of the water is fed in at the highest part of the memorial and flows down through the different textures. However, at certain moments water is added into the system, to produce very particular effects such as the section known as 'the champagne bubbles'. Working with Professor Peter Davis at Imperial College, a hydraulic engineer, Gustafson Porter and SurfDev produced a half-scale 3D CAD model (produced in hard foam) to test the relationship between location of water nozzles, water pressure, textures and effects. This testing occurred at laboratories at Imperial Collage, London and Davis's Somerset workshops.

Finding suitable stone and stonemasons presented a further challenge, with the expectation that British stone and British technology should be used to construct a memorial to a British princess. After much research to find a light-coloured stone that would sit happily in its historic landscape context, the extremely hard silver-grey De Lank granite from Cornwall was selected, along with Northern Island stonemasons McConnell and Sons.

McConnell and Sons had previous experience working with scanned regular shapes from physical models to produce matching pieces of stones.[50] However, this construction process would require their machinery to read detailed textures from a digital file.

Their OMAG S.rL. CNC production centre was reprogrammed to handle digital files. Two types of digital files were sent to the stonemasons: 549 separate files describing the shape of the blocks (the file size was small enough to be emailed), and the more complex texture files which were sent on disc. The extremely hard granite required heavy-duty equipment and tooling, with the first piece of granite wearing out the first tool after cutting just one section of stone.[51] It became clear that the OMAG could not produce the work alone, with the quarry purchasing two Terzago Macchine S.r.L saws. Vero International Software developed CNC software, hooking the circular saws up to Vero Software for the first time.[52] The saws were used to remove the bulk of the stone. To save time and energy, only half of the stone was sawn, with a sledgehammer then used to break the stone apart, ready for the finer tooling.

Manufacturing started at the end of June 2003, with the quarry in full production by the end of August. Three machines operated at a minimum of 100 hours a week, with manpower of 21 hours a day.[53]

Three shapes of finer-cutting tools were used: the saw, the bull tool and the flat-bottom tool. The hard granite continued to prove challenging, quickly wearing down diamond studded foster bronze tools. The texturing and the cutting of the stone worked in parallel with the finalisation of the digital texture files. Construction of the memorial began before the completion of the stone fabrication. Working with an accuracy of +/– 0.5mm, the completed stone blocks could be laid in sections, confident that the precision of the manufacturing process would create a final seamless finish.

The stone was 100 per cent machined, with a dolly-punch finish to the kerb, the only part of the process completed by hand-held pneumatic tools. In just 26 weeks, 520 tons of De Lank granite were cut into 549 stones.

Significantly, the manufacturing route dramatically revised the workflow of design and construction, allowing the designers (Gould, Gustafson Porter, SurfDev) to work directly with the quarry. Conventionally, a project contractor and a stone contractor would have been positioned between the designers and the quarry. For example the stone contractor would go to the quarry and purchase the stone and issue it back to the stonemasons. A more direct process not only aided accuracy, but also allowed for a far more efficient design development and construction process.

The designers and contractors all benefited from the technical knowledge gained from working on the project. While McConnell and Sons had to invest extensively in new equipment and software to complete the job, the experience developed their future capability to work on the most sophisticated stone work.[54] John Gould went on to develop other architectural stone projects such as the V&A courtyard. For Gustafson Porter, the experience confirmed the importance of landscape architects working with 3D digital models, encouraging them to employ recent graduates with digital expertise.[55] The firm became more confident in manipulating space and form on larger scales, as demonstrated in later work on phase two of *Gardens by the Bay*, Singapore.

Designed for a 200-year lifespan, the *Diana, Princess of Wales Memorial* is one of the most visited free tourist attractions in London. For landscape architecture it represents a critical precedent featuring an innovative fabrication process and manufacturing route. As John Gould concludes 'History was made when the entire structure was machined using three and five axis disc saws and milling machines directly from 3D CAD files.'[56] The extraordinary stone finishes achieved in the completed memorial fountain shown in Figure 4.16, provide clear evidence that the fabrication process did not diminish the poetics of the design. Instead the digitally driven process was essential to realising the design ambition expressed in Gustafson Porter's original competition entry.

Conclusion

Digital technologies encourage seamless and sophisticated workflow processes, bridging the gap between design and making in unprecedented ways. This presents multiple opportunities to expand the creative potential of landscape architectural practice, encouraging more comprehensive form and material explorations beyond predictable or of-the-shelf solutions.

The ability to translate designs directly from 3D digital systems into physical installation without depending on 2D abstraction, so called 'file to fabrication', opens new avenues for more efficient, automated production processes. Advancements in the engineering industries together with the development of a new generation of high-tech construction machineries, support the design and construction of complex earthworks in an extremely time and cost-efficient manner with increasing precision. These developments also facilitate a stronger appreciation of the value of landscape architecture as established in relationship to Snøhetta's *MaxLab IV* project.

Driven by a material-first design approach, digital fabrication also signals a shift in the way landscape architecture design is conceived, emphasising digital and physical prototyping to test material performance (effects and affects) and constructability. This process encourages the exploration of components as well as ecological and material systems to develop customised design solutions, where the form is no longer compromised by limited consideration of materiality or traditional construction operations. The exciting potential of a material-first approach is clearly reflected in the design qualities achieved in the *Diana, Princess of Wales Memorial* which could simply not be achieved without CAD/CAM processes.

These new workflow models are built on changing roles and responsibilities of designers and contractors, drawing on highly specialised knowledge and skills of manufacturers – often not even associated with the landscape profession – early in the design exploration and considerations of constructability. This rapidly shifting design and construction practice is evidence of an expanded collaborative environment driven by the potential of digital technologies which we explore further in our final chapter which introduces Building Information Modelling.

5 Collaboration

In recent years we have witnessed an emerging number of built projects marking an exciting turning point in landscape architecture design and construction practice. In addition to addressing the problems of our contemporary environment, complex and ambitious projects such as the *Queen Elizabeth Olympic Park*, London have inspired new documentation and construction processes. In this final chapter we focus on how these changes have reconceived the nature of collaboration, challenging hierarchical and disciplinary power structures and developing new relationships between designers, clients and contractors. As David Scheer notes we are now at a pivotal moment where the designer's role will move from the generalist to specialist, from the master builder to the collaborator.[1]

One of the most prominent advancements is the emergence of data-driven design and construction processes. This is reflected in the increasing influence of Building Information Modelling (BIM), which is currently reshaping the design and construction industries in the United Kingdom, USA, the Middle East and Australia. In general terms, BIM can be understood as a new practice model for design and construction management that departs from traditional delivery and construction protocols, for example the 'linear exchange of analogue information'[2] including the drawing-based design documentation. Instead, BIM foregrounds the collaborative sharing of building information within an intelligent, virtual model. These new processes are facilitated by emerging digital technologies, which enable the processing and management of complex data including analysis and simulation to better understand and manage the building's performance throughout all stages of the project 'well beyond the design and construction process'.[3] As Richard Garber states

5.1
The Queen Elizabeth Olympic Park, London.

The potential of building information modelling (BIM) is that a single, intelligent, virtual model can be used to satisfy all aspects for the design process including visualisation, checking for spatial conflict, automated parts and assembly production (CAM), construction sequencing, and materials research and testing.[4]

The general concepts behind BIM are not new and can be traced back to the 1970s when ideas first emerged to use computer technology to challenge the practice of 2D design and CAD-based drawing processes.[5] Influenced by the research of Charles Eastman (US), Tom Maver (UK), Arto Kiviniemi (Finland), and John Mitchell and Robin Drogemuller (Australia) this early work focused on the generation of a virtual 3D building model that could embed data in the building geometry. In his 1975 seminal paper 'The Use of Computers instead of Drawings in Building Design', Eastman outlines the capabilities of the model to assist the decision-making process stating it 'will act as a design coordinator and analyser, providing a single integrated data base for visual and quantitative analyses, for testing spatial conflicts and for drafting'.[6]

Thus, BIM utilises highly dynamic digital models generated through computable data and their interconnected and complex relationships. This means that data is coordinated and 'processed (not just stored) by computers'.[7] For many years, the practical implementations of these new workflow processes were limited, first, due to the lack of computer processing power, and second because the building industry (in comparison to automative and manufacturing industries), has been slower in revising their workflow processes. More recently the architecture, engineering and construction (AEC) industries have adopted a more progressive approach to BIM.

These changes are largely driven by dynamic market pressures, an increasing globalisation of practice, and the demand to improve economic efficiencies. However, BIM's contribution extends far beyond cost reductions and is equally recognised as an important catalyst for new modes of interdisciplinary collaboration, encouraging the 'integration of the roles of all stakeholders on a project'.[8] As Howard W. Ashcraft states 'BIM's power is enhanced by collaboration, and collaboration is made more effective through BIM'.[9] Considered in the wider context of a digital design practice, Mario Carpo suggests that BIM can be seen as 'potentially, one of the strongest manifestations of the collaborative spirit that has pervaded digital culture and technology'.[10]

Countries, such as Finland, Norway and Sweden have already widely adopted BIM processes and implementation is rapidly developing in other parts of the world.[11] For example, in the USA the number of projects developed in a BIM environment has increased by 75 per cent between 2008 and 2012.[12] However, these developments and collaborative potential have overwhelmingly focused on architectural design and construction. So far, the consequences for the landscape architecture profession have been marginal. Only a few practices have started to engage with digital technologies within their design and construction processes with many practitioners still unaware of the concepts and technological advancements of BIM. However, this position is beginning to be challenged by legislative changes, actively enforcing collaborative processes between clients, designers and contractors.

Aiming to deliver projects with more value for money, the United Kingdom is one of the first countries to mandate BIM compliance, required for all major publicly funded projects by 2016. The Government Construction Strategy, published by the Cabinet Office in 2011, signalled the beginning of a major overhaul and modernisation of the entire construction sector in the UK. This document outlined a radical shift in the design, construction and procurement of public infrastructure and will no doubt significantly impact the future practice of landscape architecture.

The proposed changes are largely driven by the intention to reduce the capital cost from the construction and operation of built projects 'by up to 20%' over 5 years.[13] Possibilities extend far beyond increasing efficiencies by managing risks, avoiding errors, or reducing the overall construction time. The aim now is to 'build the building twice. Once virtually and once on the ground',[14] eliminating the costly and wasteful redesign of buildings that occur during the design, documentation and construction phases – or even worse – after the project's completion. As Tom Armour, landscape architect at Arup outlines:

> Increasingly we will see clients and design teams having to make much better judgments than in the past on ecological and environmental issues, and in particular the use of carbon. But in the immediate future the economic problems look to be far greater. There will be much more pressure to build cheaper now and deal with the consequences later. The biggest challenge will be to save money, to understand the cost implications of what you are designing and its affordability over its whole life. But we are increasingly finding the cheapest solution is the most sustainable solution.[15]

Better commissioning and procurement processes will prove vital in achieving these targets including the simulation of the project's delivery and operation throughout its entire life cycle or 'from cradle to grave'.[16] Central to the implementation of the new workflows is the adoption of information rich BIM technologies, processes and collaborative behaviours. The UK government BIM Task Group highlights the value of this approach declaring:

> Our hypothesis is simple: that significant improvement in cost, value and carbon performance can be achieved through the use of open sharable asset information. We will also be helping the supply chain unlock more efficient and collaborative ways of work throughout the entire project and asset life-cycle end to end.[17]

Demanding more collaborative and innovative modes of practice, the new delivery standards are also conceived to challenge the contemporary industry business models, introducing competitiveness and providing opportunity for growth in the otherwise struggling building industry.

The assumed knock-on benefits of these changes provide a convincing argument for the legislative changes. First, the effects of introducing procedures for quick, efficient and carbon-reduced construction will extend far beyond the improvement of single building or project, instead providing opportunity for long-term national savings by investing in a sustainable and healthy built environment. Second, in a country where almost 90 per cent of buildings and infrastructure have been constructed, future demand in the building industry remains low. Thus, the government's investment in BIM is also conceived as a catalyst to revitalise the UK economy where knowledge of comparable standards, systems and protocols for data management will provide an important exportable commodity.[18]

Early proposals of the implementation strategy mandated only large-scale projects of more than 20 million pounds to be BIM compliant. Since then, the delivery threshold has been continuously amended, first to 10 million, then to 1 million, with the current situation requiring BIM compliance on any centrally funded project, regardless of value. The government's long-term strategy is that even the most basic planning applications would be developed within a 3D digital model suggesting that 'all construction will be in BIM in a matter of time'.[19] It is widely anticipated that the private sector will follow suit. Consequently, these government-driven propositions will have a profound impact on the landscape profession within the United Kingdom requiring landscape architects to actively engage with the emerging collaborative design and construction processes.

To maintain a prominent position in the design and delivery of projects, landscape architects need to be able to communicate their work and values to both clients and related disciplines in new digitally driven design and construction practices. This chapter documents the manner in which landscape architecture practices have been negotiating these significant changes to be able 'to sit at the table right from the word go',[20] adding 'value' to the project 'from the beginning'.[21] We begin this discussion with a focus on the *Queen Elizabeth Olympic Park* in London. As one of the most significant public projects in the UK over the last decade, the park highlights the challenges and opportunities for landscape architects to engage more effectively with the requirements of future collaborative projects encouraged by the evolution of BIM.

A changing environment for project delivery

London's Olympic Park is considered an exemplary demonstration of a large-scale infrastructure delivering the complexities of a sustainable project within strict cost and time requirements. Starting with the master plan first proposed by EDAW (now

AECOM) in 2005 and further developed by LDA Design and Hargreaves Associates, this project was not conceived within a BIM process. However, it signals a turning point for landscape architects working in complex and multidisciplinary environments, where good project management and shared values are essential in delivering quality outcomes. Similar to digital-driven BIM processes, information management and evidence-based design became the driving factors in avoiding costly errors and delays in an extremely high-profile project.

Located in east London in the former industrial areas on the border between the boroughs of Hackney, Tower Hamlets, Newham and Waltham Forest, the site was extremely challenging given the general deprivation of the area in terms of social health, economic status and environmental conditions. In this context, the 102 hectare parklands were designed with the Olympic Legacy in mind, conceiving the Games as a catalyst for the long-term regeneration of the entire Lower Lea Valley. Reflecting this larger ambition, '75 pence in every pound' that the Olympic Development Authority (ODA) spent on the project was invested 'on permanent venues and infrastructure'.[22] Aside from implementing the sporting facilities, the planning, design and development of the Olympic Park required a high level of coordination of infrastructure and engineering works to deal with the complex issues of pollution, contamination and illegal dumping of waste alongside the removal and relocation of redundant infrastructure (e.g. moving high voltage power lines underground).

Arguably one of the most significant and pragmatic decisions to achieve the desired outcomes for the park involved engaging landscape-led engineering teams, appointing Arup for developing the south park and Atkins for coordinating the delivery of the north park. Following the recommendations of John Hopkins, the project sponsor for the parklands at the ODA, each firm appointed a director-level landscape engineer in the lead position overseeing a team of engineers (including civil, structural, surface water and drainage, lighting, etc.) and other consultants. This strategic decision clearly demonstrated the ODA's commitment to design quality for the 'parklands and public realm that astonished most'[23] in this project.

The landscape engineers were key in ensuring that the design intent of the master plan and landscape design, combined with ODA's design principles, and the ambition of the Olympic Legacy project translated into the end product. This required leadership to understand design while also bringing substantial technical knowledge to the project to coordinate the landscape design with the infrastructure and architecture on site. Sitting at the intersection between design and engineering, Tom Amour from Arup points out that grounding the landscape values and qualities in an engineering environment was essential to delivering the ambitious spatial, experiential and functional qualities of the park.

This development context is influenced by a new era of metrics and data, which requires designers to be able to quantify and understand gains, efficiencies and benefits of their proposals. In this situation it becomes increasingly important to rationalise projects beyond their aesthetic value and look for evidences of performative values such as a response to pollution, reducing carbon or lowering air temperatures. These values, as Armour argues, have to be backed-up by metrics to 'prove why we are doing something'.[24]

Thus, by being able to draw upon the engineering expertise available within and dedicated to the project, the landscape engineers as lead designers played a pivotal role in shaping the course of the project and strengthening the position of landscape architecture. In 2007, LDA Design in collaboration with Hargreaves Associates was approached to develop AECOM's master plan and design for the Park (Figure 5.2). This required collaborating with both sets of landscape engineers, the permanent and temporary building architects as well as the London Organising Committee of the Olympic and Paralympic Games (LOCOG) who were responsible for the temporary overlays of structures and features required for running the Games.

The proposed landform for the park had to incorporate issues of soil contamination and specific demands for circulation and accessibility. Hargreaves's previous involvement with the Sydney Games in 2000 was influential in the designers challenging the digital crowd-flow modelling for the London Olympics which emphasised large flat concourse spaces while significantly reducing the open-space potential and limiting the engagement with the water canals running through the site. As Hargreaves states

5.2a–b
Masterplan of the *Queen Elizabeth Olympic Park*: (a) 2012 Olympic Games, and (b) 2014 transformation.

> reducing the concourse brought us the opportunity to create the 2012 Gardens that run for over half a mile. We wanted to create something horticulturally and conceptually unique that referenced the particularly British passion for collecting plants throughout the world.[25]

The structural framework was informed by bold topographic moves to ease the slope conditions along the watercourses and to improve circulation and accessibility throughout the park. The design team of LDA Design and Hargreaves Associates were working initially with a large clay model and diagrammatic sections (Figures 5.3 and 5.4), which were further developed into typological landform models using Rhino and rendering software to visualise the look and feel of the park (Figure 5.5).[26]

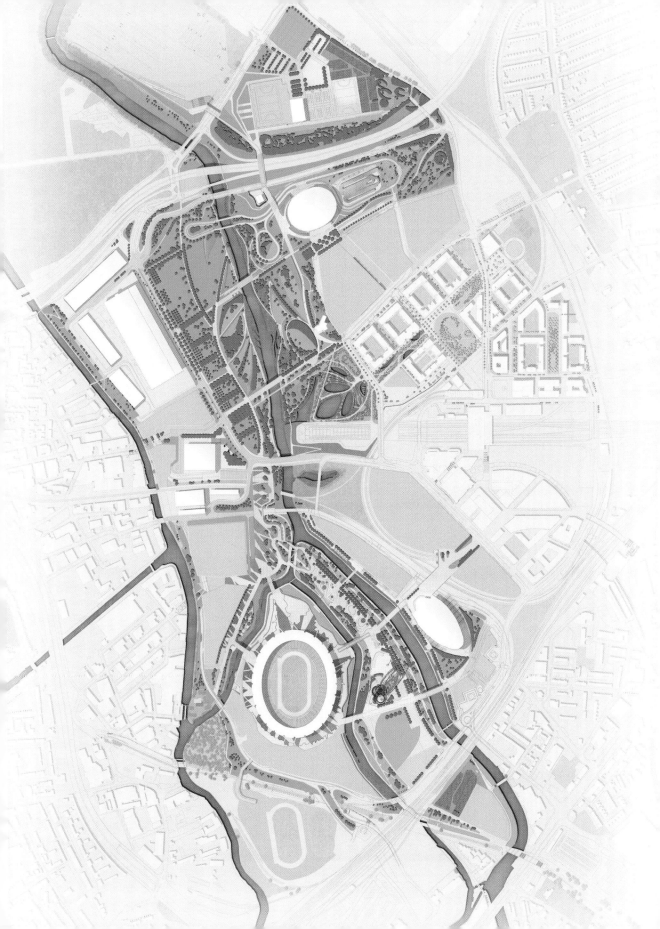

Achieving the new master plan and design development of the park in the short delivery time-frame of 6 months was only possible through a strong collaborative process. However, the new design was not accepted unchallenged. As Neil Mattinson from LDA Design outlines the landscape architects were 'challenged hard by other design teams on the landform' criticising the design 'as being way too excessive'. Demanding the landscape architects demonstrate that their proposal was 'sustainable, appropriately specified and buildable' the full scope of the design vision was only fully appreciated when construction commenced.[27]

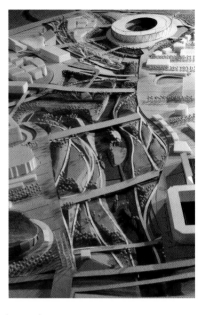

While the London Olympic Park is generally understood as a successful collaborative project, aspects of the design, development and construction processes also highlight important lessons for the landscape architecture profession. For example, the complexity and time-frame of this project required the ODA to develop an ambitious yet rigorous framework for the procurement of contractors, supported by the 'bold intention to change the way the construction industry worked'.[28] Yet, despite LDA Design and Hargreaves Associates considerable experience in documenting complex and large projects, the ODA had reservations concerning landscape architects ability to demonstrate technical command in the construction process. This is highlighted in the choice of contracts for the landscape designers.

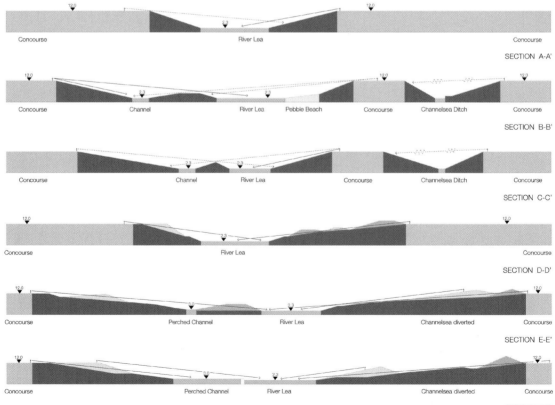

SCALE 1:1000 @ A3

5.3
LDA Design and Hargreaves
Associates developing the
masterplan in analogue
models.

New contractual obligations

Most contractors on this project operated under the New Engineering Contract (NEC3), which included all implementation works for the landscape. Assigned for the construction and procurement of infrastructure NEC3 contracts are designed to stimulate good project management by reducing conflict and managing risks and uncertainties. These contracts are built on two key concepts. First, facilitating collaboration between all involved participants in a project by establishing 'how the interfaces between all the organizations involved will be managed'.[29] And, second, by setting up early warning systems through improved information management processes. These features clearly outline the similarities between NEC contracts and BIM objectives suggesting that with the increasing acceptance of BIM we will see further applications of NEC contracts. Reflecting on the development of BIM in the UK market, Bew and Underwood suggest that these new contracts present an opportunity for change and adoption of new processes as the previous 'contractual rules of engagement have changed very little from when they were originally drafted at the end of the Victorian era'.[30] Peter Hansford, UK Government's Chief Construction Adviser in the Cabinet Office further explains:

> The Government's construction strategy is a very significant investment and NEC contracts will place an important role in setting high standards of contract preparation, management and the desirable behaviour of our industry.[31]

5.4
Design principles to address complex site conditions included the re-grading of edge condition to maximise green space for an Ecological River Park along the River Lea. Further principles included sculpting the land with recycled material from the site for recreation and habitat richness as well as integrated surface water management.

Already, NEC3 contracts have become the contract of choice in the UK, endorsed by the British Government. They have also gained traction in Hong Kong, Australia, New Zealand and South Africa.

In contrast, the LDA Design consortium was initially not part of the NEC3 contracts instead working under the Homes and Communities Agency contract (HCA). Under this contract LDA were assigned to develop the master plan and design of the park. In terms of design documentation, however, the landscape architect's responsibility was limited to the documentation and construction of the softscape. In relationship to the hardscape, they were limited to only developing the 'look and feel', with Arup and Atkins responsible for further detailing and the delivery. Consequently, the original contractual arrangements excluded the designers from having a voice in much of the implementation process.[32]

The designers eventually 'fought' their 'way into the process' and were able to provide further advice and feedback during the design development and construction phase. However, Mattinson admits that this process inevitably was 'frustrating'.[33] Fortunately, through regular cooperative working processes, Arup's and Atkins's design teams skilfully interpreted LDA's and Hargreave Associates design response into detail design and construction documentation. However this decision to favour engineers over highly experienced and skilled landscape architects

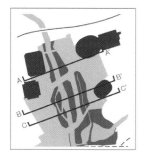

Existing Stage C Section

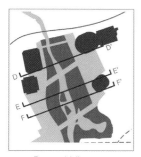

Proposed Adjustment
to Stage C Section

in the documentation and construction phase of a design project, suggests clients are less confidant of landscape architects ability to deliver complex projects.

These preconceptions place landscape architects in a vulnerable position. As this chapter will discuss in more detail, the rapidly evolving construction industry urges landscape architects to engage with new technology-driven delivery processes including BIM and evidence-based design. Otherwise, they may find themselves increasingly limited to providing the look and feel of projects, with related disciplines such as engineering and architecture charged with interpreting their designs within new modes of project delivery. In addition, a successful translation of the design intent into construction cannot always be guaranteed. In this context, a digital design practice can empower landscape architects. Understanding the new responsibilities and the role of technology especially in a BIM environment will prove vital as it 'can ultimately help the parties in the construction project work as a team with shared goals and responsibilities'.[34]

Building skills and expertise

Despite the recognised advantages of adopting BIM in the building industry, there are reservations as to whether even the architecture profession is adequately prepared for the legislative changes in the UK, suggesting that the mandated BIM standards will prove enormously challenging for many stakeholders. Within the landscape architecture profession voices have emerged expressing serious concerns that a lack of engagement with technology and BIM processes 'could effectively remove landscape architects from the supply chain'.[35] As Alastair McCapra, former chief executive of the UK Landscape Institute reflects 'BIM will

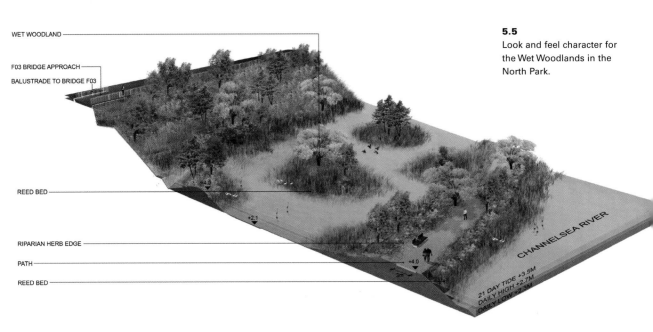

WET WOODLAND

F03 BRIDGE APPROACH
BALUSTRADE TO BRIDGE F03

REED BED

RIPARIAN HERB EDGE
PATH
REED BED

CHANNELSEA RIVER

21 DAY TIDE +3.5M
DAILY HIGH +2.7M
DAILY LOW +2.3M

5.5
Look and feel character for the Wet Woodlands in the North Park.

represent a leap forward or a jump backwards in terms of professional standing'.[36] Others go a step further suggesting the entire profession may be at risk of disappearing, calling for landscape architecture's involvement in BIM processes a necessity to 'save our profession'.[37]

Fortunately, expertise and support is emerging within the landscape architecture discipline. In preparation for the legislative changes the Landscape Institute has established a specialised BIM Working Group to build professional capabilities in the UK. These efforts are supported by Arup and LDA Design, whose experiences in the London Olympic Park project have helped landscape architects realise the opportunities of the evolving work environment.

While challenging, the level of collaboration demanded in this project provided critical insight into the future requirements of BIM-led projects. The complexity of the Olympic Park project highlights the importance of demonstrating the profession's contribution beyond design. Equally necessary is expertise in design development including rethinking engagements with the construction and engineering disciplines. For Arup the Olympic Park project marked an important cultural change in how landscape architects are valued within a team of engineers. As Armour states the project helped establish landscape architects 'as more than tree planters', demonstrating their ability to handle complexity and to establish shared values with the engineers through profound technical expertise. The success of the landscape architectural team is reflected in the increasing number of landscape architects employed in the engineering practice, rising from only six to seven prior to the Olympics, to now 30.

The Olympic Park project also demonstrates the increasing requirements and demands for rigorous information management processes. In this environment understanding the role of data will be key. Similar to advancements in other domains discussed in earlier chapters, this calls for a reconceptualisation of how landscape architects conceive, organise and work with data. For example, for LDA Design working in the collaborative environment raised awareness of the need to improve data management processes. This allowed the designers to revise their working methods and protocols leading to a more rigorous work process. These included ensuring the sharing of information at the right scale, assuring that drawings contain the right information in the correct layout, down to the pragmatics of naming layers. However, as Mattinson notes some of these processes 'should be standard practice',[38] highlighting the necessity to raise awareness in the landscape profession that the starting point for BIM compliance lies in revisiting existing work practices.

The adoption of BIM maturity level 2, mandated by 2016, does not necessarily involve the utilisation of new technologies, instead requiring more efficient workflow and data-management processes. Maturity levels have been introduced to illustrate the stages involved in achieving the government's mission by categorising 'types of technical and collaborative working to enable a concise description and understanding of the processes, tools and techniques to be used'.[39] Level 2 stands for a 'managed 3D environment' where models are 'held in separate discipline

"BIM" tools with attached data'[40] allowing the exchange of information between all members of the project team through standardised file-sharing formats. So far, the COBie format – already used in practice – is considered appropriate to manage projects at level 2 compliance. COBie stands for Construction-Operations Building information exchange, a data format that 'can be loaded on an Excel spreadsheet'[41] as it focuses on 'building information not geometric modelling'.[42]

However, the debate in the design professions, especially in relation to BIM, is often dominated by a focus on operability or appropriateness of technology. Driven by different expectations of stakeholders regarding the contribution of BIM to their respective discipline, BIM often becomes synonymous with specific software programs capable of generating the digital 3D model (e.g. Autodesk Revit, Bentley, ArchiTerra, Vectorworks). This is further amplified by the various interpretations of what the acronym BIM actually stands for, e.g. whether the emphasis lies on the *model* as outcome or *modelling* as process.

For landscape architecture as a small profession, the preoccupation with software is understandable as the upgrade of technological infrastructure often places huge financial and infrastructural burdens especially on smaller practices. However, as David Thompson, landscape architect and BIM expert at LDA Design, outlines the focus on software products is misleading. As a profession that 'doesn't fit in the Autodesk Revit world where everything is straight-lined'[43] landscape architecture will face bigger questions around workflows and operations. Similarly, Christian Hanley, Director of Technology at OLIN Studio, stresses that

> The software of today may be Revit. It's in fashion and everybody is using it. But tomorrow it could be something else. What is more important is how we come together as an orchestra, how well we know our instrument, and how we collaborate to get projects done.[44]

Thus, before reducing the discussion to software selection, it is important to consider broader conceptual questions of how landscape architecture fits within the expanded notion of collaboration afforded by digital technologies. More importantly, landscape architects need to clearly find their contribution within increasingly complex design projects and identify the discipline fit in this new environment. What is our critical contribution to the built environment and, further, what is landscape architecture's value within a revised AECL (Architecture, Engineering, Construction and Landscape) collaboration?

Hesitation to engage with new digitally driven design and construction processes are understandable considering that many landscape architects are still not fully confident working in a 3D digital environment. In addition, currently available technologies and tools, developed almost exclusively for building projects, demonstrate significant limitations in regard to landscape and infrastructure specifications. As long as the tools are not yet in place, landscape architects need to adopt more improvisational and incremental approaches to BIM. This includes exploring how technology can assist in improving the delivery of core service and developing efficiencies and better workflow processes.[45]

Professional institute responses

The UK Landscape Institute has been very proactive in encouraging the profession to 'participate in the BIM revolution'.[46] Providing a larger context for the changing collaborative environment, the Institute has set up specialised information and training events across the country. The first information tour in September 2013 focused on the conceptual and legislative underpinnings of BIM, including the pressing issue of how the profession can realign its work within the AEC technologies and project.

McCapra had already warned as early as August 2012 to 'Get ready for BIM but buy nothing'.[47] Thus, in contrast to the prevalent assumption in the profession that BIM preparedness would require purchasing of specific software, the Institute talks introduced BIM as part of changing attitudes and practices in the building environment, requiring a rethinking of roles and responsibilities in teams together with new standards for sharing data with other professions. Subsequent events in 2014 offered landscape architects 1-day master classes, focusing on more detailed aspects and techniques involved in BIM processes.

So far two schools of thought have emerged in the profession: first, enthusiastic practices who engage with the ideas behind the new processes and already invest in the exploration and adaptation of BIM, and second, practices (usually smaller firms) who are 'still scared of CAD and do things by hand drawing' and thus 'fear the new' challenges.[48] However, the hesitancy to embrace BIM extends beyond the discipline into the public sector, which is equally in need of training.

The London Olympic Park provided a steep learning curve especially for landscape architects, engineers and clients with little previous experience in collaborative, data-managed processes. Since then, the landscape architects and engineers at Arup have been involved in delivering a section for the High Speed 2 (HS2) national rail link connecting London, Birmingham, Leeds and Manchester. Utilising BIM from the start and working in a common data environment to produce a final 'asset information model', this 60 billion pound project is one of the first UK government-funded infrastructural undertakings to be fully managed in a 3D digital collaborative environment.[49]

However, beyond these large-scale national projects, examples of public and private clients demanding progressive and innovative design and construction processes remain relatively rare. Having the central government drive innovation in design quality and delivery is an essential starting point to initiate changes in the private and public sector. A so-called 'push–pull' strategy should further facilitate widespread adoption of new workflow models. This strategy involves supporting the 'Push' supply side of the industry to enable all players to reach a minimum performance in the area of BIM use in five years. This is balanced by a 'Pull' from the client side to specify, collect and use the derived information in a value adding way over a similar timescale.[50]

In this context, opportunities arise for landscape architects to adopt a more proactive approach to the new processes. For example the UK Landscape Institute conceived of their BIM events as far more than training sessions, also using them to develop leadership capability in the profession. Arguably, leadership will become even more important as the computational and operational standards for project deliveries increases to BIM maturity level 3 by 2025. This level demands a fully Integrated Project Delivery (IPD) including interoperable datasets 'managed by a collaborative model server'.[51] The IPD will further expand the conceptualisation of the current 3D model by introducing '4D construction sequencing, 5D cost information and 6D project lifecycle management information'.[52]

Collaborative digital models

Most of the practices involved in this book have either knowledge or direct experience with BIM. That said, a BIM project with a large contribution from landscape architecture is rare. Many of the UK-based firms featured in this book had expected to work with BIM during the course of our research project. However most projects that assumed to be delivered in BIM were documented using more conventional methods. Therefore the real implications of the legislative changes in the UK will not be understood for a number of years, with the profession still in the pioneering but 'exciting stage'.[53]

Within the European context Snøhetta have worked with BIM and Revit on a number of projects as have OLIN Studio in the United States. In Australia, landscape architecture has been slow to engage with BIM, however contractual shifts driven by the AEC industries are beginning to revise landscape architecture practices. In the following discussion we focus on the experience of two Australian landscape architecture firms; ASPECT Studios and HASSELL who are currently in the process of shifting their design and construction processes to work within a BIM environment.

We begin with ASPECT Studios' experience with the *Victorian Desalination Project* (introduced in Chapter 1), which reveals how working in a digital environment – irrespective of software packages – can facilitate better collaborative, and data management processes. The landscape architects investment in a 3D digital model (developed in Maya) from the very beginning of the project contributed significantly to smoother collaborative processes, while also reinforcing their role in the large design team, although they were technically 'last on the job'.[54]

The landscape model assumed an important role as the major representation for presenting the complexity of the project to the diverse stakeholder groups who included politicians, State Government Architect, engineers and government representatives. All of the consultants considered the landscape model the 'the ultimate communication tool'.[55] This model formed the basis for gaining major approvals and ensuring minimal interruptions in the complex project.[56] Reflecting on this process, ASPECT Studios comment that 'If we adopted more traditional models of presentation such as plans, sections and collages, we couldn't be sure that twenty people in the room would get it at the same time' and 'there would be enormous amount of time spent answering questions'.[57]

Thus, the 3D environment created a shared design language, making it easier for all parties (designers, consultants and clients) to evaluate the consequences of individual design actions on the larger project scale. The model also revealed emerging issues instantaneously, which could then be resolved in a collective manner. Working within digital models produced a 'conversational design process' where hierarchical and disciplinary boundaries dissolved as designers and computer specialists sit side by side, irrespective of their disciplinary roles. In this way the landscape architects could directly influence architectural design decision-making, with the unfolding design process accommodating 'multiple authorships'.[58]

Data sharing and co-location

Despite the importance of the landscape model, it is important to note that there was no singular model developed for the *Victorian Desalination Plant*. Instead, at least four digital models produced in various software were significant; the landscape architecture model (Maya), the architect's design model (3ds Max), the architect's documentation model (Revit), and the engineer's construction model (12D Civil). Consequently, the development emerged across multiple digital platforms.

As discussed at the beginning of this chapter, the possibility of BIM lies in the potential to generate one single, intelligent model that contains all spatial, geometric and performative information of the entire project. So far contemporary technology is not sufficient to allow the modelling of entire buildings or infrastructure projects within a single life model. Instead it is still more manageable and likely that each industry involved in complex project will create their own BIM models.

Consequently, individual models have to be exchanged back and forth (e.g. on a weekly basis) between the different project partners, with any changes fed into a so-called 'federated model'[59] to perform any analysis and simulation. While it is not necessary to work in the same software programs the rapidly evolving digital collaborative environment introduces new constraints and practicalities. Within this shared data environment, consideration has to be given to the nature, relevance and value of information so as to minimise information overload and conflicting data. This raises the question of who is responsible for controlling and providing information in this collaborative environment.

Another emerging issue concerns interoperability, that is 'the ability to exchange data between applications, which smooths workflows and sometimes facilitates their automation'.[60] Interoperability is managed through file-sharing formats and standards, which is increasingly moving away from simple spreadsheet formats (e.g. COBie mentioned earlier) to more complex classification standards that allow object-based geometry to be embedded within the data model (e.g. IFC, IFD or IDM). These file-sharing formats currently work well for buildings and structures but present technical limitations for landscape architecture and infrastructural projects. For example, the Industry Foundation Class (IFC), a data scheme that defines file-sharing protocols and classification of geometrical data does not contain landscape elements (e.g. trees), raising the necessity for landscape architects to 'need a voice'[61] in the development of software and file-sharing standards.

To fully embrace the potential of BIM and work within a single, intelligent model requires projects to be conceived within an Integrated Project Delivery (IPD) mode. IPD establishes a common data-sharing environment either in shared server space or from cloud/web-based servers. However, shared server environments are not always practical and cloud-based modelling still pose risks in terms of data security.[62] Co-location within a shared physical space is one way of establishing the collaborative environment required of IPD. For team members less experienced in a BIM managed process, co-location also allows resource efficient on-the-job training and integrated problem-solving by working alongside more experienced people. For example the *Victorian Desalination Project* was developed within a co-location model, with all consultants relocating to a shared office.

The *Doha City Tennis Stadium* in Qatar, currently being developed by Arup may be one of the first large-scale projects to be delivered in a fully integrated BIM environment, including a significant landscape contribution. Initially only assigned to deliver the stadium in BIM, the project has expanded to include the master plan and entire infrastructure. Further, unique to this project is the contractual requirement to co-locate the project team for the duration of the project. As Darren Hickmott outlines, this may be one of the first times that a client demanded that the team 'must work in one room'.[63]

Arup has previous experience with co-location, for example in the BIM delivery of the Manchester City Library. Working in a shared physical space with a consistent digital model significantly improved efficiencies in data management as 'problems could be solved instantly' instead of 'waiting five days for someone to reply by email'.[64] More importantly, co-location changed the dynamic and 'psychology' of the project team important to 'get the best thinking'. 'People were no longer working in silos. Once they were in that room every single person lost their hats and they became all part of one team.'[65] However, for Arup's landscape team the collaborative processes demanded in the *Doha City Tennis Stadium* project are a novelty. As one-third of the project team will be co-located to Doha for 9 months to complete the project, it will also become a test case in the feasibility of co-location for complex international projects.

Fully integrated project delivery is not just about new technology, but also fundamentally alters the relationship between contractors, clients and designers. For example lead designers and contractors will be involved in projects from the very beginning. This new process will also shift the role of project managers in the long term who may either be redundant or reframed as data managers. As stated previously, data assumes a central role in this new design and construction process requiring 'one repository of data'[66] which establishes 'a single source of truth' that transcends disciplinary boundaries. While there are advocates from within landscape architecture to establish their own landscape information modelling (LIM) process,[67] this position fails to recognise that a shared data environment and the collaborative principles of information modelling cannot be achieved by working in isolation.

Eventually, all landscape practices will need to decide their level of engagement with BIM. Some practices such as West 8 have decided at this point in time to not invest in BIM, as demonstrated in their involvement with the new British Design Museum and adjacent residential complex on the former Commonwealth Institute site in London. This project was developed as a joint venture between OMA and Allies and Morrison (architecture) in collaboration with West 8 (landscape) and Arup (structural and services engineering). The New York based firm CASE was assigned as BIM consultant to coordinate the design outcome. With only Arup having prior experience working in BIM, CASE's role expanded to assist the consultancy team to deliver the project in BIM. While the architectural firms ambitiously engaged with upskilling their staff during the project,[68] the benefits for the landscape architects to invest in this process seemed less obvious, resulting in West 8 delivering sketch drawings and Rhino models to CASE who then translated the design into their Revit model. Reflecting on the process Maarten Buijs, project manager at West 8, states that

> Considering the time and effort required to get the model together, the BIM modelling was not worth it. IT will have progressed and the BIM program may have been advanced but there is no perceived need or desire (at West 8) to engage into further use of BIM.[69]

However, large-scale multidisciplinary projects will increasingly require landscape architects to navigate between various disciplines working in BIM. If landscape architects want to remain in control of their design, it will be necessary to invest in BIM training and technology. In the following discussion, we focus on two projects where landscape architects adopted a more proactive approach to working within an integrated BIM environment. These are high-profile redevelopments in which the landscape operates as an important connecting element between the ground plane and the built form, thus requiring a significant negotiation between the landscape architects, architects and structural engineering. While HASSELL's design for the *Sydney International Convention, Exhibition and Entertainment Precinct (SICEEP)* utilised BIM for the design coordination, ASPECT Studios' involvement in the *Yagan Square* redevelopment project in Perth extended into design documentation using BIM.

Design development and coordination

In 2012, joint venture partners HASSELL + Populous won the architectural contract to design Sydney's new integrated convention, exhibition and entertainment precinct (*SICEEP*). Scheduled for completion in 2016, the project shown in Figure 5.9 is the centrepiece of a $3 billion redevelopment of Darling Harbour being delivered through a public–private partnership between the New South Wales Government and the Darling Harbour Live consortium. As landscape architects to the consortium, HASSELL has also designed the public domain for the 20 hectare precinct, featuring extensive public parklands and open space with better connections, event areas and enhanced gathering and meeting places.

The high-profile urban renewal project seeks to revitalise Darling Harbour by extending the urban fabric and reconnecting the city and surrounds with more permeable networks of streets and lanes. The landscape architecture aims to 'blend seamlessly with its surrounds and encourage permeability of the wider area'.[70] It integrates with the architecture, delivering an elevated event deck, terraced landscape, and an expansive grassland green roof.

The architectural team utilised Revit for the design, development and delivery of the architecture, whereas the landscape architects adopted BIM primarily for design coordination and clash detection. While the HASSELL + Populous architecture team of 30 included dedicated Revit modellers, the landscape architects had no previous expertise in BIM requiring the team to develop their skills during the early stages of the design process, drawing from the expertise and support available within the multidisciplinary organisation.

5.6
Circulation routes and grading options had to be carefully tested against the structural composition of the building.

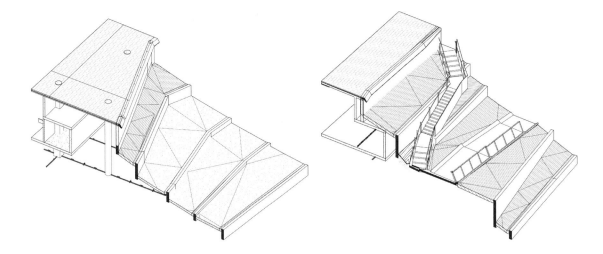

5.7
Complex interface between
architecture and landscape.
Axonometric view of north
side.

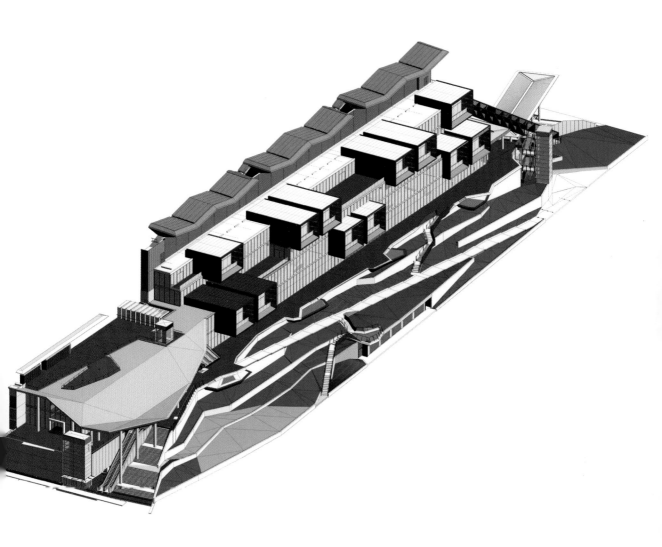

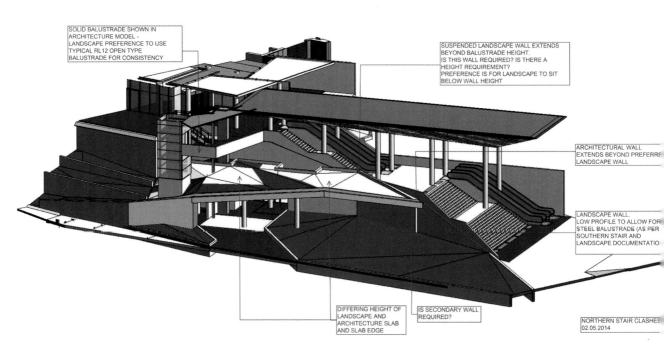

SOLID BALUSTRADE SHOWN IN
ARCHITECTURE MODEL -
LANDSCAPE PREFERENCE TO USE
TYPICAL RL12 OPEN TYPE
BALUSTRADE FOR CONSISTENCY

SUSPENDED LANDSCAPE WALL EXTENDS
BEYOND BALUSTRADE HEIGHT.
IS THIS WALL REQUIRED? IS THERE A
HEIGHT REQUIREMENT?
PREFERENCE IS FOR LANDSCAPE TO SIT
BELOW WALL HEIGHT

ARCHITECTURAL WALL
EXTENDS BEYOND PREFERRE
LANDSCAPE WALL

LANDSCAPE WALL.
LOW PROFILE TO ALLOW FOR
STEEL BALUSTRADE (AS PER
SOUTHERN STAIR AND
LANDSCAPE DOCUMENTATIO

DIFFERING HEIGHT OF
LANDSCAPE AND
ARCHITECTURE SLAB
AND SLAB EDGE

IS SECONDARY WALL
REQUIRED?

NORTHERN STAIR CLASHES
02.05.2014

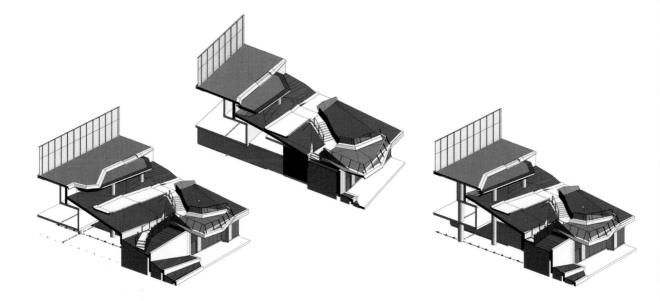

5.8
Design coordination in
Autodesk Revit. The models
were exchanged on a weekly
basis to update the design
progress, share information
and to identify clashes early
in the process.

5.9
*Sydney International
Convention, Exhibition,
and Entertainment Precinct,*
designed by Hassell and
Populous.

5.10a–c
Design development and
resolution. Testing various
iterations of the northern
interface of the Exhibition
Centre.

Initially, this process was challenging, mainly due to the fact that no shared model existed at the time with integrated information. Previously, the landscape architects worked on their own Revit model to capture information, which the architects would copy across into their model whenever that information was required. This process allowed the architecture model to move substantially quicker than the landscape architects' model, especially as the architects incorporated refinements from the structural engineers, which the landscape architects might miss out on.

The benefits of modelling in the BIM environment became evident when the multidisciplinary design team switched to a shared model space in 2014. Establishing the same processes across all disciplines facilitated a consolidated and streamlined exchange of information, resulting in regular updates and revisions that included important landscape information.

The landscape model was then used to coordinate the structural design. Modelling the landscape in more detail in Revit also led the designers to detect clashes that were previously indiscernible, despite their considerable experience working on roof projects (Figure 5.8). The complexity of the *SICEEP* project also meant that the landscape interface with architectural and structural elements would be extensive (Figure 5.10a–c). Eventually, cross-sections were cut every metre across the entire site to determine and resolve clashes; a process that would have been impossible with conventional drafting methods within the given time-frames. This not only allowed the designers to better comprehend the complex build-up of the project, but more importantly, achieve a higher level of accuracy.

The model assisted in the development of detailed plans and sections, although it was never intended for use in design documentation. Within complex and multilayered projects this delineation between design and documentation becomes a crucial consideration in risk management. When landscape information

gets absorbed into architecture and engineering models, responsibilities for key landscape components are transferred into the hands of other professions. While in multidisciplinary firms with integrated design teams this is less of a concern, in other cases this delineation can increase the risk potential for the landscape architects. Thus, for designers, engagement with BIM should ideally translate through to documentation and construction

New strategies for design documentation

Recently, ASPECT Studios have been able to test new avenues for their collaborative practice with their first project developed and documented in BIM. Together with Melbourne based architects Lyons and iredale pedersen hook (IPH) located in Perth, the team won a design competition for the reconstruction of *Yagan Square*. This project forms part of the Perth City Link initiated by the Metropolitan Redevelopment Authority to transform a former railway corridor in central Perth. Following the relocation of the train line underground in 2013, the 13.5 hectare spine is set to connect the CBD with the northern suburb Northbridge with a mix of commercial, residential and public developments.

Just over 1 hectare in size, *Yagan Square* will serve as the major civic space providing an urban mall, play areas, market hall, retail spaces and public art. Through a seamless integration of a terraced landscape with the proposed architecture, the scheme carefully navigates the complex level changes between the ground, the railway tunnel dive structure and a heritage bridge, which frames the site to the east. The key design move is a path designed as a series of 1:20 ramps that wraps around the entire site, informing the levels for each building and the terraced landscape. Sitting literally on top of the dive structure and buildings, the proximity of the structure and other services meant that the landscape design had to be carefully negotiated in relation to the architecture and railway infrastructure.

The sketch designs were developed in integrated but independent architecture and landscape models using Rhino. However, contractual obligations required the designers to deliver the entire project in BIM. While some areas covered by sub-consultants were pulled out of the contractual obligations (i.e. the artist's design of the water features and horticultural work) the landscape architects were 'thrown into the deep end'[71] and had to adopt BIM in their design development (DD) and construction documentation (CD) to achieve a LoD3. Level of Detail (LoD) is a reference guide to specify 'the content and reliability of Building Information Models

(BIMs) at various stages in the design and construction process'.[72] The levels range from LoD1 (conceptual and master planning phase), LoD2 (schematic design and design development), LoD3 (construction documentation) and LoD4 (fabrication and assembly) to LoD5 (facility management). In the *Yagan Square* project, the process for documentation and LoD for each area were guided by Lyons' BIM Strategy and Quality plan and developed in close collaboration with all key consultants at the outset of the project.

ASPECT Studios' director Kirsten Bauer initially had deep reservations about adopting BIM and Revit. However, the contractual circumstances confronted the designers with the 'realisation that landscape architects will have to have BIM skills to deal with high-end, multidisciplinary and multidimensional projects',[73] such as *Yagan Square* or the previously discussed *Victorian Desalination Project*. The necessity of having to engage with this new process prompted ASPECT Studios to radically re-evaluate their position. As Bauer states 'It did not end up as complex as originally thought. Once we got our head around that it is a different way of thinking we started to enjoy it.'[74]

Moving from sketch design into a short DD phase of only 2 months the landscape architects had to quickly transition from Rhino to Revit. Previous experience in 3D modelling and solid documentation skills proved to be vital in this process. However, with no prior experience in Revit, significant upskilling of staff was required. The first encounters were self-taught and trial-and-error explorations through following online tutorials or courses available on the education platform Lynda. To help set up the landscape model in Revit and for further support during the DD phase, ASPECT Studios hired an architectural draftsperson with Revit expertise. After a couple of weeks, this help was no longer necessary.

Lyons, one of the leading architectural design practices in Australia with extensive BIM capability, also provided essential guidance for the landscape architects to learn Revit accurately. Although co-location was discussed, this option was deemed unbeneficial to the collaborative process, in part due to the fact that half the project team was located in Perth, 3,500km west of Melbourne. Instead, the landscape architects would frequently consult in Lyons' office allowing the team to pick up skills while also assuring the best integration of the complex landscape design into the architecture models.

An essential component in these conversations concentrated on developing strategies to work around the apparent software limitations of Revit as a design and documentation tool for landscape architecture. While the exposure to the new technology required ASPECT to invest more time in achieving the level of detail they would normally have developed in a model, it is interesting to note that the architects could not provide faster solutions despite their advanced software expertise. This suggests that the modelling processes and problem-solving strategies are not easily transferable between architecture and landscape architecture, requiring the latter to develop their own processes to overcome current software shortcomings.

5.12
Workflow diagram outlining the collaborative process and various model spaces involved in the design and documentation of *Yagan Square*, with focus on the landscape design elements.

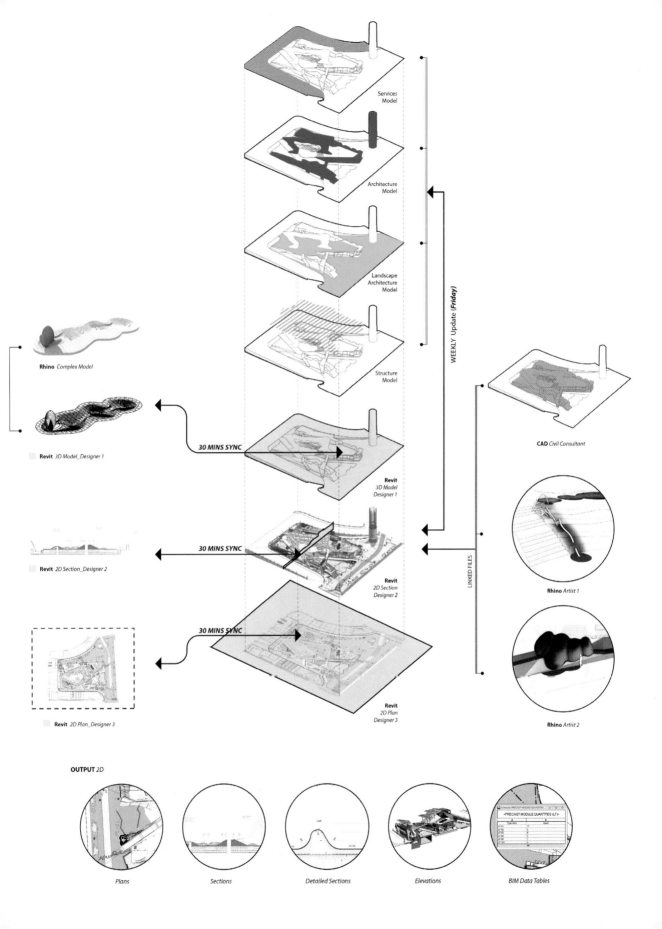

Services
Model

Architecture
Model

Landscape
Architecture
Model

Structure
Model

Rhino *Complex Model*

Revit *3D Model_Designer 1*

Revit *2D Section_Designer 2*

Revit *2D Plan_Designer 3*

30 MINS SYNC

30 MINS SYNC

30 MINS SYNC

Revit
*3D Model
Designer 1*

Revit
*2D Section
Designer 2*

Revit
*2D Plan
Designer 3*

WEEKLY Update (*Friday*)

LINKED FILES

CAD *Civil Consultant*

Rhino *Artist 1*

Rhino *Artist 2*

OUTPUT *2D*

Plans

Sections

Detailed Sections

Elevations

BIM Data Tables

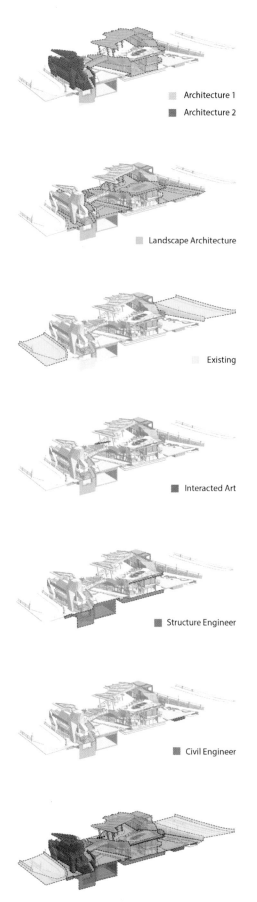

Architecture 1
Architecture 2

Landscape Architecture

Existing

Interacted Art

Structure Engineer

Civil Engineer

5.13
Diagrammatic overview of
the disciplinary intersections
within the Revit model,
demonstrating the
collaborative possibilities
of BIM in the design
and development of
multidimensional projects.

5.14
Moving from Rhino to Revit:
integration of multiple
software and representation
techniques involved in the
BIM process, focusing on
the landscape architectural
design.

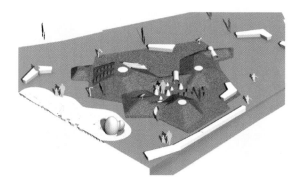

Rhino Model

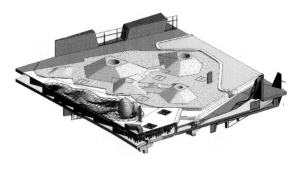

Revit Model

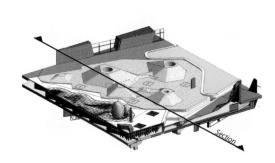

Construction Documentation

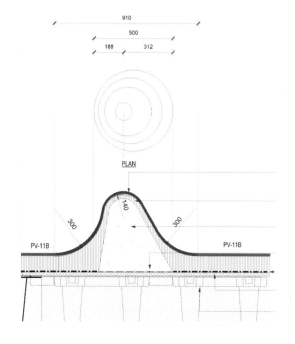

Detail

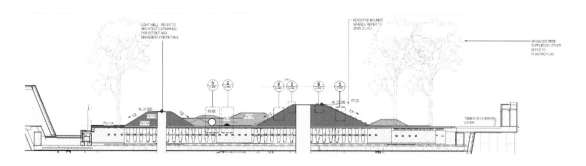

Section

Thus, the modelling process is not yet as seamless for the landscape architects as it would be for the architects. Working with placeholders in the BIM model and refining design components in other software packages (e.g. Rhino) is at this stage inevitable in order to manage program limitations in handling the complexity and irregularity of landscape geometry. In the absence of better software this means stretching to an extent the fundamental objective of BIM, namely streamlining information in one model during the entire design processes.

Although Lyons as principal consultant and BIM manager delivered a consolidated model for tender, the development process still required the consultants to work on separate models to manage the complexity of information and to handle the data relevant to each project team. For example, ASPECT would work with three models, which were consolidated into their own central model.

Despite some unresolved issues in the software environment and 'some manual work required',[75] engaging with BIM established substantial benefit for the landscape architects in this project. First, all design coordination and decision-making was managed as a team, and with the model providing a sense of immediacy, clashes could be resolved proactively. This included raising awareness for issues that would have traditionally been easily overlooked, often requiring the landscape architects to revise their design late in the process. Instead, the landscape architects now gained an equally valid and forceful voice at the design table allowing them to maintain the integrity of the landscape design and detailing by marking up clashes that other disciplines had to resolve, referring them to the landscape details already documented in the Revit model.

Most importantly, the revised workflow in BIM shifts the focus from managing communication problems to concentrating on design solutions and managing risks. As Bauer states

> For landscape architects that means there is less risk for the landscape
> to be reduced when value management occurs, as coordination has
> to happen upfront and because everyone sees clashes earlier and is
> forced to respond.[76]

This was particularly relevant in managing the multidimensional roof landscape, where the structural engineers at times had paid more attention to the architecture, resulting in clashes with the landscape.

Thus, on a pragmatic level, BIM now avoids major conflicts in projects with significant landscape and planting contribution. This is especially relevant in multi-level and multilayered projects such as green roofs, where architects are responsible for documenting the roof structure. Traditional disciplinary separation in the design process has often resulted in conflicts where architects and engineers forgot to adjust the load bearing structure of buildings or omitted the soil layer altogether. In contrast, projects that have included landscape architects in the BIM process

Clash Diagram

 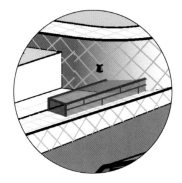 

Object Libraries and Family Structure

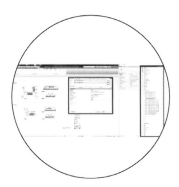  

(e.g. Snøhetta for *Annecy Congress Centre* in France, HASSELL for *SICEEP*, and ASPECT for *Yagan Square*) suggest that conceiving planting within architecture and engineering models, heightens the awareness of landscape elements within the entire project team and avoids clashes resulting from a failure to consider living systems at the beginning of projects.

Future developments

The availability of purpose-built software packages for AEC industries provide a clear advantage for those disciplines, adding to the difficulties for landscape architecture to adopt BIM processes. This further amplifies disciplinary attitudes that suggest that some software now 'gives architects and engineers the illusion to be able to do our job'.[77] However, despite the clear head start in other disciplines, BIM is still in development and even in the architecture profession the new workflow models are not adopted without hesitation.

As new forms of collaborative processes emerge, software development will proceed at an ever-faster pace. For example in May 2015 Trimble (owners of SketchUp and Tekla BIMsight – used for the construction of the Supertrees) announced an alliance with Nemetschek (owners of ArchiCAD and Vectorworks). The partnership aims to emphasise collaborative approaches to modelling, improve interoperability, integrate workflows and develop 5D construction management.[78] This development will challenges the current industry domination of Autodesk's program Revit, and demonstrates that the software industry is interested in improving BIM for a variety of disciplines, including landscape architecture.

Two critical areas have been identified where BIM-related software packages currently fail to provide smooth applications for landscape architecture. First, difficulties in generating complex, 3D geometries and topography offer one significant area for future development beneficial to landscape architecture and designers more generally. Second, and more discipline specific is the limited ability to incorporate planting and living systems within BIM. While landscape designers, as outlined in earlier discussions, have successfully navigated around the difficulties of modelling topography, planting design remains the most restricted element of landscape architectural work.

More recently, software developers have started to develop specialised software, add-on or plug-in (e.g. LandCADD for Revit, Vectorworks Landmark, Keyscape, Land F/X, Artisan, DynaSCAPE, LandARCH or Lands Design). Claiming to support landscape works, the integration of these software products into existing BIM platforms and workflows provides limited success.[79] In some case difficulties relate to issues of interoperability, while in other instances packages are simply too stripped back in scale (applicable to small projects and garden design) to make meaningful contributions to large-scale collaborative work.

Partially, the restrictions lie in the way planting design is handled within the software including the availability of plant species and specifications. More importantly, however, there is no process to accurately work with massing and planting schedules, requiring analogue, 2D measures to incorporate species and density information into the model, which in return removes its parametric capability. Alternatively, the software can translate plants as individual schedulable objects. For example, for an area massing 15,000 plants of the same species each plant will be imported as an individual object. While this process might preserve the accuracy and parametric quality of the planting design, it increases the data volume and complexity of the model beyond workability.

Following the experience with the London Olympics, which included complicated seed-mix both LDA Design and Arup have engaged with the software developer Keyscape (also part of the LI BIM Working Group) to push for better plug-in solutions for Revit. At a fundamental level more innovative and creative approaches to planting design and the representation of planting within a 3D intelligent model need to be developed. This may require a more radical reconceptualisation of planting and landscape practice within a data-driven environment, challenging current conventions. As Hickmott argues 'we have to stop saying that "we can't use that because it doesn't do what we want". Perhaps we need to change what we do and how we think about the way we do things.'[80] The incorporation of living systems and planting design into BIM is an important area for future research and PhD projects. This includes the development of 'knowledge transfer partnerships' with software companies to design landscape specific tools. Other avenues for research include explorations into programming 'data for producing algorithms for predicting plant growth',[81] and the considerable opportunities offered by BIM as post-construction management tools.

Conclusion

Some designers warn of the dangers of BIM encroaching on creativity – for example reducing design development to the assemblage of objects provided by the software toolbox – and adding a further bureaucratic layer to design.[82] The limitations of BIM in relationship to design are obvious and need to be to be taken seriously. However, it is important to note that BIM does not operate as, and should not be confused with, a 'design tool *per se*'.[83] Foremost, BIM emphasises the collaborative sharing of building information within an intelligent, virtual model.

The move towards a BIM-driven construction environment requires the reconceptualisation of the relationship between design and construction and, consequently, the role of the architect or designer. While traditionally the architect was seen inseparable to the role of the craftsman, modern architecture has lost its relationship to construction. With the introduction of Albertian humanism in the Renaissance, and the rise of the master architect as single author of the building, new emphasis was given to the mastery of drawing, marking a clear delineation between intellectual thought and the creation of the design intention on the one hand, and making and project delivery on the other.

Today's technological advancements and development of BIM provide new avenues to reconcile this separation. As Carpo argues 'The technical logic of digital tools runs counter to, and indeed negates, the Albertian principle of separation between design and making',[84] allowing the building and construction industry to generate new 'ways to reunite design and making, based not on single-actor, or single-piece, fabrication, but on a different strategy of information sharing'.[85]

As outlined in this chapter, BIM invests in a non-linear design process by embedding construction considerations early in the project and simulating building performances to avoid costly errors in the construction and operation of a building. While drawings limited the exchange in 'both the type and amount of information that could be distributed'[86] computational power now facilitates sharing of information, better collaboration and more testing of options than traditional modes of designing.

This redefinition of project requirements and deliverables suggests that future projects will no longer adopt a singular focus on the construction of buildings and landscape but instead will expand in scope to consider larger-scale performative benefits (e.g. their impact on community health). Within this context, the danger of 'over-optimisation' arises when important parts of the design (e.g. program and performance) are defined by efficiencies measures, especially when applied from outside design. Thus, in order for projects to remain design-driven, designers need to establish and communicate design values based on measurable evidence (metrics). An argument based purely on an assumed artistry or a moral high ground will not be sufficient.

Within this process, landscape architecture needs to reconsider its relationship to data, precision and performance. To stay relevant, the profession will need to actively participate in the wider AEC industry's dialogue regarding the value and contribution of landscape architecture, moving beyond generalities and 'rules of thumb' principles to offer informed data-driven analyses of landscape's value and performance.[87]

For most designers wanting to work in large-scale, complex and multi-dimensional projects in the UK, Europe, the Middle East, Australia or the USA working in BIM is increasingly becoming the norm. Currently, the exception is parts of Asia such as China, Japan and Korea, where 'the humanist tradition and the humanist authorial premises of the architectural profession, are less rooted and less influential than in the West'.[88] For example, in Japan an enduring emphasis on craftsmanship and stronger ties between design and construction has led to slower adoption of BIM. In China, Korea and other countries where construction labour is largely unskilled and thereby poorly equipped to implement complex, data and computation-heavy design and construction processes, the application of BIM is not a priority.

As we argue in this chapter, advantages in technology and BIM expand beyond efficiencies in documentation, construction and procurement. Instead, BIM is mostly an enabler for collaboration, shifting the relationships and hierarchy within the design team to significantly empower the landscape architect's position within a project. Many landscape architects will continue to work closely with low-tech consultants and contractors such as horticulturalists. Currently not all parts and sub-contractors in a project will require BIM delivery (e.g. planting design and horticulture). However, the new legal framework in the UK suggests that changing client expectations and demand for BIM compliance can no longer be ignored. The rapidly evolving construction industry enforced by new contractual obligations will inevitably require landscape architects to re-evaluate their practice modes, their role within the built environment, and their relations with engineering and construction industries.

Future directions

Over the course of this research, we have become increasingly confident that a digital design practice of landscape architecture is gaining momentum. The next decade will form an important transitional period, which we predict will mirror the growth experienced in architectural digital design practice following the millennium. More and more projects will be conceived and designed with a high level of digital input, accompanied by increased theoretical writing debating the potential of this work. We hope that our book, which presents one of the first reviews of digital practice in landscape architecture to encompass design and construction, practice and academia, will contribute to this new era of design and construction. With that in mind, in this final discussion we summarise the particular attributes of a digital design practice of landscape architecture and conclude with strategies that support the development of these new directions in teaching, practice and research.

The power of the digital model

A digital design practice presents new design logic, reflective of a different relationship between designer, information and processes. Digital techniques move from the privileging of the visual and compositional to a focus on processes of formation. Design processes are driven by explicit rather than implied knowledge, and require a high level of critical thinking and curation on the part of the designer. Those processes are dual directional — physical models can be transformed into a digital model and vice versa. Aided by computational power, the designer can work with increasingly accurate information drawn from Big Data and real-time feedback to engage with the phenomena and dynamic systems which feature prominently in a twenty-first-century practice of landscape architecture.

Digital models are central to these design processes. Our research identified four types of models used by landscape architects as part of a digital design practice. We defined these as models of formation: generation (conceptual, constraint-based and directive); simulation (testing and prototyping), and collaboration.

A *formative* approach to 3D modelling explores complex and novel form through tool-like operations that modify space in real-time onscreen. While practices such as LAAC and PARKKIM, introduced in Chapter 1 work more intuitively with this approach, the design processes of ASPECT Studios and Snøhetta present a more *generative* approach to digital modelling where the conceptualisation of the model itself becomes the primary space of design. This introduces a parametric approach to design which can be understood in both *conceptual* and stricter *constraint-based* terms. Working with hybrid techniques, ASPECT Studios applied a *conceptual* approach to parametric modelling, mixing intuitive explorations of form with a rule-based approach, including the testing of particular parameters such as slope gradients. A stricter *constraint*-based technique develops through more explicit application of rules. In both approaches the designer actively curates the generational potential of the parametric model, establishing parameters and criteria that can be tested as part of the design process.

The generative capabilities of parametric modelling can be further applied in a more *directive* rather than constraint-based design process. Working against a theoretical background of performance, the design processes evident in the Flux City and Miami Vice studios, along with PEG's design approach for their *Bellwether* scheme, develop processes situated between analysis and formation. In all cases, the designers interrogated the relationships and behaviours between form, systems and phenomena and identified changes in concentrations and intensities to inform a set of rules to apply in further design explorations. In these speculative research-driven approaches form emerges through the interrogation of information and performance.

An emphasis on the relationship between form and systems establishes a point of distinction for a landscape approach to parametric modelling, reflective of a designer's inability to definitively control and influence form, systems and phenomena. Instead the designer must intervene in systems that have their own agency and characteristics, requiring different types of design strategies and tactics.

Digital models have always been important in *simulation* processes. We identify two approaches for integrating these modelling techniques within design. The first, reflected in the design of *Gardens by the Bay*, incorporated the digital simulation of systems directly into design processes to *test* the performance of design, and follows an established positioning of modelling, as more widely applied in engineering and science. In contrast, the second approach offers a fundamental reconceptualisation of design (including the very definition of the site), where a physical and/or digital *prototyping of systems* is situated as the starting point for design, in which the designer then hacks, tests and explores design interventions. Real-time data is central to these directions, facilitating a more complex engagement with intangible phenomena and invisible forces such as heat, pollution, wind and water.

The power of digital prototyping lies in its possibility to connect the virtual with the physical space. While prototyping of systems focuses on the transfer of the physical reality into the virtual environment, prototyping for fabrication focuses instead on the exploration of the material behaviour of design. Associated more with professional design practice, digital fabrication and 'paperless' construction processes start to radically alter construction processes and workflows. Applied at scales ranging from the Snøhetta's infrastructural design for *MAX Lab IV* to the intricate stone patterns of the *Diana, Princess of Wales Memorial*, these construction processes translate data directly into form making. Together with Building Information Modelling (BIM), discussed extensively in Chapter 5, these digital models present new modes of *collaboration* which encourage greater efficiency, accuracy and communication between designers, contractors and the client.

Maximising the design and construction potential of these digital models however places new demands on disciplinary knowledge. Interviews with academics and practitioners highlighted weaknesses in landscape architecture's knowledge that limit engagement with the potential of the computational.

It becomes clear that – to varying degrees – all disciplines and professions need to revise their skills, knowledge and practices to reflect the considerable shifts in the expectations of the workforce emerging in a post-digital era. For instance, with the increasing role of data transcending into all aspects of the design and construction process, professionals will require higher skills in data analytics developed in parallel with critical thinking, to engage with the increased opportunities presented by Big Data. Christian Hanley, Director of Technology at OLIN Studio comments on how it is necessary to 'double down on data' stating that the challenge for landscape architecture is how to ask the appropriate questions for data to give back what we need as designers.[1] Similarly, as this new environment signals a radical shift from a refocus from the representation of information to an understanding of knowledge uncovered through data, the ability to break a problem down into computable information (e.g. codes and algorithms) will be valued in a vast range of jobs as technology transforms future employment.

Focusing more specifically on landscape architecture, the generality of the discipline combined with a reliance on 'rule of thumb' knowledge is acknowledged by many as a weak foundation to engage with the complexity of contemporary issues. Landscape architecture programs often offer limited curriculum concerning engineering, ecology or environmental systems, with these important areas of knowledge frequently presented as highly generalised principles or guidelines. Depth of understanding is replaced by an emphasis on landscape architecture's contribution in delivering a holistic understanding considered to be lacking in other disciplines.

In a contemporary context this assumed overview does not necessarily translate into an ability to engage with complexity. An overview in the twenty-first century is a very different proposition to the McHargian era where the ability to consider environmental systems, planning and design concurrently was novel. Now, many other disciplines have embedded greater environmental understandings and sustainable approaches into their practices.

Consequently, landscape architecture's particular strengths such as the ability to work across multiple scales and engage with the dynamic relationships between system and forms needs to evolve with more rigour. This is especially important to engage in a meaningful way with the considerable advantages that the computational offers the discipline.

Given that practice will need to shift out of necessity, how might we develop curriculum within landscape architecture programs to both deepen the discipline's knowledge base and engage with the possibilities of a digital design practice?

Transforming pedagogy

Institutions such as universities are notorious for resisting change. Academics have often taught in programs for many years and have become isolated from changes in the design and construction industries. Similarly research interests are frequently driven by personal agendas, as distinct from focusing on areas of disciplinary value. Writing in 1985 during a period of technological transition, the Dean of the Graduate School of Fine Arts at the University of Pennsylvania commented on the contra-dictory values of universities that:

> they are places where students and faculty often nurture and lead liberal reform, but they are conservative in their respect for history, bodies of knowledge, and the rigor and patience required to delve deeply, to learn, and to understand. This conservatism often manifests itself in resistance to change.[2]

Introducing new directions within universities therefore needs to be strategic and targeted to be successful. Some academics may have the opportunity to develop new programs of landscape architecture or conduct a major curriculum review along with developing new staff profiles. This presents the opportunity to fundamentally recon-ceptualise curriculum sequence and knowledge delineations to reflect design within a digital era. Few landscape architecture programs however will have the resources and ability to rapidly revise their curriculum and teaching practices. For most, change will occur through the influence of individuals and incremental processes.

As we have highlighted throughout our book, the design and construction processes associated with a digital design practice challenge the fragmentation of curriculum into a design and/or planning stream supported by technical and scientific subjects such as site analysis, communication, engineering, ecology, construction and documentation. These framings problematically delineate creativity from the pragmatic, and continue to segregate workflows into linear patterns reflective of an analogue era of production and construction. Reconceiving curriculum to reinforce the link between design and making which is so inherent to a digital design practice offers an alternative framing where the technical can be engaged more comprehensively within design processes. This repositioning also strengthens the relevance of knowledge emerging from ecology, engineering and materiality to design, repositioning it as central rather than secondary to design.

Shifting the teaching of engineering and the biological sciences to a more applied model is one way forward. Moving to a research-driven approach that includes working with metrics, data and performance establishes a more critical engagement with knowledge (as distinct from the passive application of information). Working directly with the prototyping and modelling of systems, which facilitate the simulation, testing and analysis of design, equips students with a greater understanding of how to engage this knowledge within design processes and in the evaluation of constructed projects. These subjects can be supported through workshops or laboratories as demonstrated by teaching and research initiatives such as the Landscape Morphologies Lab (LML) at the University of Southern California.

The repositioning of technical subjects extends to the manner in which materiality and construction are positioned within curriculum. These two areas are often neglected, conceived in a similar manner to site engineering as pragmatic considerations separate from the creativity of design. However, as Brian Osborn's seminar SurfaceFX demonstrated, exploration of material behaviour, facilitated by prototyping techniques, folds the consideration of material performance and detailing directly into design generation, and also introduces students to contemporary fabrication and construction techniques.

Moving more specifically to the teaching of digital technologies, one of the first steps is to liberate their delivery from the isolation of representation or communication stream to instead embed their teaching directly within design studios. Taught in isolation, students may learn aspects of software but without developing an ability to meaningfully apply these tools within design processes. Claudio Pasquero from ecoLogicStudio uses the analogy of making lasagne to explain the importance of teaching software in association with a relevant project, stating 'there is no point just learning how to make the lasagne sauce as you will never be able to make the whole lasagne'.[3]

Students find most difficulty integrating technologies into their design processes, as distinct from learning applications. This is particularly true of scripting and parametric modelling. Pia Fricker, director of the Master of Advanced Studies in Landscape Architecture at ETH comments that 'While most universities are extremely well equipped, the students often lack reflection as to the application potential of these digital tools.'[4] Consequently the ETH curriculum stresses application. Similarly the design studios featured throughout our book, are all carefully structured to embed digital workshops and skill development alongside design explorations to build capability in the application of digital techniques.

In developing these teaching approaches, academics all point to the need to push through assumptions that certain technologies are not relevant to landscape architecture and not to be discouraged by the steep learning curves required by students. Brian Osborn observes 'many of the contemporary design tools, like parametric modeling … tend to require a great deal of exposure and practice before students begin to feel comfortable with them'.[5]

Importantly, these teaching strategies support an agnostic approach to software, encouraging the development of an approach to learning software as distinct from mastering particular software. Of great value is the ability to move between different software according to their strengths and weaknesses. However, it is important to strike a balance between teaching software that might be commonly used in practice or available as open source with more expensive specialised software. For instance engineering firms predominantly use CFD programs such as ANSYS Fluent and Aquaveo SMS. However, graduating students may end up working in, or closely with engineering firms, that use these software programs, while over time attributes of these software may appear in less expensive programs.[6] It is therefore important to offer exposure to industry standard software alongside technology that may have future impact.

And, finally, landscape architecture programs need to embed a stronger engagement with data into their curriculum, which can be developed in two ways. First in the conceptualisation of the site, reconceiving traditional site analysis (conducted largely as visual surveys) to include consideration of site conditions and phenomena as recorded in data (including students recording their own site data and making their own sensors). This can be extended into the use of drones and sensors that can capture atmospheric conditions such as humidity, heat, wind and pollution to develop a more comprehensive understanding of site. And, second, through the incorporation of theoretical subjects that encourage a critical engagement with digital design theory, technological developments and data in design, construction and society more generally.

In some ways transforming practice should be an easier proposition than academia, which is inherently caught up in politics and power. Economic efficiencies and increased design capabilities offer a sound rationale to revise practice models and processes. However, as we highlight in the following section, professional discussions frequently reflect a lowest-common-denominator approach to technology – focusing on the identification of a single software program which offers 'the most bang for bucks'. For example discussions from the small-firm round table conducted as part of the 2014 ASLA conference highlighted SketchUp as the favoured program primarily because it was free.[7]

Transforming practice

Understandably discussions concerning the introduction of digital tools into practice often centre upon their appropriateness to landscape architecture. This is reflected in the discussion of BIM which has been largely dominated by debate over the appropriateness of software such as Revit. But as Christian Hanley argues software like Revit are only difficult to conceive for landscape architecture because we don't know how to use them. If landscape architects knew what software would allow them to do, comments Hanley, they 'wouldn't be using money as an excuse'.[8] He continues:

> In the implementation of new software to a studio's design workflow, the cost of the software is the cheap part. A studio must invest, both financially and intellectually, in the appropriate use and training of the software/tool. Not only as a production application, but also in how it can be leveraged to open up new design opportunities and workflows.[9]

There is also increasing evidence that companies are interested in developing software appropriate to landscape architecture's needs. Hanley, for instance, participates in a disciplinary advisory committee for Gehry Technologies presenting a landscape architecture perspective on technological development. Similarly Arup and LDA Design have consulted with the software firm Keystone regarding the challenges of incorporating planting within BIM.

All practitioners interviewed highlighted the importance of identifying a particular project to act as a catalyst for a firm to challenge themselves to work with technology in an innovative manner. Similar to teaching, software can only be understood when explored through a particular design challenge or question. Gustafson Porter for instance used the *Diana, Princess of Wales Memorial* project as a catalyst to take the practice in new directions, commenting that engaging with 'new technology only comes from a real problem'.[10] The experience and knowledge gained from the project inspired the firm's further investment in digital modelling and contributed to a growing confidence and skill in engaging with larger-scale projects such as phase two of *Gardens by the Bay*, Singapore. Similarly, Snøhetta conceived the *MAX Lab IV* project as a platform to explore parametric modelling within the context of landscape infrastructure.

Upgrading digital skills in practice can occur in a variety of ways. Multidisciplinary firms such as HASSELL and Snøhetta have the considerable advantage of knowledge transference from in-house disciplines such as architecture where the software and expertise is readily accessible. In other instances, practice can invest in professional training provided by firms such as CASE, an international building information consultancy. CASE advises designers, contractors and clients 'seeking to supplant traditional project delivery methods through technology driven process innovation'.[11] The firm promotes an incremental approach to change, focusing on how technologies improves the delivery of core services identified by the client – for instance how to produce documents more efficiently, or how to iterate faster through design. CASE then proposes strategies for aligning tool selection and process change to reflect these practice-defined goals. Online training courses offered by organisations such as Mode Lab education offer further possibilities, accessible internationally, while professional bodies such as the United Kingdom's Landscape Institute offer master classes in new technologies such as BIM.

Our research has also revealed the importance of strategically positioning technical proficiency within practice, including the conceptualisation of project teams to include 'toolmakers'. This approach differs from many practice structures which often place digitally proficient staff towards the end of design processes, restricted to more passive roles of 'visualisation' or documentation. Identifying a role for the toolmaker within project teams allows digitally capable staff to strategically apply their skills in unfolding design processes. In addition, providing staff with direct access to someone who is extremely proficient in software also encourages the transference of technical knowledge.

Acknowledging a role for a toolmaker can also contribute to the bridging of the generational divide in practice. A younger generation, comments Hanley, doesn't have the intellectual experience to understand the value of exploring a particular problem or operating at a particular urban scale that someone in practice for over 30 years might have. The challenge for the younger generation is to take these new tools and apply them in a meaningful way, rather than applying newness for the sake of newness. An effective agent for change, states Hanley, can demonstrate that any digital technique or tool they are using at the very least can deliver the same end product, and ideally adds additional value. This requires an understanding of how these techniques create more efficient workflows, offer more complex end products or shorten time-frames.

Our final recommendation for practice is to invest more in research. Many practitioners argue that all design is research. However, as Ajla Aksamija from the architecture firm Perkins + Will Tech Lab observes 'the current technological innovation and the complexity of design processes are requiring more research and integration between specialists'.[12] We began our book with a discussion of Harvard's Laboratory of Computer Graphics highlighting the valuable collaboration between universities, practice and software companies in progressing the development of theory, techniques and software. Fifty years on, and there is simply not enough landscape architecture-focused research investigating the design potential of digital technologies. This research is critical to the continued development of the discipline at a time of rapid change.

Focusing research

Currently there is no dedicated conference to a digital *design* practice of landscape architecture. Instead, interested academics and practitioners must participate in the architecture-focused digital design conference or the Digital Landscape Architecture (DLA) conferences that have been dominated by Geodesign and planning.

The responsibility to increase research is shared equally by universities and practice. Research disseminated within practice is limited predominantly to large engineering firms such as Arup, which employ landscape architects. Kieren Timberlake, a multidisciplinary design firm in Philadelphia is recognised internationally as an exemplar for embedding research into a design practice. Importantly, the dedicated research group does not operate as consultants to the firm but instead encourages everyone to conduct research. Topics can be connected to a specific project, a particular question or focused on independent ideas. A protocol guides staff on how to develop a research query through the formalisation of a question and methodology. All research must be framed to address specific goals and evaluation criteria, with emphasis on uncovering 'actionable knowledge'.[13] Some research questions may require only two days' investigation while others may require a longer-term partnership with industry.

Architect and urban ecologist Stephanie Carlisle for example developed the Green Roof research project that explores the performance of the 11 green roofs produced by the firm over the past 15 years. Carlisle proposed a research plan to measure performance which included the documentation of techniques and approaches applied in design and construction, analysis of original documentation, project visits and meetings with managers. This research, which has been disseminated through conference presentations, journal articles and featured on the firm's website, offers a rare insight into the long-term success of green roofs. The approach states Carlisle looks past 'low bar metrics of plant survival' to explore more comprehensively how decisions such as structural design and the influence of built form on micro-climate influence plant growth and emergent species.[14]

Showcasing research on the firm's website presents a very different perspective of the practice to clients than simply featuring images of finished design work. The practice's research also encourages staff to become more articulate in expressing their ideas and design approaches. Carlisle comments 'the language of communication here is very process based' encouraged by the research focus which emphasise the tools and methods involved in the practice.

This model of practice-based research offers valuable lessons on how landscape architecture firms might invest in research. Academics, trained in research, can contribute an important role in working with practice to achieve these research ambitions. Our book is one such product of this cross-over. If we had remained purely focused on the more speculative space of academia, we would have produced research of far less value to the discipline. But, as we have outlined throughout our book, to engage with the potential of technology requires a question, problem or proposition. And it is within practice that the true complexity of design is most apparent.

Notes

Preface

1   Amoroso (2012: 8).
2   Picon (2013: 126).
3   Peters (2013: 10).

Introduction

1   Coppock and Rhind (1991: 27).
2   Waldheim (2012: 446).
3   Weller and Talarowski (2014 :114).
4   Esri. Retrieved June 2013, from www.esri.com
5   Weller and Talarowski (2014: 118).
6   Coutts (1985: 5).
7   Steinitz (2012).
8   M'Closkey (2014: 125).
9   Tai (2003: 121).
10 Ibid. p. 113.
11 Shujuan and Yang (2013: 9).
12 Treib (2008).
13 Carpo (2011: 36).
14 M'Closkey (2014: 125).
15 Waldheim (2013).
16 Amidon (2005: 114).
17 Bowman et al. (2014).
18 Carpo (2014b: 41).
19 M'Closkey (2012: 213).
20 Picon (2010).
21 Picon (2013).
22 Fricker (2015).
23 Girot (2013b: 79).
24 Ibid. p. 114.
25 Cluster 18 (2015).
26 Oxman and Oxman (2014: 1).
27 Ibid. p. 1

28 Urban Code. Retrieved 30 June 2014, from http://senseable.mit.edu/urbancode
29 Kitchin (2014: 2).
30 Ibid. p. 7.
31 Benjamin (2012: 15).
32 Ibid. p. 23.
33 Dunn (2012: 20).

Chapter 1

1   Davis (2013: 1).
2   Burry and Burry (2010: 17).
3   Carpo (2014b: 38).
4   Lynn (1998: 110).
5   Carpo (2014b: 40).
6   Massumi (2013: 51).
7   Carpo (2014b: 41).
8   Oxman and Oxman (2014: 1).
9   Oxman (2008: 105).
10 Oxman (2006: 237).
11 Topological Map. Retrieved 15 January, from http://en.wikipedia.org/wiki/Topological_map
12 Burry and Burry (2010: 157).
13 Oxman and Oxman (2014: 3).
14 Woodbury (2010: 11).
15 Ibid.
16 Davis (2013: 15).
17 Ibid. p. 31.
18 Oxman (2008: 106).
19 Davis (2013: 24).
20 Kolarevic (2010: 70).
21 Corner (1999: 4).
22 Ibid.
23 Kolarevic (2005: 3).
24 Picon (2010: 104).
25 Ibid. p. 109.

26 Hensel (2013: 31).
27 Leatherbarrow (2005: 10).
28 Carpo (2013a: 57).
29 ForeignOfficeArchitects (1996: 76–7).
30 Ibid.
31 Ibid.
32 Ibid.
33 Allen (2009: 24).
34 Ibid.
35 Ibid. pp. 22–3.
36 McCullough (2013: 185).
37 Ibid.
38 Burry and Burry (2010: 61).
39 May (2012: 22–3).
40 M'Closkey (2013d: 12).
41 Hansen (2012: 25).
42 Burry and Burry (2010: 263).
43 Dunn (2012: 41–2).
44 Picon (2010: 70).
45 Tang (2014: 50).
46 Oxman (2006: 242).
47 Dutch architects to use 3D printer to build a house (2013). *Dezeen magazine* Retrieved 16 July 2014, from www.dezeen.com/2013/01/20/dutch-architects-to-use-3d-printer-to-build-a-house
48 Ishii et al. (2004: 287).
49 Hurkxkens and Munkel (2014).
50 Girot (2013a: 27).
51 Girot (2013b: 91).
52 Mertens (2010: 33).
53 Walker (2008b: 161).
54 Walker (2008a).
55 Osuldsen (2013).
56 Osborn (2014a).
57 Ibid.
58 Oxman and Oxman (2014: 1).
59 LAAC (2014a).
60 Ibid.
61 Ibid.
62 Lynn (1998: 110).
63 LAAC (2014b).
64 LAAC (2014a).
65 Ibid.
66 Tirol government (2012).
67 Free Landhausplatz. Facebook, from www.facebook.com/FreeLandhausplatz
68 Woo and Kim (1997).
69 PARKKIM. (2014).
70 Osborn (2013a).
71 Osborn (2014a).
72 Victoria (2009).
73 Ibid.

74 Bauer and Sago (2013).
75 Long (2013).
76 Bauer and Sago (2013).
77 Ibid.
78 Ibid.
79 Ibid.
80 Ibid.
81 Oxman (2006: 242).
82 Bauer and Sago (2013).
83 Larsen (2010b: 6).
84 Ibid.
85 Hallgren, M. MAX IV-Lund. *Slide Share* Retrieved September 2014, from www.slideshare.net/richardmccarthycbise/4-mikael-hallgren
86 Larsen (2010: 22).
87 Osuldsen (2013).
88 Ibid.
89 Jørstad (2012).
90 Osuldsen (2013).
91 Hasselberg (2014).
92 Kolarevic (2010: 70).
93 Oxman (2006: 243).
94 Hasselberg (2014).
95 Ibid.
96 Larsen (2010a: 10).
97 Osuldsen (2013).
98 Ibid.

Chapter 2

1 Jury Comments on the Shortlisted Entries (2011).
2 Bowring and Swaffield (2010: 150).
3 Czerniak (2002).
4 North (2012: 18).
5 Ibid. pp. 18–19.
6 Corner (2006: 32).
7 Reed and Lister (2014: 38).
8 Belesky (2013: 50).
9 Mosbach (2014b).
10 Ibid.
11 Ibid.
12 Rahm (2014a).
13 Velikov et al. (2012: 70).
14 Ibid. p. 71
15 Lambert (2012).
16 Ibid.
17 Frenzel (2014).
18 Rahm (2014b).
19 Rahm (2014a).
20 Mosbach (2014a).

21 Taichung Gateway Park International Competition Overview of the Winning Project (2013). Retrieved January 2013, from www.maa.com.tw/10037/files/introduce.pdf
22 Mosbach (2014b).
23 Mosbach (2014a).
24 Ibid.
25 Taichung Gateway Park International Competition Overview of the Winning Project (2013).
26 Rahm (2014a).
27 Ibid.
28 Taichung Gateway Park International Competition Overview of the Winning Project (2013).
29 Mosbach (2014b).
30 Mosbach (2012).
31 Ibid.
32 Mosbach (2014a).
33 Ibid.
34 Ibid.
35 Rahm (2014a).
36 Burry (2011: 231).
37 Davis (2013: 18).
38 Oxman (2008: 101).
39 Ibid.
40 Oxman (2006: 243).
41 Burry and Burry (2010: 55).
42 Ibid.
43 Ibid. p. 15.
44 Schumacher (2009: 14).
45 Carpo (2013b: 49).
46 Davis (2013: 15).
47 Ibid. p. 48.
48 Ibid. p. 210.
49 Ibid. p. 212.
50 Lorenzo-Eiroa (2013: 11).
51 Reas and McWilliams (2010: 17).
52 Chalmers and Watts (2014).
53 Ibid.
54 Davis (2013: 4).
55 Ibid. p. 63.
56 McCullough (2013: 183).
57 Davis and Peters (2013: 126).
58 Burry (2011: 9).
59 Davis and Peters (2013: 126).
60 Ibid. p. 131.
61 Hanley (2014).
62 Landau (2015).
63 Ibid.
64 Fricker (2015).
65 Fricker et al. (2013: 550).
66 Ibid.
67 Hansen (2014b).
68 GNCstaff (2014).
69 Hansen (2014a).
70 M'Closkey and VanDerSys (2013b).
71 M'Closkey (2013b: 15).
72 Ibid. p. 17.
73 M'Closkey and VanDerSys (2014a: 227–8).
74 Ibid.
75 Ibid.
76 M'Closkey and VanDerSys (2014b).
77 Ibid.
78 VanDerSys (2014a).
79 Ibid.
80 M'Closkey and VanDerSys (2013a).
81 M'Closkey and VanDerSys (2014b).
82 M'Closkey (2013b: 17).
83 M'Closkey and VanDerSys (2011).
84 M'Closkey and VanDerSys (2013a).
85 Girot (2013b: 82).
86 Ibid. p.82.
87 Ibid. p. 105.
88 Ibid. p.112
89 VanDerSys (2014a).
90 M'Closkey and VanDerSys (2013a).
91 Girot et al. (2010: 376).
92 Reed and Mah (2014).
93 Ibid.
94 M'Closkey (2013a).
95 Schnabel (2012: 58).
96 Walliss et al. (2014: 77).
97 Hong (2014).
98 Walliss et al. (2014: 77–8).
99 Reed and Mah (2014: 6).
100 Ibid.
101 Relational Urbanism (2014). Retrieved 23 September 2014, from www.bartlett.ucl.ac.uk/architecture/programmes/postgraduate/units-and-showcases/march-urban-design/cluster18/2013-2014
102 Mah (2014).
103 M'Closkey and VanDerSys (2013a).
104 Ibid.
105 Llabres and Rico (2012a: 320).
106 Zuidgeest et al. (2013: 93).
107 Ibid.
108 Steinitz (2012).
109 Llabres and Rico (2012a: 321).
110 Ibid. p. 331.
111 McHarg (1992: 196).
112 Coutts (1985: 6).
113 Llabres and Rico (2012a: 331).
114 Ball (2011).
115 esri. Esri CityEngine. Retrieved 20 September 2014, from www.esri.com/software/cityengine/features
116 Ibid.

117 Morgan (2014).
118 Ibid.
119 Ibid.
120 Ibid.
121 Ibid.
122 Ibid.
123 Armour et al. (2014).
124 Davis (2014).
125 Morgan (2014).
126 Aste and Ludlin (2014: 107–8).
127 M'Closkey and VanDerSys (2013b).

Chapter 3

1   Carlisle and Pevzner (2012).
2   Armour et al. (2014).
3   Armour et al. (2014).
4   Carlisle (2014).
5   Becker and Holmes (2014).
6   VanDerSys (2014b).
7   Hanley (2014).
8   VanDerSys (2014a).
9   Ibid.
10 Besserud et al. (2013: 86).
11 Ibid.
12 Ibid. p. 93.
13 Aish et al. (2013: 109).
14 M'Closkey and VanDerSys (2015).
15 Cantrell and Holzman (2015).
16 Bellew and Davey (2012: 26).
17 Ferguson (2014: 26).
18 Davey et al. (2010: 141).
19 Bellew and Davey (2012: 49).
20 Ibid. 49.
21 Ibid. p.56.
22 Ferguson (2014: 27).
23 Ibid. p. 30.
24 Ibid. p. 28.
25 Ibid.
26 Davey et al. (2010: 142).
27 Grant (2014).
28 Ibid.
29 Ibid.
30 Ibid.
31 Bellew and Davey (2012: 99).
32 Rossegaarde (2014).
33 Milman (2015).
34 General (2014).
35 Jones and MacLachlan (2014).
36 Engelhardt and Kessling (2013).
37 Ibid.
38 Frenzel (2014).
39 StaffReporter (2013).
40 PARKKIM, *Competition Entry*.
41 Givoni et al. (2003: 77–86).
42 M'Closkey (2013: 15).
43 Meyers (2008: 18).
44 Costanzo (2006: 62).
45 Kitchin (2014: 2).
46 Leckie (2013).
47 Ibid.
48 Eagle and Greene (2014: 2).
49 Ibid.
50 Medialab-Prado, retrieved 7 August 2014, from http://medialab-prado.es
51 Ibid.
52 Future Everything, retrieved 2 August 2014, from http://futureeverything.org
53 Tait (2012).
54 Ibid.
55 Sensable City Lab, retrieved 7 August 2014, from http://senseable.mit.edu
56 Hubcap, Sensable City Lab, retrieved 7 August 2014, from http://hubcab.org/#13.00/40.4489/-73.6118
57 One Country, Two Lungs, Sensable City Lab, retrieved 8 July 2014, from http://senseable.mit.edu/twolungs
58 Rekittke and Ninsalam (2014: 198).
59 Fraguada et al. (2012: 356).
60 Picon (2013: 127).
61 Fraguada et al. (2012: 361).
62 ETH (2014: 4).
63 Fraguada et al. (2012: 336–7).
64 Ibid. p. 359.
65 VanDerSys (2014a).
66 Girot (2013b: 80).
67 Girot (2011: 73).
68 Ibid.
69 Osborn (2014b).
70 Ibid.
71 Ibid.
72 Harris (2014).
73 M'Closkey and VanDerSys (2013).
74 Gritlab, retrieved 6 June 2014, from http://grit.daniels.utoronto.ca
75 Green Roof Innovation Testing (GRIT) Laboratory.
76 Ibid.
77 Ibid.
78 Ibid.
79 Macivor et al. (2013: 297–305).
80 Hill et al. (2015).
81 Ibid.
82 Fraguada and Melsom (2014).

83 Gubbi et al. (2013: 1646).

84 Ibid.

85 Ibid.

86 Raju (2014).

87 Townsend (2013: 303).

88 Nicholson (2014).

89 Fast Company (2014).

90 Ibid.

91 Fytogreen, retrieved 1 November 2014, from http://fytogreen.com.au

92 Galcon, retrieved 1 November 2014, from http://www.galconc.com

93 Heard (2014).

94 Foderaro (2014).

95 Llabres and Rico (2014: 55).

96 Ibid. p. 56.

97 Ibid. p. 57.

98 Landscape Morpologies Lab, retrieved 30 June 2014, from http://lmlab.org

99 Robinson (2013b).

100 Ibid.

101 Landscape Morpologies Lab, retrieved 30 June 2014, from http://lmlab.org

102 Robinson (2013a).

103 Payne and Kelly Johnson (2013: 147).

104 Ibid.

105 Dredge Research Collaborative, retrieved 30 June 2014, from http://dredgeresearchcollaborative.org

106 Ibid.

107 Cantrell and Holzman (2013).

108 Ibid.

109 Ibid.

110 Ibid.

111 Ibid.

112 Cox and Darden (2012).

113 Cantrell and Holzman (2013).

114 Ibid.

115 Ibid.

116 Cantrell and Holzman (2013).

117 Ibid.

118 VanDerSys (2014b).

119 VanDerSys (2014a).

120 VanDerSys (2014b).

121 VanDerSys (2014a).

122 Llabres and Rico (2014: 64–5).

123 RC18 (2014: 8).

124 Llabres and Rico (2014: 58).

125 RC18 (2014: 57).

126 Ibid. p. 9.

127 Fellman (2014).

Chapter 4

1 Dunn (2012: 20).

2 Kolarevic (2009: 35).

3 Ibid. p. 31.

4 Glymph (2009: 10).

5 Kolarevic and Klinger (2013: 10).

6 Ibid. p. 7.

7 Ibid. p. 6.

8 Dunn (2012: 20).

9 Ibid.

10 Tekla, Gardens at the Bay: Complex Geometry, retrieved 1 August 2014, from www.tekla.com/references/gardens-bay

11 Redevelopment of a Square in Innsbruck (2013). *Detail, 1.* p. 43

12 Ibid.

13 Petschek (2005: 1).

14 Petschek (2014: 2: 211).

15 Leong (2013).

16 Nicas (2015).

17 Osborn (2013: 4).

18 Ibid.

19 Ibid.

20 Woods (2013: 195).

21 Ibid.

22 Osborn et al. (2013: 9).

23 Ibid.

24 Ibid.

25 PEG (2014).

26 Ibid.

27 McCloskey (2013c).

28 PEG (2014).

29 Ibid.

30 Ibid.

31 Poletto and Pasquero (2012: 7).

32 Ibid. p. 6.

33 Poletto and Pasquero (2013).

34 Ibid.

35 Poletto and Pasquero (2012: 117).

36 Ibid.

37 ecoLogicStudio, retrieved 8 June 2014, from www.ecologicstudio.com/v2/index.php

38 Bullivant (2011).

39 Ibid.

40 Carlo Ratti Associati, retrieved June 2014, from www.carloratti.com/project/future-food-district

41 Urban Algae Canopy (2014).

42 Inhabitat, retrieved June, 2014, from http://inhabitat.com/incredible-urban-algae-canopy-produces-the-oxygen-equivalent-of-four-hectares-of-woodland-every-day/13-urban-algae-canopy-by-ecologic-studio-expo-milano-2015

43 Urban Algae Canopy (2014).
44 Poletto and Pasquero (2013).
45 Valldaura: Self Sufficient Lab, retrieved 1 November 2014, from www.valldaura.net/about-2
46 GOM, retrieved 27 October 2014, from www.gom.com
47 Santry (2004).
48 Bowman et al. (2014).
49 Birch and Miller (2005).
50 Santry (2004).
51 Ibid.
52 Bowman et al. (2014).
53 Santry (2004).
54 Ibid.
55 Bowman et al. (2014).
56

Chapter 5

1 Scheer (2014).
2 Garber (2009: 8).
3 Ibid.
4 Ibid.
5 Quirk (2012).
6 Eastman (1975: 50).
7 Scheer (2014: 107).
8 Azhar et al. (2012: 15–28).
9 Ashcraft (2010: 147).
10 Carpo (2014a: 13).
11 Hooper (2011).
12 Jones and Bernstein (2012: 9).
13 Cabinet Office (2011: 3).
14 Hickmott (2014).
15 Armour, cited in Hopkins and Neal (2013: 192).
16 Hickmott (2014).
17 Department for Business, Innovation and Skills (2013).
18 Cabinet Office (2011: 13).
19 Hickmott (2014).
20 Ibid.
21 McCapra (2012).
22 Hopkins and Neal (2013: 17).
23 Ibid. p. 106
24 Armour (2014).
25 Hargreaves, cited in Hopkins and Neal (2013: 116).
26 Mattinson (2013).
27 Ibid.
28 Mattinson, cited in Hopkins and Neal (2013: 172)
29 NEC (2013). How to use BIM with NEC3 contracts, from http://codebim.com/wp-content/uploads/2013/06/BIMwithNEC3guide.pdf.
30 Bew and Underwood (2010: 31).
31 Hansford (2013).
32 Landscape Institute UK (Producer).
33 Mattinson (2013).
34 Sharples (2010: 93).
35 Ahmad and Aliyu (2012: 532).
36 McCapra, (2012
37 Hickmott (2014).
38 Mattinson (2013).
39 UK Government, BIM Industry Working Group (2011: 40).
40 Bew and Underwood (2010: 34).
41 McCapra (2012).
42 East (2011).
43 Hickmott (2014).
44 Hanley (2014).
45 Hickmott (2014).
46 Slavid (2013).
47 McCapra (2012).
48 Thompson (2014).
49 Hickmott (2014).
50 UK Government, BIM Industry Working Group (2011: 3).
51 Ibid. p. 96
52 Magee et al. (2015).
53 Hickmott (2014).
54 Bauer (2013).
55 Ibid.
56 Ibid.
57 Bauer and Sago (2013).
58 Bauer (2013).
59 Scheer (2014: 107).
60 Eastman et al. (2011a: ch. 3).
61 Hickmott (2014).
62 Heier (2014).
63 Hickmott (2014).
64 Ibid.
65 Ibid.
66 Ibid.
67 Ahmad and Aliyu (2012: 531–40); Goldman, M. (2011).
68 Negro (2015).
69 Buijs (2015).
70 Infrastructure NSW (2013: 2).
71 Bauer (2015).
72 BIMForum (2013: 8).
73 Bauer (2015).
74 Ibid.
75 Fooks et al. (2015).
76 Bauer (2015).
77 Hickmott (2014).
78 Trimble (2015).
79 Schmidt (2014).
80 Hickmott (2014).
81 Thompson (2014).
82 Carpo (2013b: 49).

83 Scheer (2014: 107).
84 Carpo (2014: 9).
85 Ibid. p. 12
86 Scheer (2014: 11).
87 Fellman (2014).
88 Carpo (2014a: 13).

Future directions

1   Hanley (2014).
2   Coutts (1985).
3   Poletto and Pasquero (2013).
4   Fricker (2015).
5   Osborn (2014a).
6   VanDerSys (2014a).
7   Fellman (2014a).
8   Hanley (2014).
9   Ibid.
10 Bowman and Porter (2013).
11 CASE: BIM consulting and Building Information Modelling, retrieved 1 December 2014, from http://case-inc.com
12 Davis (2015).
13 Carlisle (2014).
14 Ibid.

Project credits

Bellwether
Taichung, Taiwan (2011)
Client: Taichung City Government – Taichung Gateway Park International Competition

Designers: PEG office of landscape + architecture
Collaborators: Josh Freese, William Wong, Meg Studer, Matt Ells

Diana, Princess of Wales Memorial
Hyde Park, London, UK (2002 – 2004)
Client: Department of Culture, Media and Sport
Sponsor: The Royal Parks

Design team: Gustafson Porter (landscape architecture); Arup (engineering); Geoffrey Osborne Ltd (main contractor); Bucknall Austin (project management); OCMIS (water feature consultants)

Consultants: Willerby Landscapes (landscape contractor); Cathedral Works Organisation (stone layers); S. McConnell and Sons (stonemasons); Texxus (stone texturing specialists); Surface Development Engineering Ltd (surface modelling)

Edaphic Effects
Philadelphia, PA, USA (2011)
2011 Boston Society of Architects Research Grant
Self-initiated research project exploring customised geo-cells

Designers: PEG office of landscape + architecture

Collaborators: Pennsylvania Horticultural Society, Philadelphia Water Department, Asociación de Peurtorriqueños en Marcha for Everyone, and Joseph's Automotive Service

Gardens by the Bay
Singapore (2006-2012)
Client: National Parks Board, Singapore

Design team: Grant Associates (landscape architecture); Wilkinson Eyre (architecture); Atelier One (structural engineering); Atelier Ten (building service engineering)

Consultants: PM Link Pte Ltd (project management); Davis Langdon and Seah (Singapore, quantity surveying); Speirs + Major Associates (lighting design); Thomas Matthews (graphic design and identity); Land Design Studio (interpretative consultants); Meinhardt Infrastructure Pte Ltd (civil and structural engineering)

Hortus Paris
presented at 'Alive: New Design Frontiers', Paris, France (26 April – 1 September 2013)
Client: Espace Fondation EDF, Paris, France
Curator: Carle Collet
Design: ecoLogicStudio

Landhausplatz | Eduard-Wallnöfer-Platz
Innsbruck, Austria (2008 – 2012)
Client: Amt der Tiroler Landesregierung, Abteilung Hochbau

Design team: Stiefel Kramer (architecture), Christopher Grüner (artist), LAAC architekten (architecture)
Architecture design: Kathrin Aste, Frank Ludin, Peter Griebel, Thomas Feuerstein. Execution: Kathrin Aste, Frank Ludin, Thomas Feuerstein, Peter Griebel

Consultants: Baumeister Ing. Stefan Heiss (construction supervision); Dipl. Ing. Alfred Brunnsteiner (structural engineering); A3 jp-Haustechnik GmbH&Co (HVAC design); A3 Jenewein Ingenieursbüro GmbH (electrical design); Halotech Lichtfabrik (light design)

Max Lab IV
Lund University, Lund, Sweden (2011 – 2015)
Client: Fastighets AB ML 4

Design team: Fojab Arkitekter AB (architecture); Snøhetta Oslo AS (landscape architects), Jenny B. Osuldsen (project leader)

Collaborators: Tyréns AB (civil engineering)

Medibank Place – 720 Bourke Street

Melbourne, Australia (2012-2014)

Client: CBUS Property; Medibank

Design team: HASSELL (landscape architecture, architecture, interior design); Brookfield Multiplex (contractor); Fytogreen Australia (green walls and façade greening)

Mud Infrastructure | Yanghwa Riverfront Park

Han River, Seoul, South Korea (2009-2012)

Design principals: Yoonjin Park and Jungyoon Kim

Designers at PARKKIM: Sujin Hong, Donghyun Sohn, Yeonhee Park, Minseo Kim, Hong –In Lee, Hansol Kang, Taehyung Park, Minji Kim, Haein Lee

Consultants: Dong Myoung (chief engineer); Taechung (civil engineer); Sam Hee Lee (hydrology advisor); Bong Ho Han (ecology advisor); Yoo Il Kim (chief of advisory board); Hanvit Construction (general contractor)

Not Garden

Philadelphia, PA, USA (2009)

Self-initiated research project exploring geotextile customisation

Designers: PEG office of landscape + architecture

Collaborators: Redevelopment Authority of the City of Philadelphia (RDA); the Urban Tree Connection

Phase Shifts Park | Jade Eco Park

Taichung, Taiwan (2012-2016)

Client: Taichung City Government

Design team: Mosbach Paysagistes, Philippe Rahm architects and Ricky Liu & Associates

Consultants competition and preliminary design: Atelier ld (rain water remediation and infrastructure engineering); Sepia conseil (rain water recycling); Transsolar (climate engineering); Bollinger-Grohmann (structure climatic devices and bridges); Rimoux lighting (green corridor installation)

Consultants detail design and executive drawing: Sino Geotechnology Inc. (rain water remediation and infrastructure engineering); C.C.Lee & Associates (HVACR consulting engineers – air conditioning engineering); Envision

Engineering (structure, climatic devices and bridges); Frontier Engineers (plumbing and electrical engineering); THI Consultants Inc. (traffic)

Queen Elizabeth Olympic Park
Stratford, East London, UK (2008-2012)
Client: Olympic Delivery Authority

Design partners: LDA Design (landscape architecture, lead consultants); Hargreaves Associates (landscape architects); Arup (landscape engineering); Atkins (landscape engineering); Sutton Vane Associates (lighting design); University of Sheffield (specialists ecology, meadow and horticulture); Sarah Price Landscapes (landscape architecture); Centre for Accessible Environments, ETM Associates (landscape management)

SICEEP – Sydney International Convention, Exhibition and Entertainment Precinct
Sydney, NSW, Australia (2014-current)
Client: Lend Lease/NSW

Design joint venture: HASSELL (architecture and landscape architecture), Populous (architecture)

Sigirino Depot
Lugano, Ticini, Switzerland (study 2003-2010, construction 2009-2020)
Client: Alp Transit Gotthard SA

Atelier Girot design team: Christophe Girot, Yael Ifrah, Ilmar Hurkxkens, Alex Prusakov

Collaborators: ITESCA Engineering and IFEC Engineering; LVML ETH Zurich (for the point cloud survey images)

The Simrishamn Regional Algae Farm
Simrishamn, Sweden (2011)
Client: Marine Centrum Department, Simrishamn Municipality

ecoLogicStudio design team: Claudia Pasquero,Marco Poletto with Andrea Bugli and Silvia Ortu

Consultants: Catherine Legrand (biology and local bio-diversity); Fredrika Gullfot (biology and algae farming); Xenia Palelouglou, Manuele Gaioni, Kwanphil Cho (interns for support in exhibition)

Sustainable Design of Power Plants
Alpine Area Exemplary, Austria (2012 – 2015)
Self-initiated research project
Project partners: alpS GmbH

Architecture team: Kathrin Aste, Frank Ludin, Bejamin Ennemoser, Peter Griebel, Marc Ihle, Clara Jaschke, Daniel Luckeneder, Allison Weiler

Thermal City | Danginri Underground Combined Heat Plant
Seoul, South Korea (2013)

Design principals: Yoonjin Park and Jungyoon Kim
Designers at PARKKIM: Sangeun Son, Sohyung Kwon, Myoungcheon Kim, Jiyong Park, Jungin Park, Chavapong Gem Phipatseritham
Project partner: Arup HK, Iris Hwang (sustainability engineer)

Urban Algae Canopy
Expo Milano, Turin, Italy (2015)

Project partner: Carlo Ratti Associati

ecoLogicStudio design team: Marco Poletto and Claudia Pasquero
Consulting team: Alt N, Nick Puckett (responsive system consultant); Taiyo Europe GmbH (ETFE design support and manufacturing); Mario Tredici (microbiologist)

Victorian Desalination Project
Lower Wonthaggi, Victoria, Australia (2009–2011)
Client: Aquasure and Thiess Degrémont JV – Parsons Brinckerhoff – Beca Joint Venture (design and construction contractor)

Design team: ASPECT Studios (landscape architecture); peckvonhartel (architecture); ARM Architecture (architecture); Ftyogreen Australia (green roof contractor); Practical Ecology (reviewed planting for ecological value); Beca (architecture, structural and hydrologic engineering), Parsons Drinkerhoff (civil engineering)

Yagan Square | Perth City Link
Perth, WA, Australia (2014-2016)
Client: Metropolitan Redevelopment Authority, Perth, WA, Australia

Design team: ASPECT Studios (landscape architecture); Lyons (principal consultant architects); iredale pedersen hook (architects), Aurecon; WSP; Jon Tarry,

Sharon Egan, Paul Carter, Helen Smith, Jeremy Kirwin Ward and Shaun Gladwell (artists)

Research Labs

The Grit Lab
University of Toronto, Canada

The GRIT Lab is made possible through grant funding from the City of Toronto Environment Office, RCI Foundation, Ontario Centres of Excellence, NSERC, MITACS, Connaught Fund, Landscape Architecture Canada Foundation and Science without Borders, as well as through contributions from industry and university partners: Tremco Roofing, Bioroof, Sky Solar, IRC Group, Carl Stahl-Decorcable, DH Water Management, Flynn, GreenScreen, Huntsman, Schletter, Scott Torrance Landscape Architect Inc., Semple Gooder Roofing Corporation, Siplast, Terragen Solar, Toro, and University of Toronto Facilities & Services.

Landscape Morphologies Lab
The University of Southern California, USA

Collaborators include investigators from the Sci-Arc, Viterbi School of Engineering, USC School of Policy, Planning and Development, USC Earth Sciences, Los Angeles Department of Water and Power, ARIDLands Institute, Army Corps of Engineering and the Los Angeles Bureau of Engineering.

Owens Lake Project: Andrew Atwood, Nicholas Barger, Alex Dahm, Kate Hajash, Yan Hou, Brendan Kempf, Jianjun Li, Steven Moody

DredgeFest
Louisiana, USA (11-17 January 2014)

Organised by the Dredge Research Collaborative: Stephan Becker, Sean Burkholder, Brian Davis, Rob Holmes, Tim Maly, Brett Milligan and Gena Wirth.

Partners included the Robert Reich School of Landscape Architecture at Louisiana State University, the Coastal Sustainability Studio at Louisiana State University, the Center for Land Use Interpretation, Gulf Coast Public Lab, and Scenario Journal.

Design Studios

Landscape Architecture Department
School of Architecture, University of Virginia

Groundwork LAR 6010, Fall 2013
Foundation Studio 1

Instructor: Brian Osborn

Teaching assistants: Rachel Stevens and Sarah Miller

Surveillance Practices ALAR 7010/8010, Fall 2014

Graduate Option Studio

Instructor: Brian Osborn

Surface *FX* SARC, Spring 2013

Instructor: Brian Osborn

Research assistants: Gwendolyn McGinn and Katherine Jenkins

Department of Landscape Architecture

Harvard Graduate School of Design

Flux City Spring 2014

GSD1212 Landscape Architecture Design IV

Coordinators: Chris Reed and David Mah

Studio faculty: Leyre Asensio Villoria, Silvia Benedito, Leena Cho and Sergio
    Lopez-Pineiro

J-term workshop faculty: Zaneta Hong

Mid-term workshop faculty: Eduardo Rico and Enriquetta Llabres-Valls

Teaching assistants: Daekwon Park, Christina Antiporda, Takuya Iwamura, Difei Ma,
    Taehyung Park

Landscape Architecture Department

School of Design, University of Pennsylvania

Miami Vice: Selling the Sunshine State

LA 701-001, Fall 2013

(also delivered at GSD, Harvard in 2014)

Instructors: Karen M'Closkey

Simulated Natures

LARP 740 *Topics in Digital Media*, 2014

Instructors: Keith VanDerSys and Joshua Freese

Edaphic Ecologies

LARP 740 *Topics in Digital Media*, Spring 2012

Instructors: Keith VanDerSys and Joshua Freese

School of Architecture and Design
RMIT University, Melbourne

Design Studio: Tideland
Bachelor of Architectural Design, Semester 1, 2014
Lower Pool Design Studio – coordinator: Anna Johnson
Instructor: Tom Morgan

Department of Architecture
ETH, Zurich, Swiss Federal Institute of Technology
Master of Advanced Studies in Landscape Architecture (MAS LA) modules

Field Oriented Programming
Instructors: James Melsom and Luis Fraguada (invited guest)
Theoretical Programming
Instructors: Pia Fricker, Georg Munkel and Karsten Droste (invited guest)

Robert Reich School of Landscape Architecture
Louisiana State University

Studio: Synthetic Urban Ecologies, 2013
Instructors: Bradley Cantrell and Justine Holzman
Collaborators: Urban Biofilter, a non-profit ecological design firm based in Oakland,
        California

Bartlett School of Architecture
University College London (UCL)

Proxy Modelling
Relational Urbanism Research Cluster 18, 2012-2013
UDII (Urban Morphogenesis) MArch Urban Design, B-Pro Programme

Tutors: Eduardo Rico, Enriqueta Llabres-Valls and Zach Flucker
Creative Coding: Iker Mugarra and Immanuel Koh
History and Theory: Emmanouil Zaroukas and Molly Claypool
Students: Waishan Qiu, Yanxiu Chen, Guanghui Luo, Jia Zhang
B-Pro Director: Frederic Migayrou
B-Pro Deputy Director: Andrew Porter
Programme leader MArch Urban Design: Adrian Lahoud
UDII (Urban Morphogenesis) coordinator: Claudia Pasquero

Image credits

Cover Image

Cover   Darren Chin Siau Ming

Introduction

I.1	John Gould / Wah Poon / Texxus
I.2–3	Gustafson Porter
I.4	research Wendy Walls, graphic design Tom Harper

Chapter 1

1.1	Matthew Scarnaty
1.2a–b	Wendy Walls
1.3	Heike Rahmann
1.4	Jack Langridge Gould
1.5	(a) Daniel Widis and Andrew Boyd (b) Melany Masel (c) Xinyu Yan
1.6	ETH Zurich
1.7–1.8	LAAC
1.9–1.10	Gunter Wett
1.11–1.14	PARKKIM
1.15	Scott Shinton
1.16	ASPECT Studios, peckvonhartel and ARM Architecture
1.17	peckvonhartel and ARM Architecture
1.18–1.20	ASPECT Studios
1.21–1.24	Snøhetta
1.25–1.26	Snøhetta and Fojab arkitekter

Chapter 2

Chapter 3

References

Ahmad, A. M. and Aliyu, A. A. (2012). 'The Need for Landscape Information Modelling (LIM) in Landscape Architecture', in Buhmann, Ervin and Pietsch (eds), *Proceedings Geodesign, 3D Modelling and Visualisation* (pp. 531–40).

Aish, F., Davis, A. and Tsigkari, M. (2013). 'Ex Silico Ad Vivo: Computational Simulation and Urban Design at Foster +Partners'. *Architectural Design: Systems City, 04*(224).

Allen, S. (2009). 'From the Biological to the Geological', in S. Allen and M. McQuade (eds), *Landform Building*. Hong Kong: Lars Muller.

Amidon, J. (2005). *Moving Horizons: The Landscape Architecture of Kathryn Gustafson and Partners*. Basel: Birkhauser.

Amoroso, N. (2012). *Digital Landscape Architecture Now*. London/New York: Thames & Hudson.

Armour, T. (2014). Interview at Arup office, London.

Armour, T., Armour, S., Hargrave, J. and Revell, T. (2014). *Cities Alive: Rethinking Green Infrastructure*. Arup.

Armour, T., Hickmott, D. and Rico, E. (2014). Interview with Arup, London Office.

Ashcraft, H. W. (2010). 'Furthering Collaboration', in P. Deamer and P. G. Bernstein (eds), *Building (in) the Future: Recasting Labor in Architecture* (pp. 145–58). New York: Yale School of Architecture, Princeton Architectural Press.

Aste, K. and Ludlin, F. (2014). 'Sustainable design of alpine infrastructures'. Paper presented at the Peer Reviewed Proceedings of Digital Landscape Architecture ETH Zurich.

Asuni (2011). 'Land's Blog – Landscape Information Modeling (LIM)'. Retrieved from http://en.blog.asunilands.com/index.php/landscape-information-modeling-lim

Azhar, S. et al. (2012). 'Building Information Modeling (BIM): Now and Beyond'. *Australasian Journal of Construction Economics and Building*, 12(4), 15–28.

Ball, M. (2011). 'Esri Adds 3D Design Tools with Procedural Acquisition', *Spatial Sustain: Promoting Spatial Design for a Sustainable Tomorrow*. Retrieved 22 September, 2014, from www.sensysmag.com/spatialsustain/esri-adds-3d-design-tools-with-procedural-acquisition.html

Bauer, K. (2013). Interview at Aspect Studio office, Melbourne.

Bauer, K. and Sago, J. (2013). Interview at Aspect Studio office, Melbourne.

Becker, S. and Holmes, R. (2014). 'Landscape Information Modeling', *Mammoth*. Retrieved 2 August 2014, from http://m.ammoth.us/blog

Belesky, P. (2013). 'Adapting Computation to Adapting Landscapes'. *Kerb: Journal of Landscape Architecture*(21), 50.

Bellew, P. and Davey, M. (2012). *Green: House Green: Engineering: Environmental Design at Gardens By the Bay*. Novato, CA: Oro Editions.

Benjamin, D. (2012). 'Beyond Efficiency', in S. Marble (ed.), *Digital Workflows in Architecture*. Switzerland: Birkhauser.

Besserud, K., Sarkisian, M., Enquist, P. and Hartman, C. (2013). 'Scales of Metabolic Flows: Regional, Urban and Building Systems Design at SOM'. *Architectural Design: Systems City, 04*(224).

Bew, M. and Underwood, J. (2010). 'Delivering BIM to the UK Market', in J. Underwood and U. Isikdag (eds), *Building Information Modeling and Construction Informatics: Concepts and Technologies* (pp. 30–65). Hershey: IGI Global.

BIMForum. (2013). 'Level of Development Specification-2013'. Retrieved 4 April 2015 from http://bimforum.org/lod

Birch, A. and Miller, V. (2005). 'Meet the Masterminds'. *Building.co.uk*. Retrieved 1 June 2014, from www.building.co.uk/meet-the-masterminds/3051382.article

Bishop, I. and Lange, E. (eds) (2005). *Visualisation in Landscape and Environmental Planning Technology and Applications*. London: Taylor & Francis.

Bowman, M., Gould, J. and Williams, N. (2014). Interview at Gustafson Porter office, London.

Bowman, M. and Porter, N. (2013). Interview at Gustafson Portor offico, London.

Bowring, J. and Swaffield, S. (2010). 'Diagrams in Landscape Architecture', in M. Garcia (ed.), *The Diagrams of Architecture*. Chichester, UK: Wiley.

Buijs, M. (2015). Email response to questions.

Bullivant, L. (2011). 'Algae Farm'. *Domus*. Retrieved 1 April 2014, from www.domusweb.it/en/architecture/2011/09/16/algae-farm.html

Burry, J. and Burry, M. (2010). *The New Mathematics of Architecture*. London: Thames & Hudson.

Burry, M. (2011). *Scripting Cultures: Architectural Design and Programming*. Chichester, UK: Wiley.

Cabinet Office (2011). *Government Construction Strategy* (pp. 1–43). London: TSO.

Cantrell, B. and Holzman, J. (2013). 'Synthetic Urban Ecologies'. Retrieved 7 June 2014, from http://reactscape.visual-logic.com/teaching/synthetic-urban-ecologies

Cantrell, B. and Holzman, J. (2015). *Responsive Landscapes*: Abingdon, Oxon: Routledge.

Carlisle, S. (2014). Interview at Kieran Timberlake Architects office, Philadelphia.

Carlisle, S. and Pevzner, N. (2012). 'NYC High Performance Landscape Guidelines'. *Scenario 02: Performance* (spring).

Carlo Ratti Associati (2014). Retrieved June 2014, from www.carloratti.com/project/future-food-district

Carpo, M. (2011). *The Alphabet and the Algorithm*. Cambridge, MA: MIT Press.

Carpo, M. (2013a). 'The Digital and the Global', in M. Carpo (ed.), *The Digital Turn in Architecture 1992–2012*. Chichester, UK: Wiley.

Carpo, M. (2013b). 'Digital Indeterminism: The New Digital Commons and the Dissolution of Architectural Authorship', in P. Lorenzo-Eiroa and A. Sprecher (eds), *Architecture in Formation: On the Nature of Information in Digital Architecture* (pp. 47–52). Abingdon, Oxon: Routledge.

Carpo, M. (2014a). 'Foreword', in R. Garber (ed.), *BIM Design: Realising the Creative Potential of Building Information Modelling* (pp. 8–13). Chichester, UK: Wiley.

Carpo, M. (2014b). 'Ten Years of Folding', in R. Oxman and R. Oxman (eds), *Theories of the Digital in Architecture*. Abingdon, Oxon: Routledge.

CASE: BIM consulting and Building Information Modelling. Retrieved 1 December 2014, from http://case-inc.com

Chalmers, J. and Watts, T. (2014). 'Kids should code: why "computational thinking" needs to be taught in schools'. *Guardian*, 21 December. Retrieved from www.theguardian.com/commentisfree/2014/dec/19/kids-should-code-why-computational-thinking-needs-to-be-taught-in-schools

CIBSE BIM Steering Group (2015). 'BIM Talk'. Retrieved 20 February 2015, from http://bimtalk.co.uk/bim_glossary:level_of_maturity

Cluster 18 (2015). 'The Bartlett School of Architecture'. Retrieved 30 January 2105, from www.bartlett.ucl.ac.uk/architecture/programmes/postgraduate/units-and-showcases/march-urban-design/cluster18/2014–2015

Coppock, J. T. and Rhind, D. W. (1991). 'The History of GIS'. In D. J. Maguire, M. F. Goodchild and D. W. Rhind (eds), *Geographical Information Systems: Principles and Applications* (vol. 1). New York: Wiley.

Corner, J. (1999). 'Introduction: Recovering Landscape as a Critical Cultural Practice', in J. Corner (ed.), *Recovering Landscape: Essays in Contemporary Landscape Architecture*. New York: Princeton Architectural Press.

Corner, J. (2006). 'Terra Fluxus', in C. Waldheim (ed.), *The Landscape Urbanism Reader*. New York: Princeton Architectural Press.

Costanzo, M. (2006). *MVRDV: Works and Projects 1991–2006*. Milan: Skira editore.

Coutts, J. (1985). 'Computers: A Revolution at the GSFA?'. *Penn In Ink: The Annual Review of the Graduate School of Fine Arts* (spring).

Cox, S. and Darden, P. (2012). 'Metabolic Forest'. Retrieved 7 June 2014, from http://responsive-landscapes.com/2013/12/10/metabolic-forest-2

Czerniak, J. (ed.) (2002). *CASE: Downsview Park Toronto*. Munich: Prestel Verlag.

Dangermond, J. (2010). 'GeoDesign and GIS – designing our futures'. Paper presented at the Digital Landscape Architecture Anhalt University of Applied Science, Germany.

Davey, M., Bellew, P., Er, K. and Kwek, A. (2010). 'Garden by the Bay: High Performance through Design Optimization and Integration'. *Intelligent Buildings International*, 2.

Davis, D. (2013). *Modelled on Software Engineering: Flexible Parametric Models in the Practice of Architecture*. RMIT University Melbourne.

Davis, D. (2014). 'What's next for Autodesk is what's next for architects', at www.danieldavis.com

Davis, D. (2015). 'Three Top Firms That Are Pursuing Design Research'. *Technology*. Retrieved 4 April 2015, from www.architectmagazine.com/technology/three-top-firms-that-are-pursuing-design-research_

Davis, D. and Peters, B. (2013). 'Design Eco-systems'. *Architecture Design Computation Works: The Building of Algorithmic Thought* (March/April).

Department for Business, Innovation and Skills (2013). BIM Task Group: About Us. Retrieved 20 February 2015, from www.bimtaskgroup.org/about

Dredge Research Collaborative. Retrieved 30 June 2014, from http://dredgeresearchcollaborative.org/

Dunn, N. (2012). *Digital Fabrication in Architecture*. London: Laurence King.

Dutch architects to use 3D printer to build a house. (2013). *Dezeen magazine*. Retrieved 16 July 2014, from www.dezeen.com/2013/01/20/dutch-architects-to-use-3d-printer-to-build-a-house

Eagle, N. and Greene, K. (2014). *Reality Mining: Using Big Data to Engineer a Better World*. Boston, MA: MIT Press.

East, E. W. (2011). COBie Frequently Asked Questions. Retrieved 4 March, from www.wbdg.org/resources/cobiefaq.php

Eastman, C. M. (1975). 'The Use of Computers Instead of Drawings in Building Design'. *AIA Journal, March*, 46–50.

Eastman, C., Teicholz, P., Sacks, R. and Liston, K. (2011a). *BIM Handbook: A Guide to Building Information Modeling for Owners, Managers, Designers, Engineers, and Contractors*. Hoboken, NY: Wiley.

Eastman, C., Teicholz, P., Sacks, R. and Liston, K. (2011b). 'Interoperability', in C. Eastman, P. Teicholz, R. Sacks and K. Liston (eds.), *BIM Handbook: A Guide to Building Information Modeling for Owners, Managers, Designers, Engineers, and Contractors*. Hoboken, NY: Wiley.

ecoLogicStudio. Retrieved 8 June 2014, from www.ecologicstudio.com/v2/index.php

Engelhardt, M. and Kessling, W. (2013). 'Design for Outdoor Comfort'. *Transsolar*, www.transsolar.com/blog/design-for-outdoor-comfort/index.html

ETH (2014). Master of Advanced Studies in Landscape Architecture, ETH Zurich.

Fast Company (2104). 'How the "Internet of Things" Is Turning Cities into Living Organisms'. Retrieved 10 July 2104, from www.fastcompany.com/biomimicry/how-the-internet-of-things-is-turning-cities-into-organisms

Fellman, C. (2014). Interview at Snøhetta office, New York.

Ferguson, H. (2014). 'Singapore's Supertrees'. *Ingenia*, March (58).

Foderaro, L. W. (2014). 'In real time, compiling picture of urban ecology'. *New York Times*, 3 December.

Fooks, M., Schwabe, N., Lundh, C. and Hays, J. (2015). Interview at ASPECT Studios office, Melbourne.

ForeignOfficeArchitects (1996). 'Yokohama International Port Terminal'. *Architecture on the Horizon AD 66* (July–August).

Fraguada, L., Girot, C. and Melsom, J. (2012). 'Synchronous horizons: redefining spatial design in landscape architecture through ambient data collection and volumetric manipulations'. Paper presented at the ACADIA Synthetic Digital Ecologies. Retrieved from http://lvml.net

Fraguada, L. and Melsom, J. (2014). 'Urban pulse: the application of moving sensor networks in the urban environment: strategies for implementation and implications for landscape design'. Paper presented at Digital Landscape Architecture 2014, ETH, Zurich.

Free Landhausplatz *Facebook*, from www.facebook.com/FreeLandhausplatz

Frenzel, C. (2014). Personal communication.

Fricker, P. (2015). Email communication

Fricker, P., Girot, C. and Munkel, G. (2013, September). 'How to teach "new tools" in landscape architecture in the digital overload'. Paper presented at the Computation and Performance – Proceedings of the 31st eCAADe Conference, Faculty of Architecture, Delft University of Technology, Delft, the Netherlands.

Future Everything (2014). Retrieved 2 August 2014, from http://futureeverything.org

Fytogreen (2014). Retrieved 1 November 2014, from http://fytogreen.com.au

Galcon (2014). Retrieved 1 November 2014, from www.galconc.com

Garber, R. (2009). 'Optimisation Stories: The Impact of Building Information Modelling on Contemporary Design Practice'. *Architectural Design*, 79(2), 6–13.

Garber, R. (ed.) (2014). *BIM Design: Realising the Creative Potential of Building Information Modelling*: Chichester, UK: Wiley.

General, V. A. (2014). *Heatwave Management: Reducing the Risk to Public Health*.

Girot, C. (2011). 'Sigirino Depot-Switzerland: Large Artificial Mound of Excavation Material'. *Topos-European Landscape Magazine* (74).

Girot, C. (2013a). 'About Topology'. *Topos*, 82, 7.

Girot, C. (2013b). 'The Elegance of Topology', in C. Girot, A. Freytag, A. Kitchengast and D. Richter (eds), *Topology: Topical Thoughts on the Contemporary Landscape*. Berlin: jois Verlag GmbH.

Girot, C., Bernhard, M., Ebnöther, Y., Fricker, P., Kapellos, A. and Melsom, J. (2010). 'Towards a meaningful usage of digital CNC tools: within the field of large-scale landscape architecture'. Paper presented at eCAADe 28.

Givoni, B., Noguchi, M., Saaroni, H., Pochter, O., Yaacov, Y., Feller, N. et al. (2003). 'Outdoor Comfort Research Issues'. *Energy and Buildings*, 35(77–86).

Glymph, J. (2009). 'Evolution of the Digital Design Process', in B. Kolarevic (ed.), *Architecture in the Digital Age: Design and Manufacturing* (pp. 102–20). New York: Taylor & Francis

GNCstaff (2014). 'Atlanta and Code for America website improves court operations', *GCN: Technology, Tools and Tactics for Public Sector IT*. Retrieved September 9, from http://gcn.com/blogs/pulse/2014/05/atlcourt.aspx

Goldman, M. (2011). Landscape Information Modelling. *Design Intelligence*. Retrieved 18.12.2012, from www.di.net/articles/landscape_information_modeling

GOM (2014). Retrieved 27 October 2014, from www.gom.com

Grant, A. (2014). Interview with Grant Associates, Bath.

Green Roof Innovation Testing (GRIT) Laboratory. *Research 2013 ASLA Professional Awards* from www.asla.org/2013awards/394.html

Gubbi, J., Buyya, R., Marusic, S. and Palaniswami, M. (2013). 'Internet of Things (IoT): A Vision, Architectural Elements and Future Directions'. *Future Generation Computer Systems*, 29.

Hallgren, M. (2014) 'MAX IV-Lund', *Slide Share*. Retrieved September 2014, from www.slide-share.net/richardmccarthycbise/4-mikael-hallgren

Hanley, C. (2014). Interview at Olin office, Philadelphia.

Hansen, A. (2012). 'From Hand to Land: Tracing Procedural Artifacts in the Built Landscape'. *Landscape Urbanism* (autumn), 25.

Hansen, A. (2014a). 'Datascapes: Design for Changing Cities and Shifting Lands'. Retrieved 3 August 2014, from http://datascapessymposium2014.tumblr.com

Hansen, A. (2014b). Interview, GSD, Harvard.

Hansford, P. (2013). 'Foreword'. *How to Use BIM with NEC3 Contracts*, at http://codebim.com/wp-content/uploads/2013/06/BIMwithNEC3guide.pdf

Harris, J. (2014). *Drawing the [0]rganic [Soil] Layer*. University of Virginia, School of Architecture.

Hasselberg, P. E. (2014). Interview at Snøhetta office, Oslo.

Heard, G. (2014). Interview at Medibank Building, Melbourne.

Heier, A. (2014). Interview at Snøhetta office, Oslo.

Hensel, M. (2013). *Performance-Oriented Architecture : Rethinking Architectural Design and The Built Environment*. Chichester, UK: Wiley.

Hickmott, D. (2014). Interview at Arup office, London.

Hill, J., Perotto, M. and Yoon, C. (2015). 'Processes of quantifying the hydrological performance of extensive green roofs'. Paper presented at Proceeding of the RCI 2015 Building Envelope Technology Symposium San Antonio, TX.

Hong, Z. (2014). Interview, Harvard GSD.

Hooper, M. (2011). 'A Review of BIM-Guidelines: Content, Scope and Positioning'. Lund University, presentation for Interreg Öresund-Kattegat-Skagerrak European Regional Development Fund.

Hopkins, J. C. and Neal, P. (2013). *The Making of the Queen Elizabeth Olympic Park*. Hoboken, NY: Wiley.

Hubcap (2104). *Sensable City Lab*. Retrieved 7 August 2014, from http://hubcab.org/#13.00/40.4489/-73.6118

Hurkxkens, I. and Munkel, G. (2014). 'Speculative precision: combining haptic terrain modelling with real-time digital analysis for landscape design'. Paper presented at Digital Landscape Architecture 2014, ETH, Zurich.

Infrastructure NSW (2013). 'Project brief: high level output specification'.

Inhabitat (2104). Retrieved June 2014, from http://inhabitat.com/incredible-urban-algae-canopy-produces-the-oxygen-equivalent-of-four-hectares-of-woodland-every-day/13-urban-algae-canopy-by-ecologic-studio-expo-milano-2015

Ishii, H., Ratti, C., Piper, B., Wang, Y., Biderman, A. and Ben-Joseph, E. (2004). 'Bringing Clay and Sand into Digital Design – Continuous Tangible User Interfaces'. *BT Technology Journal*, 22(4).

Jones, L. and MacLachlan, B. (2014). *2014 Heatwave Business Impacts – Social Research Co.* Melbourne: City of Melbourne.

Jones, S. A. and Bernstein, H. M. (2012). 'The Business Value of BIM in North America: Multi-Year Trend Analysis and User Ratings (2007–2012)', in M. Construction (ed.), *Smart Market Report* (pp. 1–70). New York: McGraw-Hill.

Jørstad, P. (2012). *Vibration Reduction by Shaping the Terrain Topography*. LTH, Lund University.

Kitchin, R. (2014). 'Big Data, New Epistemologies and Paradigm Shifts'. *Big Data and Society*, April–June.

Kolarevic, B. (2005). 'Prologue', in B. Kolarevic and A. M. Malkawi (eds), *Performative Architecture: Beyond Instrumentality*. London: Spon Press.

Kolarevic, B. (2010). 'Between Conception and Production'., in P. Bernstein and P. Deamer (eds), *Building (in) the Future: Recasting Labor in Architecture*. New York: Princeton Architectural Press.

Kolarevic, B. (ed.) (2009). *Architecture in the Digital Age: Design and Manufacturing*. New York: Taylor & Francis.

Kolarevic, B. and Klinger, K. (2013). 'Manufacturing/Material/Effect', in B. Kolarevic and K. Klinger (eds), *Manufacturing Material Effects: Rethinking Design and Making in Architecture*. New York: Taylor & Francis.

LAAC (2014a). Interview with LAAC, Innsbruck Office.

LAAC (2014b). Practice notes: Landhausplatz. Retrieved 30 June 2014, from www.laac.eu/en/presskit

Lambert, L. (2012). 'Architectural Theories: A Subversive Approach to the Ideal Normalized Body'. *The Funambukist: Bodies, Design and Politics*. Retrieved 2 December 2013, from http://thefunambulist.net/2012/04/29/architectural-theories-a-subversive-approach-to-the-ideal-normatized-body

Landau, C. (2015). Email communication.

Landscape Institute UK (Producer) (2012). 'Delivering the Olympic Park: An interview with Neil Mattinson of LDA Design'. *Landscape Legacy of the Olympics* [video]. Retrieved from www.youtube.com/watch?v=DSyQVSA9xUM

Landscape Morphologies Lab (2104). Retrieved 30 June 2014, from http://lmlab.org

Larsen, S. (2010a). *Highlights and Activities 2011–2012. Max IV Laboratory*: Lund University.

Larsen, S. (2010b). 'Stability and Tolerances'. *Detailed Design Report on the Max IV Facility. Max IV Laboratory*: Lund University.

Leatherbarrow, D. (2005). 'Architecture's Unscripted Performance', in Branko Kolarevic and Ali M. Malkawi (eds), *Performative Architecture: Beyond Instrumentality*. New York: Spon Press.

Leckie, C. (2013). 'The "big data" gold rush: mining data for a smarter Melbourne'. *Professorial Lecture Series*. Retrieved 2 December 2013, from http://eng.unimelb.edu.au/events/professorial/chris-leckie

Leong, M. (2013). Interview at Thiess office, Melbourne.

Llabres, E. and Rico, E. (2012a). 'In Progress: Relational Urban Models'. *Urban Design International*, 17(4).

Llabres, E. and Rico, E. (2014b). 'Proxi Modelling: A Tacit Approach to Territorial Praxis'. *Journal of Space Syntax*, 5(1).

Long, M. (2013). Interview at Thiess office, Melbourne.

Lorenzo-Eiroa, P. (2013). 'Form:In:Form on the Relationship between Digital Signifiers and Formal Autonomy', in P. Lorenzo-Eiroa and A. Sprecher (eds), *Architecture in Information: On the Nature of Information in Digital Architecture*. New York: Routledge

Lynn, G. (1998). 'Architectural Curvilinearity: The Folded, the Pliant and the Supple'. *Folds, Bodies and Blobs: Collected Essays*. Brussels: La Lettree Voleé.

M'Closkey, K. (2012) *Digital Landscape Architecture Now*. London/New York: Thames & Hudson.

M'Closkey, K. (2014). 'Structuring Relations: From Montage to Model in Composite Imaging', in C. Waldheim and A. Hansen (eds), *Composite Landscape: Photomontage and Landscape Architecture*. Berlin/Boston: Hatje Cantz/Isabella Stewart Gardner Museum.

M'Closkey, K. (2013a). *Miami Vice: Selling the Sunshine State*. Department of Landscape Architecture University of Pennsylvania.

M'Closkey, K. (2013b). 'Synthetic Patterns: Fabricating Landscapes in the Age of "Green"'. *Journal of Landscape Architecture* (spring).

M'Closkey, K. (2013c). Lecture at American Academy, Rome.

M'Closkey, K. (2013d). *Unearthed: The Landscapes of Hargreaves Associates*. Philadelphia, PA: University of Pennsylvania Press.

M'Closkey, K. and VanDerSys, K. (2011). 'Bellwether'. Retrieved March 2014, from www.peg-ola.com/project.php?id=1

M'Closkey, K. and VanDerSys, K. (2013a). Email response to questions (1).

M'Closkey, K. and VanDerSys, K. (2013b). Interview at the American Academy, Rome.

M'Closkey, K. and VanDerSys, K. (2014a). 'Interview'. In R. Weller and M. Talarowski (eds), *Transects: 100 Years of Landscape Architecture and Regional Planning at the University of Pennsylvania*: Applied Research + Design Publishing

M'Closkey, K. and VanDerSys, K. (2014b). Response to email questions (2).

M'Closkey, K. and VanDerSys, K. (2015). 'Simulating Nature', from www.design.upenn.edu/landscape-architecture/events/simulating-natures

McCapra, A. (2012). 'Get Ready for BIM But Buy Nothing'. *Landscape Institute News*. Retrieved 11 March 2015, from www.landscapeinstitute.org/news/get_ready_for_bim_but_buy_nothing

M'Cullough, M. (2013). '20 Years of Scripted Space', in Carpo (ed.), *Digital Turn in Architecture 1992–2012*.

McHarg, I. L. (1992). *Design with Nature*. New York: Wiley.

Magee, M., Ferla, L.-M., Miller, S. and Scanlon, L. (2015). 'Building Information Modelling'. Retrieved 20 February 2015, from www.out-law.com/en/topics/projects–construction/projects-and-procurement/building-information-modelling

Mah, D. (2014). Interview at the GSD, Harvard.

Massumi, B. (2013). 'Becoming Architectural: Affirmative Critique, Creative Incompletion'. *Architectural Design, The Innovation Imperative: Architectures of Vitality* (January/February).

Mattinson, N. (2013). Interview at LDA Design office, London.

May, K. (ed.) (2012). *Clog: Data Space*. Canada.

Medialab-Prado (2104). Retrieved 7 August 2014, from http://medialab-prado.es

Mertens, E. (2010). *Visualising Landscape Architecture: Functions, Concepts, Strategies*. Basel: Birkhauser.

Meyers, E. K. (2008). 'Sustaining Beauty. The Performance of Appearance. A Manifesto in Three Parts'. *Journal of Landscape Architecture* (spring).

Milman, O. (2015). 'Climate change will hit Australia harder than the rest of world, study shows'. *Guardian*. Retrieved from www.theguardian.com/environment/2015/jan/26/climate-change-will-hit-australia-harder-than-rest-of-world-study-shows

Morgan, T. (2014). Email communication

Mosbach, C. (2012). 'Performations'. *Architecture and Ideas Entropic Territories XI*.

Mosbach, C. (2014a). Email communication

Mosbach, C. (2014b). 'Landscape vs Technologies?'. *l'Observatorie des Tendancies du Jardin (OTJ)*.

NEC (2013). 'How to use BIM with NEC3 contracts'. http://codebim.com/wp-content/uploads/2013/06/BIMwithNEC3guide.pdf.

Negro, F. (2015). Telephone interview with CASE, New York.

Nicas, J. (2015). 'Drones' next job: construction work'. *Wall Street Journal*, www.wsj.com/articles/drones-next-job-construction-work-1421769564

Nicholson, C. (2014). 'Q & A : Marcus Quigley on How the Internet of Things Is Automating City Systems'. *Smart Planet*. Retrieved 12 July 2014, from www.smartplanet.com/blog/pure-genius/qa-marcus-quigley-on-how-the-internet-of-things-is-automating-city-systems

North, A. (2012). 'Processing Downsview Park: Transforming a Theoretical Diagram to Master Plan and Construction Reality'. *Journal of Landscape Architecture* (spring).

One Country, Two Lungs (2104). *Sensable City Lab*. Retrieved 8 July 2014, from http://senseable.mit.edu/twolungs

Osborn, B. (2013a). *Groundwork*: University of Virginia

Osborn, B. (2013b). 'Introduction', in Brian Osborn, K. Jenkins and G. McGinn (eds), *Surface FX*. Landscape Architecture Department: University of Virginia.

Osborn, B. (2014a). Email communication.

Osborn, B. (2014b). *Surveillance Practices: Graduate Option Studio*. University of Virginia, School of Architecture.

Osborn, B., Jenkins, K. and McGinn, G. (2013). 'Tecmat: Temporary Erosion Control Mat', in Brian Osborn, K. Jenkins and G. McGinn (eds), *Surface FX*. Landscape Architecture Department: University of Virginia

Osuldsen, J. (2013). Interview at Snøhetta office, Oslo.

Oxman, R. and Oxman, R. (2014). 'Introduction: Vitrivius Digitalis', in R. Oxman and R. Oxman (eds), *Theories of the Digital in Architecture*. Abingdon, UK: Routledge.

Oxman, R. (2006). 'Theory and Design in the First Digital Age'. *Design Studies*, 27.

Oxman, R. (2008). 'Digital Architecture as a Challenge for Design Pedagogy: Theory, Knowledge, Models and Medium'. *Design Studies*, 29.

PARKKIM. (2014). Interview with PARKKIM at their Seoul office.

Payne, A. O. and Kelly Johnson, J. (2013). 'Firefly: Interactive Prototypes for Architectural Design'. *Architectural Design, Computation Works: The Building of Algorithmic Thought* (March/April).

PEG (2014). Edaphic Effects. Retrieved 12 December 2013

Peters, B. (2013). 'The Building of Algorithmic Thought'. *Architecture Design March/April*.

Petschek, P. (2005). 'Terrain modelling with GPS and real time in landscape architecture'. Paper presented at Digital Landscape Architecture (DLA) Conference: Trends in Real-Time Landscape Visualization and Participation, Anhalt University of Applied Sciences.

Petschek, P. (2014). *Grading: LandscapingSMART, 3D Machine Control Systems, Stormwater Management* (vol. 2). Basel: Birkhäuser.

Petschek, P. and Mach, R. (eds). (2006). *Visualisation of Digital Terrain and Landscape Data: A Manual*. Berlin: Springer.

Picon, A. (2010). *Digital Culture in Architecture : An Introduction for the Design Professions*. Basel, Switzerland: Birkhauser.

Picon, A. (2013). Substance and Structure II: The Digital Culture of Landscape Architecture. *Harvard Design Magazine* (36).

Poletto, M. and Pasquero, C. (2012). *Systemic Architecture: Operating Manual For The Self-Organising City*. Abingdon, Oxon: Routledge.

Poletto, M. and Pasquero, C. (2013). Interview at ecoLogicStudio, London.

Quirk, V. (2012). 'A Brief History of BIM/Michael S Bergin'. *ArchDaily*. Retrieved 3 March 2015, from www.archdaily.com/?p=302490

Rahm, P. (2014a). Interview at GSD, Harvard.

Rahm, P. (2014b). *Institute for Advanced Architecture Lecture Series*. Retrieved 24 August 2014, from www.youtube.com/watch?v=_cMWGqfVvro

Raju, P. (2014). 'IBM to Provide Smart City Tech for Palava Project'. *Urban Update*.

RC18 (2014). *The Metropolis of Alberta Tar Sand Extraction* Bartlett School of Architecture: University College London.

Reas, C. and McWilliams, C. (2010). *Form + Code in Design, Art, and Architecture*. New York: Princeton Architectural Press.

Redevelopment of a Square in Innsbruck (2013). *Detail, 1*.

Reed, C. and Lister, N.-M. (2014). 'Parallel Genealogies', in C. Reed and N.-M. Lister (eds), *Projective Ecologies*. New York: Harvard University Graduate School of Design and Actar Publishers

Reed, C. and Mah, D. (2014). Flux City studio brief. GSD. Harvard.

Rekittke, J. and Ninsalam, Y. (2014). 'Head in the point clouds – feet on the ground'. Paper presented at Digital Landscape Architecture 2014, ETH Zurich.

Relational Urbanism (2014). Retrieved 23 September 2014, from www.bartlett.ucl.ac.uk/ architecture/programmes/postgraduate/units-and-showcases/march-urban-design/ cluster18/2013–2014

Robinson, A. (2013a). Email communication.

Robinson, A. (2013b). 'Genius ingenium: Near Adjacencies to the Owens Lake'. *Arid: A Journal of Desert Art, Design and Ecology*. Retrieved 6 June 2014, from http://aridjournal.com/ genius-ingenium-alexander-robinson/

Rossegaarde, D. (2014). Smog Free Project, from www.studioroosegaarde.net/uploads/ files/2014/08/10/194/PLAN%20The%20Smog%20Free%20Project%20by%20 Studio%20Roosegaarde.pdf

Santry, C. (2004). 'Diana, Princess of Wales Memorial Fountain, London'. *The Edge: Stone Business*. Retrieved 1 October 2014, from www.stonebusiness.net/index. php?option=com_content&view=article&id=660&Itemid=67

Scheer, D. (2014). *The Death of Drawing: Architecture in the Age of Simulation*. Abingdon, Oxon: Routledge.

Schmidt, L. (2014). 'LandCADD: An Unecessary Revit Add-In'. Retrieved 4 April 2015, from http://landarchbim.com/2014/02/19/landcadd-an-unecessary-revit-add-in

Schnabel, M. A. (2012). 'Learning Parametric Designing', in G. Ning and W. Xiangyu (eds), *Computational Design Methods and Technologies Applications in CAD, CAM, and CAE*. Hershey, PA: IGI Global.

Schumacher, P. (2009). 'Parametricism: A New Global Style for Architecture and Urban Design'. *Digital Cities AD*, 79(July–August).

Sensable City Lab (2104). Retrieved 7 August 2014, from http://senseable.mit.edu

Sharples, C. D. (2010). 'Technology and Labour', in P. Deamer and P. G. Bernstein (eds), *Building (in) the Future: Recasting Labor in Architecture* (pp. 90–9). New York: Yale School of Architecture, Princeton Architectural Press,.

Shujuan, L. and Yang, B. (2013). '3D digital graphics in landscape architectural professional practice: current conditions in a nutshell'. Paper presented at CELA Landscape Research Record.

Slavid, R. (2013). 'Practice 2: BIM for Landscape'. *Landscape: Journal of the Landscape Institute* (spring).

StaffReporter (2013). 'POSCO E&C to Build World's First Underground Combined Cycle Power Plant'. *Asianpower*. Retrieved 20 September 2014, from http://asian-power.com/project/ news/posco-ec-build-worlds-first-underground-combined-cycle-power-plant

Steinitz, C. (2012). *A Framework for Geodesign: Changing Geography by Design*. Redlands, CA: Esri Press.

Tai, L. (2003). 'Assessing the Impact of Computer Use on Landscape Architecture Professional Practice: Efficiency, Effectiveness, and Design Creativity'. *Landscape Journal* 22(2).

Taichung Gateway Park International Competition Overview of the Winning Project (2013). Retrieved January 2013, from www.maa.com.tw/10037/files/introduce.pdf

Tait, J. (2012). 'Open Data Cities'. Retrieved 7 August 2014, from http://futureeverything.org/ news/open-data-cities

Tang, M. (2014). *Parametric Building Design: Using Autodesk Maya*. London/New York: Routledge.

Tekla (2104) 'Gardens at the Bay: Complex Geometry'. Retrieved 1 August 2014, from www. tekla.com/references/gardens-bay

Thompson, D. (2014). Interview at LDA Design office, London.

Tirol government (2012). Treffpunkt Landhausplatz.

Topological Map (2105). Retrieved 15 January 2105, from http://en.wikipedia.org/wiki/ Topological_map

Townsend, A. M. (2013). *Smart Cities: Big Data, Civic Hackers and the Quest for a New Utopia.* New York: Norton.

Treib, M. (ed.). (2008). *Representing Landscape Architecture.* London/New York: Taylor & Francis.

Trimble (2015). 'Trimble and Nemetschek Group Partner to Expand Adoption of Building Information Modeling Across Building Design, Construction and Operation'. *PRNewswire.* Retrieved from www.prnewswire.com/news-releases/trimble-and-nemetschek-group-partner-to-expand-adoption-of-building-information-modeling-across-building-design-construction-and-operation-300076511.html

UK Government BIM Industry Working Group (2011). *BIM Management for value, cost and carbon improvement: Strategy Paper for the Government Construction Client Group.*

Urban Algae Canopy (2014). *Domus.* Retrieved 20 October, 2014, from www.domusweb.it/en/news/2014/04/30/urban_algae_canopy.html

Urban Code (2104). Retrieved 30 June 2014, from http://senseable.mit.edu/urbancode

Valldaura (2104). 'Self Sufficient Lab'. Retrieved 1 November 2014, from www.valldaura.net/about-2

VanDerSys, K. (2014a). Interview at the University of Pennsylvania, PA.

VanDerSys, K. (2014b). *Simulated Natures.* Department of Landscape Architecture: University of Pennsylvania, School of Design.

Velikov, K., Thun, G. and Ripley, C. (2012). 'Thick Air'. *Journal of Architectural Education,* 65(2).

Victoria, S. G. (2009). *Partnerships Victoria: Project Summary – Victorian Desalination Project.* Department of Sustainability and Environment. Capital Projects Division in conjunction with the Department of Treasury and Finance.

Waldheim, C. (2012). 'Digital Landscape 3.0 (2013–2037)', in M. Mostafvi and P. Christensen (eds.), *Instigations: Engaging Architecture Landscape and the City.* Germany: Lars Muller.

Waldheim, C. (2013). 'Landscape as Digital Media: Notes Towards a Digital Landscape 3.0'. *Thinking the Contemporary Landscape – Positions and Oppositions.* Retrieved September 2013, from http://girot.arch.ethz.ch/blog/thinking-the-contemporary-landscape-memo

Walker, P. (2008). 'Foreword', in P. Petschek (ed.), *Grading for Landscape Architects and Architects,* . Basel: Birkhäuser.

Walker, P. (2008). 'Modeling the Landscape', in M. Treib (ed.), *Representing Landscape Architecture.* London/New York: Taylor & Francis.

Walliss, J., Rahmann, H., Sieweke, J. and Hong, Z. (2014). 'Pedagogical Foundations: Deploying Digital Techniques in Design/Research Practice'. *Journal of Landscape Architecture,* 3.

Weller, R. and Talarowski, M. (2014). *Transects: 100 Years of Landscape Architecture and Regional Planning at the University of Pennsylvania.* China: Applied Research + Design Publishing Gordon Goff Publisher.

Woo, H. and Kim, W. (1997). 'Floods on the Han River in Korea'. *Water International,* 22(4).

Woodbury, R. (2010). *Elements of Parametric Design.* Abingdon, Oxon: Routledge.

Woods, C. (2013). 'Thermal Bench', in Brian Osborn, K. Jenkins and G. McGinn (eds), *Surface FX.* Landscape Architecture Department: University of Virginia

Zuidgeest, J., Van der Burgh, S. and Kalmeyer, B. (2013). 'Planning by Parameters'. *Architectural Design Computational Works: The Building of Algorithmic Thought* (March/April).

Index